KNOWLEDGE
OF THE
MOST HIGH

GREG AMUNDSON

KNOWLEDGE OF THE MOST HIGH

PRAISE FOR THE WORK OF GREG AMUNDSON

"Greg Amundson is a true warrior leader and monk. His deep commitment to his faith, and ability to communicate that faith through his passion for the warrior mindset, is unparalleled. *The Good Soldier* is another lighted path that Greg has provided for those searching for Truth."

— *Mark Divine*, U.S. Navy SEAL (Retired) *New York Times* bestselling author of *The Way of the SEAL, Unbeatable Mind* and *Staring Down the Wolf*

"Greg's ability to transcend boundaries and speak to the essence of spirituality is profound and encouraging."

— *Scott McEwen*, #1 *New York Times* bestselling co-author of *American Sniper*, national bestselling *Sniper Elite* series, and the new *Camp Valor* series of novels

"I often tell people at my seminars, 'We don't need more Buddhists in the world, we need more Buddhas. We don't need more Christians, we need more Christ-like beings.' And such is the case with my amazing, breathing brother Greg Amundson. He's not one of those wishy-washy, praise the Lord, in-your-face, superficial Christians: He is a former SWAT Operator, DEA Special Agent, U.S. Army Captain, and CrossFit athlete and coach. He is a spiritual warrior, and he carries God in his heart. Greg's sermons, lectures and books teach the principles of spiritual development that can change your life."

— *Dan Brulé*, world renowned lecturer and international bestselling author of *Just Breathe*

"Greg Amundson is the epitome of a modern day warrior. He leads in all aspects of his life: as a warrior, as a Christian, and as a fitness expert. He writes with magical simplicity, yet is rigorous in his research and reasoning. As a leadership and motivation coach, when I need my own motivation I look to Greg Amundson. His track record of proving the validity of his message in his own life, and the lives that his message touches, is astounding."

— *Jason Redman*, Navy SEAL (Retired) and *New York Times* bestselling author of *The Trident: the Forging and Reforging of a Navy SEAL Leader*

"Greg Amundson is one of the most prolific author's and speakers of our time, and his work will profoundly bless your life."

— **Dr. Gabrielle Lyon**, DO, Special Operations, Task Force Dagger

"Greg Amundson's new book *The Good Soldier* contains a visionary message on leadership, self-mastery, and walking the path of a modern day warrior. This is a profound and encouraging read that has reinvigorated my desire to be of service to others. Hooyah!"

— **Joe De Sena**, Spartan Founder & CEO and #1 *New York Times* bestselling author of *Spartan Up!*

"Greg Amundson has the ability to weave the warrior mindset and biblical message in a way that cuts to my heart. His sermons and books encourage me to put God first, strive for self-mastery, and be of greater service to others."

— **Jay Dobyns**, ATF Special Agent (Retired) *New York Times* bestselling author of *No Angel* and *Catching Hell*

ALSO BY GREG AMUNDSON

Published Books

Your Wife is NOT Your Sister – (And 15 other love lessons I learned the hard way)
Robertson Publishing – 2012

Firebreather Fitness – Work Your Body, Mind and Spirit into the Best Shape of Your Life
(with TJ Murphy) Velo Press – 2016

The Warrior and The Monk – A Fable About Fulfilling Your Potential and Finding True Happiness
Robertson Publishing – 2018

Above All Else – A Year of Increasing Wisdom, Stature, and Favor
Eagle Rise Publishing – 2018

Victory! – A Practical Guide to Forging Eternal Fitness
Eagle Rise Publishing – 2019

The Good Soldier – How to Fight Well, Finish the Race and Keep the Faith
Eagle Rise Publishing – 2019

CrossFit® Journal Articles

A Chink in My Armor

Coaching the Mental Side of CrossFit

CrossFit HQ – 2851 Research Park Drive, Santa Cruz, CA.

Diet Secrets of the Tupperware Man Vol. I

Diet Secrets of the Tupperware Man Vol. II

Forging Elite Leadership

Good Housekeeping Matters

How to Grow a Successful Garage Gym

Training Two Miles to Run 100

ACKNOWLEDGMENTS

First and foremost, I am exceedingly grateful for the everlasting love and embrace of God and His Son, Jesus Christ. For my beloved parents, Raymond and Julianne Amundson, who encouraged me from a young age to develop my mind, body, and spirit in such a manner that I could be of greater service to others. A great deal of appreciation is extended to Brooklyn Taylor for her brilliant layout and design contributions to this book. I am indebted to the great pastoral mentors and educators whose leadership has deeply influenced my understanding of doctrine and theology: Mark Divine, Dan Brulé, Ken Gray (in memoriam), Chaplain Richard Johnson, Pastor Dave Hicks, Dr. Deepak Chopra, Raja John Bright, Dr. Gary Tuck, Dr. Steve Korch, Dr. Adam Nigh, Pastor René Schlaepfer, Pastor Max Lucado, Bishop Robert Barron, and Dr. Charles Stanley. Finally, to the students and exemplary teaching staff at Western Seminary, may you continue to experience "Gospel Centered Transformation" in every area of your life.

DEDICATION

This book is dedicated in loving memory
to my mom and dad, who provided me with the greatest
example of a "Heart like Christ" I have ever known.

"God is more worthy of your pursuit, attention, and love than
all the other passions of the world combined."

— Dr. Raymond Amundson

"God is entirely devoted to your personal advancement."

— Julianne Amundson

TABLE OF CONTENTS

INTRODUCTION

INTRODUCTION

IN DECEMBER 2001, I WALKED a small CrossFit® Box, experienced the thrill of my first workout, crumbled into a heap on the floor, and thought that I was doing to die. Although physically crushed, my spirit was elated—by the grace of God I had uncovered the Holy Grail of fitness, and my life would never be the same.

Although the physical rewards of CrossFit and martial arts training have been extremely gratifying, I often wondered if there yet remained an untapped reservoir of potential that transcended my temporal score on a leaderboard or colored belt around my waist. In other words, I couldn't help but think that there was more to physical training than just physical adaptation, and that I had to challenge any preconceived notion that life was limited to the objective realm of my senses. I soon realized that it was high time that I started to focus on the spiritual unseen reality. This Spirit-led awakening and newfound enthusiasm for the unseen realm led me into a three-year Masters Degree program at Western Theological Seminary in San Jose, California.

I learned very quickly that when we exclusively focus on the temporal matters of the world, then we become subject to the longstanding admonishment that "people look at the outward appearance, but God looks at the heart" (1 Samuel 16:7). Nearly a lifetime of athletic and martial arts training, in addition to 20 years of service in law enforcement, has led me to understand that what happens within our minds and hearts is truly the greatest expression of all that God made us to be. However, unlike the physical skills we learn and practice within the gym, a law enforcement academy, or military training environment, the Bible teaches that there are some things we cannot do on our own. In the gym we need a spotter—in life we need a Savior.

By way of illustration, consider the attendees at a basic weightlifting clinic: They are taught that the key to increasing in their athletic capacity is adhering to the formula of moving large loads, long distances, very quickly! And how is this achieved? The attendee learns they must follow one of the universal principles of functional movement: The athlete is instructed to accelerate the object through a relay of contractions from core to extremity. This powerful and controlled series of contractions allows the athlete to produce power—and power is defined as intensity—and intensity is the independent variable most commonly associated with maximizing the rate of return on favorable adaptation.

And herein we arrive at the cornerstone of the biblical solution to every problem that we will ever face. We must focus on the spiritual equivalent of the physical independent variable, which is our True Core—reconciliation with God through a saving relationship with Jesus Christ. When we "seek first the Kingdom of God," we allow for God's grace to positively and constructively influence all the extremities of our life (Matthew 6:33). In other words, when God is in first place (our Core), then all the other pieces of our life fit perfectly into place (the extremity). In the words of C.S. Lewis, "When we look for Christ we will find Him, and with Him everything else thrown in."[1]

Here is the main point I want to make: God is the independent variable of our life. By grace through faith in Christ, the believer is reconciled with God, indwelt by the Holy Spirit, and equipped to maximize our life in a supernatural way (Ephesians 2:8-9; Acts 1:8, 2:4-39).

In the event it is not already painfully obvious, I love the methodology of rigorous physical training, and everything that the warrior professions stand for. However, I also fear that for many people—myself included—physical training and professional work can become a form of idolatry. Biblically speaking, "idol worship" means to put something other than God into the rightful place reserved for God alone. If God is that to which we give all of our time, energy, thought, and attention, then many of us are clearly engaged in worshipping things that are the idol of our own creation. When idolatry happens in any degree, our entire world begins to revolve around what we worship, and speaking from experience, this inherently sinful act of disobedience to God can creep into our life in unexpected and ensnaring ways.

That being said, God has an amazing way of putting Christian leaders in the right place, at the right time, to help change the course of history. I believe that you can be a catalyst for the Gospel message right between the four-walls of your home, place of work, gym, or martial arts dojo—and it's my prayer that this book can help you accomplish that awesome mission. In other words, you can learn to preach the Gospel within the micro-nation right in your own backyard.

When preaching to the micro-nation that God has entrusted to you, it is imperative that you are able to relate the Gospel within the context and

1 C.S. Lewis. *Mere Christianity.* (Collier Books, New York, NY. 1963), p. 175.

framework of the unique environment that you are in. As a first step, you need to ground yourself in a solid understanding of the Bible and systematic theology. Biblical revelation treats God's attributes and qualities not in a speculative way, but rather in an objective and practical manner.[2] There is a vital connection between the God of the Holy Bible, and the way we are called to relate to Him. Furthermore, there is a direct relationship between who God is, what God does as revealed within His Word, and what God perfectly demonstrates in the life of His Son, Jesus Christ. In the life of Jesus, we see that the attributes and qualities of God that are revealed by what Jesus said and did are the supreme representation of what God does, and are therefore both quantitative and qualitative evidence of who He is (Hebrews 1:1-3).

The Bible teaches that God's actions are not random, spontaneous, or erratic. Rather, they are outflows of His nature and essential Being. Therefore, by increasing our knowledge about God, we can correctly relate to God by aligning our thoughts and actions in accordance with what Scripture says that God is like. Additionally, we can best equip ourselves to confidently and competently teach others about the God we have come to know, to trust, and most importantly, to "love with all our heart, all our mind, and all our soul" (Matthew 22:37).

When we fully understand who God is, we will see Him, relate to Him, and love Him as the One True God, the God of Heaven and Earth. We will make Him our Lord and Savior, the one whom we aim to please, and whose will we are desirous of fulfilling during our lifetime. Increasing knowledge of God will encourage us to fashion ourselves after the Prophet Samuel, whose response when the Lord called him was, "Speak LORD, for your servant is listening" (1 Samuel 3:10). Samuel did not capitalize on this opportunity to pour out his needs to the Lord by saying, "Listen, LORD, your servant speaks." When we adopt this inverted theology and approach to our relationship to God, we in effect presume to know what is best for our lives and sinfully construct a god onto ourselves. But we must remember, as the Bible so emphatically seeks to teach, that it was God who created us, as opposed to the idolatrous design of a god created after our own fashion and needs.[3]

---

2 Millard Erickson. *Christian Theology* (Grand Rapids, MI: Baker Academic, 2013), p. 720. The chapter in *Christian Theology* on *The Goodness of God* was instrumental in helping me frame and conceptualize the ideas in the preface of this book.

3 William Barclay, *The Acts of the Apostles New Daily Study Guide* (Louisville, KY: Westminster John Knox Press, 1953), p. 155.

God created us in His image, and He therefore knows what is best for us in the long run. We will stand before God in the final judgment, not God before us (Romans 14:11). As we increase in the wisdom, knowledge, and revelation of what God does and who He is, we will join with Jesus in proclaiming, "Holy is your name. Your kingdom come, your will be done, on earth as it is in heaven" (Matthew 6:10). I pray that the following exposition of Holy Scripture contained within this book would educate and inspire you to boldly share your love of God with others.

GREG AMUNDSON
Santa Cruz, CA

CHAPTER
ONE

THE GOAL OF INTERPRETATION (HOW TO READ THE BIBLE)

IN ALL BRANCHES OF THE United States Military and Public Safety entities, successful communication is exceedingly important. Success in communication, regardless of the environment or type of message being conveyed, should always be the goal. However, oftentimes in a Military and Public Safety setting, the sender's communication is relating matters of life and death, and thus the receiver's responsibility to accurately decode the sender's intended meaning is absolutely critical. Furthermore, the sender's means of communication, their location, and level of duress may prevent the interpreter from asking the sender questions or making clarifications. The implications of communication in Military and Public Safety professions provide an excellent backdrop to understanding the inherent role and responsibility of the interpreter, in all matter of interpretation, to discern the sender's intended meaning.

Having once received the text of the communication, the receiver now has the responsibility of accurately interpreting the message and discerning the sender's intended meaning. In order for this task to be accomplished, it becomes imperative that the interpreter not focus solely on the text of the message (text-centric interpretation), or on their judgments, feelings, ideas, or independently formulated conclusions (receiver-centric interpretation). As this essay will outline, in order for successful interpretation to take place, the receiver has the responsibility of attempting to understand the sender's intended meaning.

THE MIND OF THE SENDER

THE TASK OF DECODING THE sender's intended meaning is accomplished by moving beyond both receiver-centric and text-centric analysis and interpretation of the message, directly to the heart of the matter, which is striving to answer the question, "What was in the mind of the sender during their encoding of the message?" In order to discern what the sender of the message intended to communicate, the interpreter must penetrate the mind of the sender. This is no simple task, yet it is a critical one, and necessary for the interpreter to achieve. To reverse engineer the message once received becomes the goal of the interpreter. Reverse engineering a communication is a two-step process, which moves backward through space and time from the receiver, through the text, into the sender's mind and their very thoughts.

**SENDERS INTENDED
MEANING**

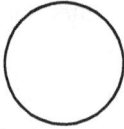

TEXT CENTRIC   RECEIVER CENTRIC

In order to understand the sender's intended meaning, the interpreter must lay down their individual judgments, perspectives, and biases (receiver-centric interpretation). In addition, the interpreter must move even beyond the substance of the text itself (text-centric interpretation). A text centric or receiver centric focus fails to appreciate and honor the original ideas of the sender. The highest aspiration of the interpreter should be to know the very thoughts the sender had in mind as their communication was being made. In the context of Scripture, this high aspiration is of supreme importance, for the original thoughts in the sender's mind were the very thoughts of God.

As outlined in a lecture by Dr. Gary Tuck, interpreting the sender's intended meaning leads to congruency between the sender and receiver.[4] One example would be a driver's interpretation of a stop sign several hundred feet before an intersection. Rather than immediately or randomly stopping upon observance of the sign, the driver correctly interprets the sender's intended meaning and stops only at the limit line.[5] Furthermore, once fully stopped, the driver once again interprets the sender's intended meaning and does not remain permanently stopped, but rather safely proceeds along the roadway in accordance with the safe flow of traffic.[6]

In all manner of communication, the interpreter must appreciate that the sender's inherent goal was to be understood. From the perspective of the sender, what matters even more than the text of their message, or the interpretative biases of the receiver, is that their original ideas be understood and valued. By striving to decode the sender's intended meaning, the interpreter demonstrates appreciation for the inherent human need to be understood, accounted for, and

---

4   Tuck, Dr. Gary. "Goal of Interpretation." Lecture, Western Seminary, Milpitas, California, September 25, 2017.
5   Ibid.
6   Ibid.

valued. In order to achieve congruency, alignment, harmony, and understanding in communication, the interpreter must come to know the mind and thoughts of the sender. This high aspiration can only be achieved through the art and science of decoding the sender's intended meaning.

GO FLY THE FLAG
The Danger of Text-Centered Interpretation

DURING MILITARY AND PUBLIC SAFETY communication training, the task of decoding the sender's intended meaning is referred to as "commander's intent." In these professions, mission success is paramount, and should harm befall the sender, the receiver would still be able to execute the orders, directions, and "commanders intent," ensuring that even without clear leadership, the meaning of the sender's communication would be achieved. Any other focal point on behalf of the interpreter, in particular an overemphasis on the specific text of the communication, could easily lead to a misunderstanding of the sender's intended meaning. I learned this principle the hard way.

In the summer of 2001, I was serving as a Deputy Sheriff for the Santa Cruz County Sheriff's Office in Santa Cruz, California. One morning during a patrol briefing, my supervisor, Sgt. Robert Pursley, told me, "Go fly the flag at the top of Red Robin Road." Using my issued map-finder, I discovered Red Robin Road was a remote roadway in a secluded part of Southern Santa Cruz County.

I departed the Sheriff's Office Headquarters and eagerly drove to Red Robin Road. Up and up the road crisscrossed through thick forests, until I finally arrived at a dead end overlooking a deep valley. Not immediately observing a flagpole, I got out of my patrol vehicle and walked around the hilltop, looking everywhere in a desperate attempt to locate the flagpole, and fly the flag. I was completely focused on the specific text of Sgt. Pursley's communication, and had incorrectly interpreted his intended meaning. A more senior Deputy later explained to me that the term "Go fly the flag" simply meant to drive a marked patrol vehicle through a particular geographic area.

SO, YOU'RE SAYING THERE'S A CHANCE!

The Problem with Receiver-Centric Interpretation

WHEN AN INTERPRETER decodes a text by relying solely on their own understanding, feelings, biases, or perspectives, the sender's intended meaning can be easily misunderstood. In the movie, "Dumb and Dumber," the character Lloyd Christmas asks the character Mary Swanson what his chances are for a romantic relationship.[7] Their interaction depicts an exaggerated example of how an interpreter can incorrectly decode a message based on personal bias and expectations.

Lloyd: "So, what are my chances?"

Mary: "Not good."

Lloyd: "You mean not good, like one out of 100?"

Mary: "I'd say more like one out of one-million."

Lloyd: "So, you're saying there's a chance!"

Renowned martial artist and Law Enforcement defensive tactic instructor Tony Blauer commented that "good information does not need to displace other good information."[8] In the Law Enforcement tactical community, preconceived opinions and conclusions on techniques and best practices are common, and it can be extremely challenging for new information to be interpreted independent of a bias. Any difference between information the receiver currently has, and new information they are receiving, can create confusion and a failure to correctly decode the sender's meaning.

In romantic relationships, the problem of receiver-centric interpretation can ultimately lead to significant breakdown of communication. When the receiver of a communication projects what they think the sender means or *should mean* onto the message, the receiver essentially interprets the message in a self-serving manner. On the other hand, intimacy can be increased between parties in communication when the receiver inquires into the intended meaning of a message. For example, a husband who thoughtfully asks himself, "What did my wife really mean when she said that?" extends love and consideration for his wife by not subjecting her to his personal opinions, assumptions, or prejudices.

---

7   Farrelly, Peter, Bennett Yellin, Bobby Farrelly, Todd Rundgren, Jeff Daniels, and Lauren Holly. Dumb & Dumber. Mask. n.d., 1994.

8   Blauer, Tony. "Be Your Own Bodyguard." Law Enforcement Seminar, Drug Enforcement Administration, San Diego, 2010

Receiver-centric interpretation may lead to false conclusions based on the expectations of the interpreter. For example, in vehicle code enforcement, officers are frequently greeted by a defense from the offender with regard to a receiver-centric interpretation of posted signs for offenses related to speeding at night. An offender in this instance might try to explain they interpreted the sign "Speed Limit – 55 MPH" to mean limited to 55 MPH during daylight hours, or in inclement weather, or during heavy traffic conditions; but certainly not late at night when the roadway was clear. Regardless of the receiver's individual bias, prejudices, or pre-conceived convictions, the sign "Speed Limit – 55 MPH" was in fact the sender's intended meaning.

CONCLUDING THOUGHTS

SUCCESSFUL INTERPRETATION OF A MESSAGE is dependent upon the receiver's ability to understand the sender's intended meaning. Any other means of interpretation, such as text-centric or receiver-centric, neglects the essential human element of communication, which is the fact that a human being formulated an idea, and attempted to express that idea to another person. Only by seeking to understand the sender's thought process and original ideas can the receiver successfully interpret the meaning of the message.

CHAPTER
TWO

TELLING THE STORY OF SCRIPTURE

WHEN STUDYING THE BIBLE, it is always a good idea to begin at the beginning. Although the Bible is comprised of several individually written books, all the books fit within a single narrative and serve the purpose of telling an integrated and seamless story about God. The following 21 lessons will help shape your understanding of the big picture of God's Word and provide context and reference points for a deeper study of the Scriptures. To assist your understanding of the biblical narrative, each lesson contains a specific scope in addition to my rationale for its inclusion. Furthermore, each of the 21 lessons fit within the framework of one of the most exciting and intriguing themes of the Bible, and that is the theme of spiritual warfare.

LESSON ONE: *In the Beginning* (Genesis 1:1-4)

Scope of Lesson One: Lesson One sets the stage for the entire story of the Bible. We begin by welcoming God on the scene as a creator of everything that is good. God enacts two powerful principles for victory in spiritual warfare, which are the establishment of order and the separation between light and darkness, a metaphor for good and evil.

Rationale for Lesson One: In the context of understanding our biblical theme of spiritual warfare, we are introduced to a God who confronts a world "formless and empty" and out of this formlessness, creates order. Due to the human tendency to be dismayed by the apparent chaos, meaninglessness, and out-of-control nature of the world, it is extremely important to understand that the intention of God, from the very beginning, was to establish order, and for everything within His creation to abide within that state of order.

LESSON TWO: *In His Image* (Genesis 1:26-28)

Scope of Lesson Two: In Lesson Two, we discover that God made humans in His image. Two of the specific qualities of God's image we are designed to share with God are creation and rule.

Rationale for Lesson Two: The proposition in Lesson Two is monumental: We are made in the image of God. Specifically, God intended for man and woman to share in His ability to create ("Be fruitful and multiply") and to create order through the establishment of rule ("Fill the earth and subdue it") and dominion. As we weave our way through the biblical narrative, it is extremely important to understand our ordained right to creativity, authority, order, and rule.

LESSON THREE: *The Fall* (Genesis 2:15-17 – Genesis 3:6-12)

Scope of Lesson Three: In Lesson Three, we are introduced to the first question God asks of His creation: "Do you trust me?" We discover that instead of trusting God's wisdom, creation chose to be independent from God, and autonomous in its ability to know right from wrong, and good from evil.

Rationale for Lesson Three: Lesson Three is significant for it highlights the tendency for the human experience to include the following:

1. Listening to our internal voice of negativity rather than the voice of God. (Genesis 3:11)
2. Blaming external conditions for our choices and experiences. (Genesis 3:12)
3. The temptation of external gratification and worldly reward. (Genesis 3:6)

As we continue to navigate our way through the biblical narrative, specifically with the theme of spiritual warfare, we learn the solution and key to victory is to seek God and trust His Word.

LESSON FOUR: *Rebellion to Blessing* (Genesis 11:1-9 – Genesis 12:1-3)

Scope of Lesson Four: In Lesson Four, we are introduced to a key aspect of God's relationship with humans: God's desire to enter into agreements and covenants and to make promises with His creation.

Rationale for Lesson Four: Lesson Four establishes the enduring love that God has for His creation. Despite the human tendency to deny God, to rebel, and to disobey, God's love for us remains constant. God loved His creation so much that He devised a plan to restore humanity through the family of Abraham. Understanding the nature of God to make promises with humanity in a compassionate attempt to restore His creation becomes a key aspect of the continuing biblical narrative.

LESSON FIVE: *The People of Israel* (Exodus 19:1-6)

Scope of Lesson Five: In Lesson Five, we are introduced to a further development in the original promise that God made to the family of Abraham: God extends the covenant promise through Moses to the entire people of Israel.

Rationale for Lesson Five: Lesson Five presents a reoccurring theme of God asking His creation, "Do you believe me?" In Lesson Five, we specifically see this question in the form of Exodus 19:5: "Now, if you will obey Me and carefully keep My covenant... Then you will be My holy nation." This type of promise is very important to understand, for the promise of blessing is made conditional upon people believing and trusting in God. We learn that God always keeps His promise; it is humans who break the conditions of the agreement.

LESSON SIX: *The Commandments and Laws* (Exodus 20-23)

Scope of Lesson Six: God establishes the rules of the covenant by giving the Ten Commandments and other laws His people must keep.

Rationale for Lesson Six: In Lesson Six, we learn that when God makes a promise or enters into a covenant agreement, He is always explicitly clear on the rules of the agreement. This theme of establishing rules and laws further extends the biblical theme of spiritual warfare through our narrative. We specifically learn the initial rules of the agreement were dealing with the actions of humans. Lesson Six continues to teach us about the nature of God: He is merciful and wants partnership with His creation. By establishing the framework of rules and laws, He provides creation with a means to live in peace and under God's favor.

LESSON SEVEN: *The Battle is the Lord's* (Joshua 5:13-15 – Joshua 21:43-45)

Scope of Lesson Seven: After the death of Moses, Joshua is declared the "New Moses" and leads God's people into the Promised Land. We learn that when we are in agreement with God's plan, no opposition can possibly stand in our way.

Rationale for Lesson Seven: As we continue our theme of spiritual warfare through the biblical narrative, a key advantage for God's creation to be victorious is presented: We learn the battle is the Lord's. This is very important to understand, for the human tendency is to feel overwhelmed by the "battle" and to believe we have to do things on our own. Lesson Seven helps us see that when we are in agreement with God's promises, agreements, covenants, and laws, then God will partner with us, and will even fight our battles on our behalf, ensuring our victory. At the end of Joshua, we learn that not only will God fight our battles for us, after His victory, God will fulfill His promises.

LESSON EIGHT: *A Mighty Warrior* (Judges 6:12 - 7:1-8 - 21:25)

Scope of Lesson Eight: Even in the midst of Israel's failure to uphold their covenant agreement, God remains faithful by continuing to build up warriors in His name.

Rationale for Lesson Eight: Following the death of Joshua, power was divided between tribal leaders, chieftains, and judges. The people of Israel, without clear and single-pointed leadership, began to spiral out of control, becoming corrupt and breaking the covenant agreement with God. However, we also learn that God takes steps to rise up warriors in His name, to unify the people of Israel in remembering their promise. Following the spiritual warfare theme through the biblical narrative, we discover that when God spoke over Gideon ("The Lord is with you, mighty warrior"), he was transformed, and became that which God had declared. Finally, we learn the reason for the failure of the people of Israel: they lacked a King (Judges 21:25).

LESSON NINE: *King David* (1 Samuel 16:13 - 17:45 - 17:47 – 2 Samuel 7)

Scope of Lesson Nine: Lesson Nine picks up on the theme of failure due to a lack of leadership. God now rises up King David to unify the people of Israel and reestablish their promise to God. Finally, we are introduced to a new covenant that God establishes with David.

Rationale for Lesson Nine: Continuing the theme of spiritual warfare through our biblical narrative, we are introduced to the character of David, a mighty warrior for God. Once again, the notion that God will fight our battles for us is proven through the epic battle of David and Goliath. We further learn the importance of leadership, and are introduced to the notion that our ultimate leader, through the covenant God makes with David, will be Jesus Christ.

LESSON TEN: *From Conquered to Conquest* (Daniel 6:10-26 - 7:27)

Scope of Lesson Ten: In Lesson Ten, we discover that despite King David and his son King Solomon's best attempt, they ultimately succumbed to temptation, resulting in the conquest of Israel by Babylon. However, we are given hope of a new King that will reign with God over all the nations.

Rationale for Lesson Ten: Once again, we discover that through faith in God, all things are possible. In the context of spiritual warfare, this is a message of great hope and courage. By studying the faith of Daniel, and God's ability to "shut the mouths of the lions," we find inspiration that even the rulers of the world (i.e., King Darius) are no match for God. Finally, we find through the vision of Daniel the hope in a "Son of Man" whose Kingdom will be an everlasting one.

LESSON ELEVEN: *The Hope of a New King* (Haggai 2:21-23 – Malachi 4:1-3)

Scope of Lesson Eleven: As we transition from the Old Testament to the New Testament, we meet two Prophets of God who continue to provide the people of Israel with hope in a bright future, a new Kingdom, and a new King.

Rationale for Lesson Eleven: Despite the failures of the people of Israel and of their leaders, God is committed to remaining faithful to His covenants and promises. We learn through the prophetic word of the prophets, that a new King will soon reign over both heaven and earth, and that His Kingdom will have no end. This hope for the future sets the stage for the Messiah, Jesus Christ, who is the ultimate fulfillment of the Old Testament.

LESSON TWELVE: *Our Savior Jesus Christ* (Matthew 1:17 – 1:23 - 4:17)

Scope of Lesson Twelve: We learn in Lesson Twelve the greatest fulfillment of God's covenants is through His son, Jesus Christ. In Matthew 1:23, the brilliant plan of God is presented when Matthew wrote, "They will call Him Immanuel," which means, "God with us." Rather than speaking through a prophet or delegating His supreme authority, God became man through Jesus Christ.

Rationale for Lesson Twelve: In Lesson Twelve, we are introduced to the fulfillment of God's promise to Abraham, for through the genealogy of Matthew 1:1-3, we discover that Jesus Christ is a "Son of David and a Son of Abraham" and that Jesus will fulfill God's promise to "Bless all the nations." We learn that Jesus' central teaching was: "The Kingdom of God is near," and this was central to God's plan of rescuing His people from the despair they were experiencing at the closing of the Old Testament.

LESSON THIRTEEN: *The Sermon on the Mount* (Matthew 5)

Scope of Lesson Thirteen: Lesson Thirteen introduces us to the first public ministry of Jesus Christ, referred to as the Sermon on the Mount. The parallel between this historic ministry of the "New Law" and Moses' famous sermon on Mount Sinai of the Ten Commandants and "Old Law" becomes apparent.

Rationale for Lesson Thirteen: While the Old Testament, Commandments, and Laws dealt with the external world and the specific actions the Israelites were to take, Jesus taught a new Law that dealt with the mind and the heart. We quickly discover that a central theme in the ministry and teaching of Jesus Christ was his warning to not simply focus on actions (You have heart it said, do not COMMIT adultery) with the word "commit" clearly being the overt act, and Jesus' new teaching, "But I tell you, everyone who looks at a woman to lust for her has already committed adultery with her in his heart" (Matthew 5:28). Therefore, Jesus Christ continues our theme of spiritual warfare, inspiring us to see there is a battle within our own mind that can only be won with God.

LESSON FOURTEEN: *According to Faith* (Matthew 8:23-27 – 9:27-31)

Scope of Lesson Fourteen: Lesson Fourteen is key to understanding that faith in God and in Jesus Christ is absolutely critical for God's blessing in our life.

Rationale for Lesson Fourteen: In the covenants of the Old Testament, we discovered that God's blessing was dependent upon the people of Israel upholding their agreement and promises. These promises were delivered through Moses as the Commandments and Laws. However, in the New

Testament and through the life of Jesus Christ, we learn something profound: In order to receive God's blessing, we must believe and have faith in Jesus Christ. This was beautifully chronicled in Matthew 9:27-31 in the healing of the blind man, whose healing was based upon his faith in Jesus. "Let it be done for you according to your faith" (Matthew 9:29).

LESSON FIFTEEN: *Out of the Mouth* (Matthew 15:10-20 – James 3:1-12)

Scope of Lesson Fifteen: In continuing the theme of tracing spiritual warfare through our biblical narrative, we discover Jesus' teaching a key to our victory: We must overcome the evil nature of our mind through focusing on God.

Rationale for Lesson Fifteen: Continuing the theme of Jesus expanding upon the teachings of the Old Testament, we are introduced to one of the most profound insights that Jesus professed: "It's not what goes into the mouth that defiles a man, but what comes out of the mouth" (Matthew 15:11). This insight is incredibly important, for the focus on the Laws and Commandments of the Old Testament dealt mainly with the overt actions of men and women. However, Jesus was teaching that in order to prevent evil actions in the first place, we must uproot evil thoughts, for thoughts always preceded actions. We now begin to see that many terms of the Old Testament for the "dwelling place of God" were in fact metaphors for the mind and heart of God's creation.

LESSON SIXTEEN: *Death and Resurrection Predicted* (Matthew 16:21-23 – 17:22 – 20:18-19)

Scope of Lesson Sixteen: The apostles of Jesus Christ were familiar with the prophecies of the Old Testament, and believed Jesus was their messiah, and would reign over the coming Kingdom of God. When Jesus predicted his own death, their hope and understanding of the Old Testament was greatly challenged.

Rationale for Lesson Sixteen: The apostles and Jews felt certain, based on Old Testament prophecies, their coming messiah would rule "all the nations" and would live among them. When Jesus predicted his own persecution, death and resurrection, his apostles were greatly troubled, in particular Peter, who said, "Oh no Lord, this could never happen to you" (Matthew 16:22). Jesus' response teaches the key to this lesson, which is humans' tendency to be concerned with the problems of the world, instead of focusing on God and His plan.

LESSON SEVENTEEN: *A New Covenant Proposed* (Matthew 26:26-30)

Scope of Lesson Seventeen: Lesson Seventeen introduces us to the significance of the first Lord's Supper, where Jesus Christ established a new covenant with his disciples.

Rational for Lesson Seventeen: Lesson Seventeen continues the covenant theme through the Bible, reviewing Lessons Five and Six, from the original covenant in the Garden of Eden, to the new covenant established by Jesus Christ. It is very important to understand the new and final covenant with Jesus Christ, for this covenant allows Christ to be with us eternally in God's Kingdom.

LESSON EIGHTEEN: *Greatness in the Kingdom of God* (Luke 22:24-29 – 22:39-46)

Scope of Lesson Eighteen: In Lesson Eighteen, we see Jesus completely turn upside down the commonly held perspective of authority, power, and "greatness." We learn what will truly be considered great in the Kingdom of God is not the standard of greatness in the world of man.

Rationale for Lesson Eighteen: One of the key lessons we learn through the life of Jesus Christ is the importance of seeking God first. From the very beginning, this was the question first posed by God to Adam, "Will you trust Me?" In other words, can we trust that God is greater than anything we could ever hope to achieve or acquire in the world? This age-old question is now posed to the disciples by Jesus, along with a specific solution to avoid the temptation of the world. In Luke 22:46, Jesus says, "Get up and pray, so that you won't enter into temptation." Through prayer, we can keep our minds focused on God, and on seeking Him first.

LESSON NINETEEN: *Death and Resurrection* (Matthew 27:32-37 – 27:50-54 – 27:64-66 – 28:1-7)

Scope of Lesson Nineteen: Lesson Nineteen continues the biblical theme of spiritual warfare in a triumphant and victorious way, for Jesus Christ overcame death through his resurrection.

Rationale for Lesson Nineteen: The theme of spiritual warfare that we have been tracing through the Bible now provides the believer with hope and faith for guaranteed victory over the challenges of the world. In continuance of the new covenant and Lesson Seventeen, we hear the very words of Jesus to his 11 disciples: "And remember, I am with you always, to the end of the age" (Matthew 28:20). This hope in our future, based on the presence of Jesus Christ with us, is a key aspect of the entire Bible story. We no longer have to wait for the arrival of God's Kingdom or a King, for Jesus is now always with us.

LESSON TWENTY: *The Great Commission* (Matthew 28:18-20 – Revelation 5:1-7)

Scope of Lesson Twenty: Lesson Twenty is a milestone in our journey, which now takes the theme of spiritual warfare, and issues the followers of Jesus Christ marching orders to lead the way.

Rationale for Lesson Twenty: Following the resurrection of Jesus Christ, we are presented with a beautiful scene from Scripture in which Jesus tells his disciples that "all authority has been given to me" (Matthew 28:18). Through this authority, Jesus then commissions his disciples, and all those who follow Him, to observe everything that Jesus taught. We discover that not only is Jesus now always with us (Lesson Nineteen), but that Jesus directs those who believe in Him to engage in "spiritual warfare" over the temptations and evils of the world through faith in Him, and by following his teachings. Because Jesus died for our sins, the traditional sacrifices of the Old Testament are no longer required. Rather, we now are called to sacrifice the way of the world for a greater good, which is Jesus Christ and the Kingdom of God.

LESSON TWENTY-ONE: *Union with Christ* (Acts 2 – Colossians 2:9 – Hebrews 1:1-3)

Scope of Lesson Twenty-One: Lesson Twenty-One is the final step of our journey, which is a succinct recapitulation of the Gospel message, and theological foundation for the union with Christ believers can enjoy.

Rationale for Lesson Twenty-One: In Acts 2, the Apostle Peter teaches that Jesus Christ walked the earth in "the fullness of the deity in bodily form" (Col. 2:9) and was "the radiance of God's glory and the exact representation of His being" (Heb. 1:3). Peter's declaration will be echoed throughout the remainder of the New Testament—Jesus was the God-Man to whom all religions point (Jn. 14:6) and to whom all the prophets testified (Heb. 1:1-3). Peter explains that according to God's plan and "with the help of wicked people" Jesus was put to death on the cross (Acts 2:23). However, far from being the end of the story, God raised Jesus from the dead in fulfillment of Old Testament prophecy (Acts 2:24-31; cf. Rom. 8:11-13) and exalted Him to the right hand of the Father (Acts 2:32-33; cf. Rom. 8:34). Peter teaches that the result of the Spirit-empowered confession of sin is a fundamental change of heart about who God is (Acts 2:38). Far greater than a mere change of mind, the new believer's *change of heart* results in an *outward change of behavior* that springs from *an inward change of desires* (1Sa. 16:7; Prov. 4:23; Ezk. 36:26-27).

Through the propitiatory death of Jesus, all who call on His name in faith receive forgiveness of sins (Acts 2:38; cf. Ro. 10:13). The subsequent result is the gift of the Holy Spirit and the new life and heart of Christ (2Cor. 3:18; cf., Col. 3:10). The regenerated Spirit-empowered heart is given for the purpose of living a new life as a Christian and participation in the body of Christ (Acts 2:41-47; cf. 1Co. 12:12-27). A believer whose "heart" is changed through the power of the Holy Spirit will never be the same again (Ps. 51:10; Ezk. 36:26-27).

CHAPTER
THREE

UNDERSTANDING BIBLICAL COVENANTS

IN THE OLD TESTAMENT, the term "covenant" occurs on 285 occasions[9] in which its use represents specific commitments, promises, and obligations between two or more parties. Within the scope of the Bible, the term was most importantly used in agreements between God and His creation. However, the term was also used to establish agreements between humans, to include the holy covenant of marriage, and in a figurative context, even for promises made to oneself.[10] Outside the scope of the Bible, a covenant was historically utilized to govern the international relations between a great king and a vassal king.[11] Therefore, in their historical context, covenants adopted a standardized and structured form in which the promises, stipulations, signs, and witnesses were defined and recorded. For our purposes, it is of immense importance to understand covenants, for God choose to use this format and historical framework to reveal Himself as the Great King, and His creation as vassal kings.[12]

A covenant began with a preamble, which identified the great king who would author the covenant, and who would be responsible for establishing the scope and framework of the agreement to be reached. Next, the covenant included a historical prologue, which served to justify and substantiate the reasons why the vassal king should be obedient to the great king. Next, and of significant importance to the vassal king, the covenant would establish the stipulations that the vassal king would be obligated to perform and uphold. The covenant also included the blessings and benefits the vassal king would enjoy for keeping the covenant, as well as the curses and punishments they should expect for disobedience and breaking the covenant.[13] Finally, witnesses before the agreeing parties and a specific sign of the covenant were formally established.

---

9   *The New Dictionary of Biblical Theology (Downers Grove, IL: InterVarsity Press, 2000). Covenants, p. 420.*
10   Ibid., p. 420
11   Lawrence, Michael. *Theology in the Life of the Church (Wheaton, IL: Crossway, 2010), p. 55.*
12   Ibid., p. 56.
13   This paragraph is largely taken from the section "What is a Covenant" in the book Biblical Theology in the Life of the Church, pg. 56.

THE NOAHIC COVENANT AND THE CULTURAL MANDATE GIVEN TO ADAM

OUR INVESTIGATION INTO BIBLICAL COVENANTS begins with God's initial creation of man and subsequently continues in a more formal manner through God's relationship with Noah. In the creation story of Genesis, the word "covenant" is not used, and therefore many scholars base the covenant agreement between God and Adam in the Garden of Eden on the implied nature of God's gift of life to humanity, and humanity's task of cultivating the garden and trusting God's sovereign rule.[14]

In Genesis 1:26-28, God established His part of the covenant, assigning His creation dominion over the earth, with the specific task to "be fruitful, multiply, fill the earth, and subdue it."[15] It should also be noted that Genesis makes explicitly clear that "God blessed them" through His grace, not by the works of His creation. The stipulation that God established through His first covenant with creation, in addition to "working and watching over the garden of Eden,"[16] was not to eat from the tree of the knowledge of good and evil. The overarching blessing God established with His creation through the first covenant was His grace and the promise of life in Eden in partnership with God. The curse, in the event God's creation violated the covenant, was severe; God said that if man were to eat from the tree of the knowledge of good and evil, he would certainly die.[17]

Following the establishment of God's first covenant with creation, we are introduced to the severe repercussions Adam and Eve experienced for breaking their part of the agreement. However, in Genesis 3, we also note that although Adam and Eve were cast out of Eden, and would experience the consequences of their actions as outlined in Genesis 3:8-19, their lives were spared. This balance of God's continual grace and mercy and creation's continual disobedience against God is a consistent theme through the entire biblical narrative. Furthermore, as Romans 5:12-14 substantiates, the initial covenant established between God and Adam, the first of His creation, extended through the entire world. Therefore, when Adam and Eve disobeyed God, sin entered their individual lives and spread throughout the entire human race.[18]

---

14 *The New Dictionary of Biblical Theology, p. 421.*
15 New King James Bible, Genesis 1:28.
16 Ibid., 2:15.
17 Genesis 2:17.
18 *The New Dictionary of Biblical Theology, p. 49.*

GOD'S COVENANT WITH NOAH

FOLLOWING GOD'S BANISHMENT OF ADAM AND EVE from the garden of Eden, the human race began a downward spiral of sin and wickedness. The extent of evil that God's creation had succumbed to ultimately resulted in "the Lord regretting that He had made man on earth, and He was grieved in His heart."[19] Genesis 6:5 elaborates on the nature of man as observed by God, in that "man's wickedness was widespread on the earth and that every scheme his mind thought was nothing but evil all the time."

In Genesis 6:18, we see the first mention of the word "covenant" in the Bible. God explains to Noah that He is going to bring a flood, and that the floodwaters will destroy every creature "with the breath of life in it. Everything on earth will die."[20] However, through the establishment of a covenant, God promised that Noah, his family, and "two of all living creatures"[21] would be spared.

In Genesis 8 and Genesis 9, we again see the specific use of the word "covenant" in addition to stipulations and promises on behalf of God and His creation. After the floodwaters receded, Noah built an alter to the Lord, and made burnt offerings upon it.[22] When God smelled the "pleasing aroma, He said to Himself, 'I will never again curse the ground because of man ... I will never again strike down every living thing as I have done.'"[23] God then blessed Noah and commanded Noah to be fruitful, and to multiply and fill the earth. The promise that God established with Noah was made abundantly clear in Genesis 8:22, in which God promised that "day and night will never cease."[24]

In the context of continuity with God's initial covenant with Adam, it is interesting to note the similarity in God's commands to Noah and Adam. On both occasions, God called His creation to rule and establish dominion over the earth. God specifically placed every living creature under the rule and authority of both Adam and Noah. Furthermore, God provided Adam and Noah the right to eat with great discretion, with the exception for Adam being the tree of the knowledge of good and evil, and for Noah, the restriction of not eating meat

---

19   Genesis 6:6.
20   Genesis 6:17.
21   Genesis 6:19.
22   Genesis 8:20.
23   Genesis 8:21.
24   Genesis. 8:22.

with its lifeblood in it. Also, in the context of continuity, God established in His covenant with Noah a covenant with all of mankind, for God said, "I am confirming My covenant with you and your descendants after you."[25]

In the context of discontinuity, God established a very clear sign of His covenant with Noah. However, a covenant sign was not established with Adam. In the case of Noah, God placed "His bow in the clouds"[26] and promised that every time He observed His bow in the clouds, He would remember His covenant, and that "water will never again become a flood to destroy every creature."[27] God spoke to Noah, and acknowledged for the certainty and remembrance of them both, that the rainbow would serve as a sign of their covenant.

THE ABRAHAMIC COVENANT

GOD'S FIRST CALL TO ABRAM (who subsequently became known as Abraham) is recorded in Genesis 12. Following the fall and scattering of the nations at Babylon, the Lord told Abraham to go to the land He would show him. The initial covenant story between God and Abraham thus begins at this part in the biblical narrative. It is important to note that God makes the majority of the initial promises. Abraham's first and only obligated requirement is to trust God and follow His direction.

In Genesis 12, although the word "trust" is not used in the text, the stipulation made upon Abraham by God is to trust His leadership and direction. In Genesis 12.1, God tells Abraham to "go out from your land"[28] and to leave his relatives and his father's house. This requirement of trust is further substantiated by the fact Abraham was already 75 years old.[29] With the exception of the implied requirement to trust God and follow His directions, there are no further specific stipulations on Abraham's part at this point in the biblical narrative.

Immediately after telling Abraham to go to the land that He would show him, God made several promises to Abraham. The specific unilateral promises

---

25   Genesis 9:9.
26   Genesis 9:13.
27   Genesis 9:15.
28   Genesis 12.1.
29   Genesis 12:4.

God made to Abraham in the first call were:

1. Making Abraham into a great nation;
2. Making Abraham's name great;
3. Abraham would be a blessing;
4. God would bless those who bless Abraham;
5. God would curse those who treated Abraham with contempt;
6. God would bless all the peoples on earth through Abraham.[30]

In Genesis 15, we see a continuance of the promises between God and Abraham, in addition to the explicit language of the covenant recorded in Genesis 15:18. In Genesis 15:1, God promised Abraham that his reward would be very great. Telling Abraham to look at all the stars in the sky, the Lord promised Abraham that his offspring would be that numerous.[31] In addition to promising Abraham an extensive offspring, the Lord also promised to give Abraham "this land that he possessed."[32]

In Genesis 15:8, Abraham asked God for a sign so that he would know with certainty what God had promised. Although not necessarily a sign of the covenant (subsequently articulated in Genesis 17 through circumcision), God answered Abraham in Genesis 15:9, commanding Abraham to bring Him "a three year old cow, a three year old female goat, a three year old ram, a turtledove, and a young pigeon."[33] Abraham split them down the middle and laid the pieces opposite each other. In Genesis 15:17, we discover "a smoking fire pot and a flaming torch appeared and passed between the divided animals." Immediately thereafter, Genesis records that on that specific day, God made a covenant with Abraham.

Many scholars believe the initial covenant established between God and Abraham in Genesis 15 was unilateral in nature. This claim is substantiated by the fact that as the Spirit of God passed between the divided animals, Abraham remained only a spectator; it was God alone who took on obligations.[34] However, as the initial covenant of Genesis 15 is expanded upon throughout the book of Genesis, the bilateral nature of the promises and stipulations between God and Abraham become more evident and further shaped.

In Genesis 18:19, God explained that in order for blessing to extend through

---

30   Unilateral promises 1–6 identified in Genesis 12:1-3.
31   Genesis 15:5.
32   Genesis 15:7.
33   Genesis 15:9.
34   *The New Dictionary of Biblical Theology, p. 423.*

Abraham to all the nations of the earth, Abraham must "teach his children and his house after him to keep the way of the Lord by doing what is right and just."[35] Further evidence of the bilateral nature of the Abrahamic covenant is subsequently seen in Genesis 22:18 when God specifically explained that because Abraham obeyed God, all the nations of the earth would be blessed by his offspring. Therefore, in the context of continuity between the covenant first established at the creation of man through Noah and Abraham, we see the overarching theme of God requiring humankind to trust Him and remain obedient.

The requirement of obedience to God on humankind's part was put to the ultimate test in Genesis 22. Because Abraham completely trusted God and remained obedient to Him, the Lord declared, "Because you have done this thing" Abraham would be blessed. This part of the biblical covenant story, and indeed the very use of the word "because," is of immense importance, for we see that God's blessing upon Abraham was absolutely dependent upon Abraham's trust and obedience to God. Following Abraham's confirmation of obedience, God promised, "All the nations of the earth will be blessed by your offspring because you have obeyed My command."[36]

It should also be noted the manner in which the initial promises God made to Abraham were expanded through Genesis. For example, in Genesis 15, the promises God made with regard to Abraham's possession of land was restricted to specific geographic territories.[37] However, in Genesis 17, God was much more expansive and unrestrictive in His promises. For example, in Genesis 17:5, when God changed Abram's name to "Abraham" God bestowed the title, "Father of all nations," onto him. Furthermore, in 17:6-7, God extended the territory of Abraham's rule to "Many nations," and promised that "nations and kings will come through you." God's promise as defined in Genesis 17:8 was also noted as being an "eternal possession."

An area of continuity between the Noahic and Abrahamic covenants was God's establishment of a covenant sign. God's sign of the covenant for Noah was His "bow in the clouds." In the covenant God made with Abraham, God required Abraham to circumcise every one of his males at eight days of age.[38] These covenant signs were established both as a reminder for God to uphold His promise, and for Noah and Abraham to remain faithful and in agreement to their promises to God.

---

35   Genesis 18:19.
36   Genesis 22:18.
37   Genesis 15:18-21.
38   Genesis 17:10-12.

THE MOSAIC COVENANT

AS WE CONTINUE OUR GOAL of understanding biblical covenants, we now turn our attention to the Mosaic Covenant established in Exodus 20-25. The redemptive and historical context takes shape with God observing the "afflictions of His people" and delivering them out of "the hands of the Egyptians."[39] We discover almost immediately the bilateral nature of the Mosaic Covenant in God's declaration: "Now, therefore, *if* ye will obey my voice indeed, and keep my covenant, *then* ye shall be a peculiar treasure onto me above all people."[40] This verse in particular highlights the relationship of the Covenant in the context of "If – Then." In order for Moses and the people of Israel to receive God's blessing, they must keep His covenant and uphold specific stipulations that God will give to Moses.

It is important to note, as was common practice in the establishment of a covenant between a great king and vassal king, that Exodus includes a formal review of the favor and blessing the Great King (God) had already provided to Israel. For example, in Exodus 19:4, God spoke to Moses and said, "You have seen what I did unto the Egyptians, and how I bear you on eagles' wings, and brought you onto myself."[41] Following the recapitulation of God's favor, God immediately continues to build upon the former blessing with an even more profound promise. God declared to Moses, "*If* you will obey my voice, and keep my covenant, *then* you shall be a particular treasure onto Me above all people."[42] Therefore, Exodus 19:4 and 19:5, in the context of understanding the Mosaic Covenant, are extremely significant for they outline the bilateral nature of the covenant and provide encouragement for the magnitude of blessing that God had in store for Israel if they would love and obey God and keep their promises.

After outlining the general bilateral nature of the covenant, God continued to expand upon the stipulations that Israel must keep in order to remain in God's favor. The specific commandments given by God at Mt. Sinai were meant to ensure obedience to God and to firmly establish Israel as a "holy Nation." God spoke to Moses and articulated the following commandments and stipulations:

39 Exodus 3:7-8 – my emphasis of "*If – Then.*"
40 Exodus 19:5.
41 Exodus 19:4.
42 Exodus 19:5 – my emphasis of "*If – Then.*"

1. The people of Israel were to have no other gods before God;
2. They were not to make a "graven image, or any likeness of any thing" and worship it;
3. They were not to take the name of the Lord in vain;
4. They were to remember the Sabbath day and keep it holy;
5. They were to honor their mother and father;
6. They were not to kill;
7. Nor commit adultery;
8. Nor steal;
9. Nor bear false witness against their neighbor;
10. Nor covet their neighbors house, or wife, or other property.[43]

If God's covenant was kept, then God promised the establishment of a "kingdom of priests, and a holy nation."[44] In the context of continuity with the Abrahamic Covenant, we see an extension of God's promise in Genesis 15 of making Israel a "Great Nation." However, through the Mosaic Covenant, the "greatness" is now elaborated upon and takes the distinct shape of a holy and "Priestly" people and nation. Furthermore, we see continuity in the context of God requiring obedience to specific behaviors in order to remain within the blessing of the covenant.

In the context of discontinuity with the previous covenant, the obligations and stipulations of the Mosaic Covenant create a distinct framework of privilege and responsibility between God and His people.[45] Furthermore, the stipulations were extensively increased and required greater obedience on Israel's part. For example, God made it abundantly clear His expectation was that Israel remained a distinct nation in order to retain their occupation of the promised land. Although the sign of the covenant through circumcision was retained through the Mosaic Covenant, there was an additional sign that was established through the Sabbath: the requirement to honor the Sabbath, and keep it holy.

---

43   Exodus 20:3-1.7.
44   Exodus 19:6.
45   *The New Dictionary of Biblical Theology (Downers Grove, IL: InterVarsity Press, 2000). Covenants, p. 423.*

THE DAVIDIC COVENANT

THE BIBLICAL REDEMPTIVE STORY now continues to unfold and we discover that God would establish David as a king over Israel, and that the promises made to Abraham would be extended and ultimately fulfilled through David's royal line.[46] The Davidic Covenant is established in 2 Samuel 7 and carries within it several close connections to the Abrahamic Covenant. We immediately take notice of the transference of responsibility to reflect God's glory from the nation to a king, namely the line of David. This is a key progression from the former covenant, in that David, as the king, represents the entire nation. Therefore, the relationship between the Great King (God) and vassal king (David) becomes clearly defined.[47]

There are several areas of continuity between the Abrahamic and Davidic Covenants. We begin by taking note that in Genesis 12:2 and 2 Samuel 7:9, God promised both Abraham and David a "great name." Furthermore, in Genesis 22:17 and 2 Samuel 7:11, we observe both Abraham and David were promised "victory over their enemies."[48] Finally, both Abraham and David were required to keep God's laws, although we now observe a unique maturation between God's law and David's obligations begins to take shape.

In 2 Samuel 7:10-16, we observe several additional and significant promises that God made to David in their newly established covenant. First, God promised to appoint a place for His people where they will "move no more."[49] In addition, in 2 Samuel 7:10, God also promised a clearly defined progression from the "Wickedness" that Israel had experienced before, to a state of blessing and favor. God also promised that David's "Seed" would be established on a throne that would "rule his kingdom forever." This is also a beautiful and monumental part of scripture, where we observe insight into the permanent rule of David's seed through the "son of God."

The stipulations between God and David were outlined in 2 Samuel 7:14 and Psalm 132:12. We first observe the "If – Then" type language that was also noted in the Mosaic Covenant. God declared, "If he commit iniquity" then God would "chasten him with the rod of men, and with the stripes of the

---

46   The Bible Project, Study Guide for Covenants, p. 7.
47   *The New Dictionary of Biblical Theology, p. 425.*
48   Ibid., p. 425.
49   2 Samuel 7:10.

children of men."[50] In Psalm 132:12, we note that David clearly established the bilateral nature of the covenant, for he acknowledged that *if* his children kept the covenant with God, *then* his children would remain on the throne. In this context, both God and David utilize the "If – Then" language to clearly establish the bilateral nature of the covenant, and to bring attention to the promise and consequences of disobedience.

The sign of the Davidic Covenant was the birth of a son that would continue David's line or rule, even after his death. As noted earlier, this beautiful and foretelling verse of the coming Son of God was brought to our attention in 2 Samuel 7:14, when God declared, "I will be his father, and he shall be my son." In 2 Samuel 7:16, within the same verse, God reiterated that David's kingdom and throne would be established forever. In this context, we also observe a key area of discontinuity from the former covenant with Moses and Abraham. Rather than promising blessing to a specific region and people, through David and "His seed" we now discover that God's blessing would be extended through all nations and all people. For example, in Psalm 72:11, we observe that "all kings shall fall down before him, and all nations shall serve him."[51] This promise was then expanded upon in verse 17 and served to clarify the "worldly rule" of David's line: "His name shall endure forever, his name shall be continued as long as the sun."

In a final and foretelling area of continuity with the Noahic and Mosaic covenants, we sadly observe the theme of failure to maintain "irreproachable behavior."[52] Although God's promise to bless the nations through Abraham's seed would be fulfilled through David's line, we soon discover this would be accomplished *supernaturally* and not merely biologically.[53]

THE NEW COVENANT

THE BIBLICAL REDEMPTIVE STORY continues to unfold through the conclusion of the Old Testament, and we discover Israel failed to maintain the terms of the covenant established in the Davidic covenant. Furthermore, the

---

50 1 Samuel 7:14.

51 Psalm 72:11.

52 *The New Dictionary of Biblical Theology, p. 426.*

53 *The New Dictionary of Biblical Theology, p. 426.*

kings and rulers who were acting in the capacity of vassal kings with God were unfaithful to their covenant made with David. In 2 Kings 17, we read, "For so it was, the children of Israel had sinned against the Lord their God."[54] It is important at this point in the biblical story to observe the specific violation of the covenant agreements that Israel made, many of which had been established during the Mosaic covenant.

In this context, we see the continuity of the previous covenant stipulations through the Davidic covenant, and also note the continued failure of God's people to uphold their commitments. In 2 Kings 7:12, we discover that despite God's commandment that Israel not serve idols, this was exactly what they had succumbed to doing. 2 Kings 17 also uses the specific covenant language, for in verse 15 we read, "They rejected his statues, and his covenant that he made with their fathers." As a result of Israel's failure to uphold their covenant agreement, and the blatant disregard and violation of their promises, we read that "the Lord was very angry with Israel, and removed them out of his sight."[55] The culmination of Israel's continual tendency to "walk in the way of sin" resulted in Israel being "carried out of their own land" and sent into exile into Babylon.[56]

Despite Israel's exile, we discover that Israel's prophets remained optimistic and foretold of a day when all of God's covenant promises would be fulfilled for all the nations. In Isaiah 9, we discover God's covenant would ultimately be fulfilled through "God's Son" and the "government will be upon his shoulder." We further discover the newly established covenant would "have no end, upon the throne of David, and upon his kingdom, and to establish it with judgment and with justice from henceforth even forever."[57]

One of the first specific mentions of a "new covenant" took place in Jeremiah 31. We discover that despite Israel's exile and failure to uphold their promises, through God's continual grace, another opportunity to receive His blessing still awaited His people. It is interesting to note, in the context of continuity and discontinuity with previously established covenants, that God also addressed this very issue. In Isaiah 31:32, God declared that "not according to the covenant that I made *in that day* I took them by the hand to bring them out of the land of Egypt, which my covenant they broke." In

---

54   2 Kings 17:7.
55   2 Kings 17:18.
56   2 Kings 17:22-23.
57   Isaiah 9:6-7.

this verse, we discover God specifically addressed the Mosaic covenant, and the fact that Israel had violated their promises. Yet we also take note in the following verse that God would extend previously enacted covenant promises into a new covenant of everlasting proportion.

In Isaiah verse 33, we read that God would establish a new covenant, and that God would "put His law in their inward parts, and write it in their hearts; and I will be their God, and they shall be my people." The mighty declaration of God in verse 33, "I will be their God and they shall be my people," clearly served the function of a "covenant formula" and thus maintained continuity with previous covenants.[58] This magnificent verse also brings awareness to God's intention, through the new covenant, to effect change in Israel's "Inward parts" and their "Heart" and not simply their actions.

In the Gospel of Matthew, we further discover the new covenant would be an eternal and everlasting covenant with God and the people of all nations. In this context, the new covenant encompassed all the promises of the Old Testament, such as physical inheritance; a divine-human relationship between the Great King (God), the vassal king, and all the nations' people; and blessing on a national and international scale.[59] The promises of the covenants God made with Noah, Abraham, Moses, and David would find their ultimate fulfillment through Jesus Christ in the new covenant.[60]

The new covenant with Jesus Christ was expressly stated in Matthew 26:28, during the Lords supper, when Jesus said, "For this is my blood of the new testament, which is shed for many for the remission of sins." The blessing and promise through Jesus Christ in the new covenant was the "forgiveness of sins" and entrance into the Kingdom of God, which essentially served to release God's people from the curse of violating the stipulations of the previous covenants.

The promises extended through the new covenant were now made accessible and available to all those who believed in Jesus Christ. This was a clear progression and area of discontinuity from previous covenants, which focused more on "heirs" of Abraham's seed in the biological context.[61] In Romans 11:26, the saving grace of the new covenant was clearly presented to all of Israel. The new covenant with Jesus Christ was chronicled in Hebrews as being superior to all previous covenants. Hebrews 7:22 declared, "By so

---

58   The New Dictionary of Biblical Theology, p. 427.
59   Ibid., p. 427.
60   Ibid., p. 427.
61   Ibid., p. 427.

much was Jesus made a surety of a better testament." Furthermore, in Hebrews 8:6, we discover, "Jesus now hath obtained a more excellent ministry, by how much also he is the mediator of a better covenant, which was established upon better promises."

In Hebrews 8:9-12, it is interesting and significant to note Old Testament covenant scripture (Jeremiah), which further substantiated the fact that Jesus was the fulfillment of all previously established covenants. Additionally, we note that the covenants of the Old Testament were "remembered no more" through the establishment of the new covenant with Jesus Christ. The sign of the new covenant was baptism, which would provide for the forgiveness of sins and serve to create a true heart and faith in Jesus Christ.[62] These promises are of truly magnificent proportion, for through Jesus Christ and the new covenant, all who believe in Him are able to receive forgiveness for their sins and receive everlasting life in the Kingdom of God.

CONCLUSION

UNDERSTANDING THE COVENANTS is of immense importance in tracing God's promise of eternal salvation through the entire biblical narrative. The covenants express God's intention to establish both sovereign rule and harmonious partnership with His creation. Ultimately, through Jesus Christ, God chooses to live among us in order to completely fulfill His promises, and to bring His people into the Kingdom of God.

---

62   Hebrews 10:22.

CHAPTER
FOUR

THE BOOK OF HAGGAI AND PUTTING FIRST THINGS FIRST

CONTEXT

THE BOOK OF HAGGAI is a series of four messages, occurring over an approximate four-month time span, which serve to challenge and encourage the people of Israel to "go up into the mountains and bring down timber and build the house of the LORD" (Haggai 1:8). Each message serves to progressively build momentum within the mind of the reader, effectively leading the Israelites out of their present poverty (Haggai 1:5-6, 9-11) to a renewed state of promise and blessedness (Haggai 2:10-19, 2:20-23). The specific text for purposes of my investigation and exposition (Haggai 2:10-19) occur during Haggai's third message, and contain a promise of blessing for the people of Israel once their spiritual priorities had been correctly established.

Haggai teaches the Israelites a key spiritual principle with resounding implication for their present state of poverty (Haggai 1:5-6, 9-11). The principle is beautifully illustrated by a metaphor that explains the fact that spiritual uncleanness contaminates the temporal matters of the world (Haggai 2:11-14).[63] Haggai's third message is also notable for a sharp rebuke by the LORD, "Whatever they do and whatever they offer is defiled" (Haggai 2:14). The metaphor of contamination, presented by Haggai in his third message, offers wonderful insight into his first message, which contrasted the Israelites "expecting much, yet returning little" (Haggai 1:9).

Haggai's third message also contains a key passage with immense historical and cultural ramification. In the book of Deuteronomy, Moses foretold of two specific curses the Israelites would experience for "not obeying the LORD" (Deuteronomy 28:15). These curses included "being struck with blight and mildew" (Deuteronomy 28:22) and were therefore identical to the curses spoken by Haggai (Haggai 2:17).[64] This particular verse, supported by the entirety of Haggai's third message, served to teach the Israelites the agricultural curse they were experiencing was the direct result of "not returning to God" (Haggai 2:19). Although the Israelites certainly felt the

---

63   This observation and subsequent principle were discovered within the text of Haggai 1:9a: "You expected much (temporal matters of the world), but it turned out to be little." The explanation for the worldly poverty is juxtaposed within the same verse, "because of my house (in ruin, resulting in spiritual uncleanness) which remains in ruin, while each of you is busy with your own house" (Haggai 1:9b).

64   Haggai also included the curse of hail (Haggai 2:17), which would have a devastating effect on the Israelites' vineyards.

hand of God against them (Haggai 1:5-6, 9-11, 2:15-17), they had failed to "return to God" by not repenting of their sin, not reestablishing their spiritual priorities, and neglecting to rebuild the temple (Haggai 1:9).

Haggai's third message is also notable for the trajectory of the text, which is the magnificent promise to exalt Israel through Zerubbabel (Haggai 2:20-23). Were the book of Haggai to end with his third message, the reader would be left desiring more context and greater insight into the verse, "From this day on I will bless you" (Haggai 2:19). As the reader continues into Haggai's fourth and final message, the discovery is made, and the most demanding and hopeful expectations are met. The enemies of God will be overthrown (Haggai 2:22) and Zerubbabel is promised a place in God's future kingdom (Haggai 2:23), which is a promise that extends beyond Zerubbabel to the Davidic line that he represents.[65]

SETTING

THE HISTORICAL SETTING and backdrop for Haggai's prophecy was the reign of King Darius I, the King of Persia from 521 – 486 BC. Following the overthrow of the Babylonian empire by the Medo-Persian alliance in 539 BC, Cyrus issued a decree that displaced peoples, including the Israelites, could return to their homelands (Ezra 1:1-4).[66] The first wave of displaced people to return to Jerusalem was led by Sheshbazzar (Ezra 1:5-11) and numbered 42,360 Israelites, plus an additional 7,337 servants and 200 male and female singers (Ezra 2:64-65). Sheshbazzar was a prince of Judah, and through his governorship the foundation of a new temple was laid during the early stages of his administration (Ezra 5:16).

Although the first wave of emigrants to Jerusalem were able to lay the foundation of the temple, the people's response upon the observance of the completed work had mixed emotions. "No one could distinguish the sound of the shouts of joy from the sound of weeping, because the people made so much noise" (Ezra 3:13). The temple rebuilding project and initial momentum soon faded, largely due to the fact that the Israelites faced the challenges of living in a city surrounded by hostile foreigners (Ezra 4:4), and were further plagued by drought and crop failure (Haggai 1:6, 1:9-11).[67] To make matters worse, rather than focusing on rebuilding

---

65   Laney, Dr. Carl. *Essential Bible Background (CreateSpace, 2016)*, p. 147.

66   Tuck, Dr. Gary. *The Arguments of the Books of the Old Testament (Dr. Gary Tuck, 2011)*, p. 279.

67   Hill & Walton. *A Survey of the Old Testament (Zondervan, 2009)*, p. 679.

the temple, the people had become preoccupied with rebuilding their personal lives.[68] "Because of my house, which remains a ruin, while each of you is busy with your own house" (Haggai 1:9).

The second group of displaced people to return to Jerusalem was led by Zerubbabel and Jeshua, who arrived in Jerusalem in approximately 522 BC. Zerubbabel became the new governor and Jeshua the high priest (Haggai 1:1). Jeshua and the people became inspired by the prophet Haggai (Haggai 1:13-14) and subsequently mobilized for a second reconstruction effort. The rebuilding of the temple was finally finished in 515 BC (Ezra 6:15), approximately 17 years after the inception of the project led by Sheshbazzar.

The historical setting contributes to my understanding of the text by illustrating that although the hardship the Israelites were facing was physical in nature (Haggai 1:5-7), the cause of the hardship was in fact spiritual (Haggai 2:14). This distinction is important in the context of teaching and preaching God's Word, for oftentimes people are preoccupied with seeking personal comforts (Haggai 1:3, in his reference to living in a "paneled house"), rather than seeking to please God. The text provides sharp contrast between the curse that results from neglecting God (Haggai 1:6, 1:9-11) and the blessing that results from serving Him (Haggai 2:18-23).

PURPOSE

THE APOSTLE PAUL WROTE, "All Scripture is God-breathed and is useful for teaching, rebuking, correcting, and training in righteousness, so that the man of God may be complete, equipped for every good work" (2 Timothy 3:16-17). God intends His Word to "complete" us, so that we can serve His purposes. Since God designed the Bible to complete us for the purpose of His glory, the implication within Paul's verse is that in some sense, we are incomplete without His Word. From this perspective, all Scripture was inspired within the mind of the biblical author by the Holy Spirit in order to address a specific human concern, sin, transgression, or condition of brokenness, and to "correct, rebuke, and encourage" humankind to return to God (2 Timothy 4:1-2).

The purpose of the book of Haggai is to succinctly teach the progressive manner in which God's Word can address a fallen condition (rebuke), mandate thoughtful

---

68   Laney, Dr. Carl. *Essential Bible Background (CreateSpace, 2016), p. 144.*

consideration for the present conditions of life (correction), and then to encourage and teach the necessary steps for reconciliation with God. The book of Haggai is a brilliant case study that historically depicts the purpose of God's Word to empower humankind "for every good work" (2 Timothy 3:17, Haggai 2:9).

The book of Haggai presents four interrelated messages, which challenge the Israelites to initiate the reconstruction of the temple of God that had been destroyed by the Babylonians nearly 70 years earlier.[69] Over a 3½-month period, Haggai rebuked, challenged, and encouraged the Israelites to complete the temple project that had initially been commissioned to Sheshbazzar (Ezra 5:16). In addition to rebuilding the physical structure of the temple, Haggai also called the people back to proper worship of God, and to remain in faithful covenant with Him (Haggai 2:5).

The first message (Haggai 1:2-11) confronted the people's compliancy and failure to rebuild the temple, which had resulted in famine and infertility (Haggai 1:6, 9-11). The people's response (Haggai 1:12-15) demonstrated their faithful acknowledgement and admittance of the accusations of Haggai and proved their obedience to God's Word. The second message (Haggai 2:1-9) offered encouragement to the people that despite the humble appearance of the temple (Haggai 2:3) there would come a time when "the glory of this present house will be greater than the glory of the former house" (Haggai 2:9).

The third message (Haggai 2:10-19) continued to offer encouragement in the form of a present-promise that "from this day on I will bless you" (Haggai 2:19). The fourth and final message (Haggai 2:20-23) provided a future and divine promise to Zerubbabel (Haggai 2:20-23) and ensured the preservation of the Davidic line until the coming of Jesus Christ.[70]

THEME

THE TEMPLE REPRESENTED God's abiding presence with His people and served as a tangible reminder of His covenant with Israel (1 Kings 6:13). The temple of Yahweh was closely associated with the Davidic monarchy, and may be traced to David's heartfelt desire to build a temple for God, which contrasted with God's promise to build a dynasty for David (2 Samuel 7:2, 10-16). The temple symbolized

---

69   Hill & Walton. *A Survey of the Old Testament (Zondervan, 2009)*, p. 680.
70   Laney, Dr. Carl. *Essential Bible Background (CreateSpace, 2016)*, p. 147.

the Israelites' peace with God, and also peace within the land (1 Kings 5:3-4).[71] Furthermore, the physical structure of the temple was an objective measure of God's favor on His people, and provided the Israelites with the assurance that "God would live among the Israelites and will not abandon my people Israel" (1 Kings 6:13).

The prophet Haggai arrived on scene against the backdrop of a destroyed and looted temple (2 Kings 25:8-17). In this context, the enthusiasm of Haggai for completing the construction of the temple may be understood and appreciated (Haggai 1:8). The new temple would once again represent God's presence with His people (Haggai 1:13, 2:4) and provide a renewing of covenantal blessing for the Israelites (Haggai 2:19). It is extremely important to note that in addition to rebuilding the physical structure of the temple (Haggai 1:13), the prophet Haggai also mandated proper and true worship of God (Haggai 1:5). The distinction between worshiping God and remaining obedient to Him, and simply having faith in a temple-building, was also a key message of the prophet Jeremiah (Jeremiah 7:4).[72]

Based on this evidence, the rebuilding and completion of the temple is the major theme of the book of Haggai. However, it is important to note that the theme of rebuilding the physical structure of the temple (Haggai 1:4) served to illustrate the complementary theme of misplaced priorities. The Israelites were overly concerned with matters pertaining to "business within their own house" (Haggai 1:9), rather than focusing on proper worship of God. The Israelites' misplaced priorities resulted in their "expectation of much, but fulfillment of little" (Haggai 1:9). Haggai encouraged the people to understand that through obedience and proper worship of God, the completed temple would ensure their renewed blessing and favor in the eyes of God (Haggai 2:19).[73]

THEOLOGY

THE BOOK OF HAGGAI INCLUDES several themes and concepts from Israel's rich theological heritage that serve the purpose of advancing God's redemptive plan for His creation through the work of Jesus Christ. Within the text of Haggai 2:10-19, three specific and major theological points are made: the "Lord

---

71   Hill & Walton. *A Survey of the Old Testament (Zondervan, 2009)*, p. 683.

72   This observation was brought to my attention in M. J. Evans' article *Blessing and Curse*, in *The New Dictionary of Biblical Theology*, (InterVarsity Press, 2000), p. 399.

73   Hill & Walton. *A Survey of the Old Testament (Zondervan, 2009)*, p. 683.

Almighty," the divine blessing of God, and the purpose of the temple for God's people. These three theological points ultimately converge in the emphasis placed by Haggai upon rebuilding the temple.

The history of the temple dates to Moses, who declared that God would establish a place for proper worship of His name (Deuteronomy 14:23-25). During the era of the tribal league, the interim site for Yahweh's presence was within the tabernacle at Shiloh (Joshua 18:1). King David obtained the permanent site for Yahweh's name when he purchased the threshing floor of Araunah near Jerusalem (2 Samuel 24:18-25) and collected the material needed for the temple construction (1 Chronicles 22:1-16). Under the leadership of David's son Solomon, the temple project was completed, and the glory of Yahweh entered the sanctuary upon Solomon's prayer of dedication (1 Kings 8). The completed temple symbolized Israel's peace with God and peace within the land (1 Kings 5:3-4). In addition, the physical existence of the temple served as a tangible reminder of God's covenant with Israel.[74]

The destruction of the temple of God in 587 BC by King Nebuchadnezzar and the Babylonians symbolized the alienation of Israel from God, the apparent end of the reign of David's line, and the loss of the Promised Land to invading nations (2 Kings 25:8-21).[75] Therefore, the enthusiasm of Haggai for rebuilding the temple can be understood, as the new temple would represent a renewing of God's favor and presence among His chosen people (Haggai 1:13, 2:4). Haggai's use of the phrase, "Lord Almighty," in verse 2:11 linked his message with Israel's past (2 Samuel 6:2, 7:8) and indicated that the great covenant God of Israel's history was the same God who spoke to the post-exilic community.[76]

The theological point of divine blessing may be traced all the way to the creation account of Genesis, in the context of perfect harmony between God and humanity (Genesis 1:22).[77] Haggai encouraged the people to understand that rebuilding the temple would result in the beginning of renewed harmony with God, and usher in a new era of blessing (Haggai 2:19). The combination of the completed temple and the ensuing blessing that would follow helped pave the way for the work of Jesus Christ.

The ministry of Jesus Christ revealed the beautiful and ultimate theological truth the temple of God was intended for. Throughout the Old Testament, the temple represented God's reconciliation and presence with His people. However, the work of Jesus Christ made reconciliation between humankind

---

74 Ibid.
75 Alexander & Rosner, *The New Dictionary of Biblical Theology*, *(InterVarsity Press 2000), p. 257.*
76 Ibid. The term "Lord Almighty" is used nearly 300 times in the Old Testament, with 14 occurrences in Haggai.
77 Ibid.

and God a present reality through his sacrificial death at Calvary (Matthew 12:6). Through Jesus Christ's death and resurrection, the theology of the temple transitioned from a physical structure to the indwelling presence of Christ's Spirit within the body of each individual believer. Furthermore, through the sacrificial death of Christ, the individual believer is now permanently reconciled to God, and becomes an heir of the blessing promised to Abraham (Galatians 3:10-14).

APPLICATION

THE BOOK OF HAGGAI IS A BRILLIANT case study that historically depicts the purpose of God's Word to empower humankind "for every good work" (2 Timothy 3:17, Haggai 2:9). The Apostle Paul wrote that "all scripture is God-breathed and is useful for teaching, rebuking, correcting, and training in righteousness, so that the man of God may be complete, equipped for every good work" (2 Timothy 3:16-17). From this perspective, the Holy Spirit inspired within the mind of Haggai certain biblical principles that require both "thinking about such things" and "putting such things into practice" (Philippians 4:8-9). In my close study of the book of Haggai, I discovered four key biblical principles that have immense relevance and application to life.

The first biblical principle is that disobedience to God results in unfavorable consequences. Haggai helped the people of Israel realize that their failure to rebuild the house of God equated to disobeying Him, and was the cause of the famine and infertility they were now experiencing (Haggai 1:6, 9-11, 2:14). The first truth principle reveals that the fallen condition of mankind is to focus on the material goods of the world (Haggai 1:4). In many respects, rather than *seeking righteousness with God*, the tendency of humanity is to seek *right conditions* in the world. However, God calls us to seek Him first and the spiritual benefits of His Kingdom, which result in "everything else being added to us as well" (Luke 12:31, Haggai 2:19).

The second biblical principle discovered in the book of Haggai is that obedience to God results in His encouragement and Spirit upon us (Haggai 1:14, 2:4-5, 2:19). The relevance of this specific truth principle is immense: When we are obedient to God, He empowers us for His purposes in our life, and we become capable of doing more for His Kingdom than we could ever achieve on our own (Philippians 4:13). Haggai provides the people of Israel with the motivation to labor under difficult conditions by assuring them that "the glory of this present house will be greater than the glory of the former house" (Haggai 2:9).

The third biblical principle discovered within the book of Haggai is that misplaced priorities result in the demands of the world crowding out our worship of God. The ensuing result and relevance to life is that when God becomes second place, we end up working harder and harder, while achieving less and less (Haggai 1:9, 2:14-16). In the case of Haggai, the people had become consumed with rebuilding their paneled houses, while the house of God remained a ruin (Haggai 1:4). The Israelites' misplaced priorities had resulted in painful consequences: "Whatever they do and whatever they offer is defiled" (Haggai 2:14). Even today, the "paneled houses" of our lives oftentimes lead to temporally urgent matters crowding out spiritually eternal priorities.[78] Haggai teaches the futility of seeking comfort and fulfillment in anything other than God.

The fourth and final truth principle discovered within the book of Haggai was revealed to me through the power of the Holy Spirit in the form of a mathematical equation:

WITH	GOD'S SPIRIT	PLUS	WORK	OVER TIME	EQUALS VICTORY

The proof text for this equation has three distinct parts that work in a linear and progressive manner. When *God's Spirit* is with us (Haggai 1:14a) and we are willing to subject ourselves to *Work* (Haggai 1:14b, 2:4), the sum of the two parts (*God's Spirit* + *Work*), over a period of *Time* (Haggai 2:1, Haggai 2:10), results in God's glory being made manifest in the ensuing *Victory* in our life (Haggai 2:19).[79]

---

78   Laney, Dr. Carl. *Essential Bible Background (CreateSpace, 2016), p. 147.*
79   Approximately nine weeks transpired between the message contained in Haggai 2:1-9 and the message contained Haggai 2:10-19.

CHAPTER
FIVE

ALL THE HEAVENS DECLARE

An Exegetical Analysis of Creation in Psalms

CREATION AS A BIBLICAL DOCTRINE is a theme that is immediately presented in the early chapters of Genesis. At eight points throughout Genesis 1, God spoke and the ensuing results "declared the glory of God" (Psalm 19:1).[80] By using speech as a metaphor, the biblical authors encourage the reader to understand that God's creation was voluntary, effortless, and majestic.[81] God is presented as absolutely sovereign and independently responsible for the fulfillment of His Word. God commanded and it was so. The broad and general creative injunctions presented in the creation account of Genesis present God as a Creator-King who rules over both heaven and earth.[82]

Throughout the Bible and particularly in Psalms, the theme of creation focuses on the invocation of praise for the wonderful Creator-God.[83] The psalmist encourages the reader to stare in sheer wonder and amazement through the looking glass of what has been created to the *Source of the creation.* The psalmist repeatedly directs the reader to meditate on the "work of God's fingers" (Psalm 8:3) by beholding the revelation of God's glory through His creation. The general revelation of God is made manifest as the "skies proclaim the work of his hands" (Psalm 19:1) and all of creation "pours forth speech" (Psalm 19:2) of the knowledge of God. Through the comparative exegetical analysis of Psalms 8, 19, and 104, in addition to other select verses from the Old and New Testaments, this chapter will focus on the unequivocal revelation of God through His creation within nature, mankind, and covenantal law.

---

80   In Genesis 1, God spoke creatively on eight occasions: Genesis vv. 3, 6, 9, 11, 14, 20, 24, and 26. The immediacy of creation doctrine in Genesis was discovered in *The New Dictionary of Biblical Theology (Downers Grove, IL: InterVarsity Press, 2000). Creation, p. 429.*

81   Ibid., p. 429.

82   Ibid., p. 429.

83   Longman, Tremper III and David E. Garland. *The Expositors Bible Commentary on Psalms, p. 137.*

THE REVELATION OF GOD IN NATURE

IN THE BOOK OF ROMANS, THE AUTHOR presents one of the most striking and pointed accusations against "godless and wicked people" (Romans 1:18) who refuse to bow to the Glory of God. "For since the creation of the world God's invisible qualities—his eternal power and divine nature—have been clearly seen, being understood from what has been made, so that people were without excuse" (Romans 1:20). The very splendor, wonder, and "divine nature" of God the author of Romans so passionately speaks of is made abundantly clear throughout Psalms.

In Psalm 8 the psalmist focuses the reader's attention on the opening and closing verses on the glory of the Creator-God who is the object of celebration. The psalmist's use of the title "our Lord" encourages the reader to see Yahweh as King and ruler over all of His creation.[84] Therefore, the psalmist seems to conclude within the very first verse of the Psalm that in the observance of creation, God should be the ultimate focus of praise. "LORD our Lord, how majestic is your name in all the earth!" (Psalm 8 vv. 1, 9). The underlying argument of the psalmist is that praise of creation independent of the Creator is in vain. "Pantheism defies and glorifies nature as a separate entity from the Creator; theism joyfully looks at God as the good Creator, Ruler, and Sustainer of the world."[85] The directed praise of God as the true source of creation is further identified in the verse, "You have set your glory in the heavens" (Psalm 8:1). Additionally, as the psalmist beholds the glory of God's creation, he points the reader's attention to the "work of God's fingers" to include the "moon and the stars," which God has independently set in place (Psalm 8:3). This verse seems to emphasize the Kingship and independence of Yahweh's sovereignty in all of His creation.

The psalmist seems to encourage the reader to appreciate that creation itself is a revelatory aspect of God. The psalmist achieves this in Psalm 8 by helping the reader understand the praise for the revelation of Yahweh originates "in all the earth" (Psalm 8:1). However, in Psalm 19 the psalmist utilizes a different strategy by bringing the reader's attention to the heavenly inception of praise

---

84 Longman, p. 138.
85 Longman, p. 137.

for Yahweh as the "heavens declare the glory of God" (Psalm 19:1).

The wondrous qualities of creation "go out into all the earth" (Psalm 19:4) and present themselves for all to see. "God has pitched a tent for the sun" (Psalm 19:4), which then "rises at one end of the heavens and makes its circuit to the other; nothing is deprived of its warmth" (Psalm 19:6). In this particular verse, the psalmist connects the creation account of Genesis in which "God created two great lights—the greater light to govern the day and the lesser light to govern the night" (Genesis 1:16) to the praise of God for His very creation. The creation account of Genesis therefore serves as a background for the psalmist's praise of God, and encourages the reader to meditate on the fact that the entire work of creation rests exclusively in the hands of God.

Furthermore, the praise and celebration of creation within Psalms complements the creation account of Genesis in the focus upon "effects rather than cause" and was meant to help Israel praise God as the independent creator of the entire universe.[86] The psalmist seems to point in hopeful anticipation of the conclusive creation-verse of Hebrews: "By faith we understand that the universe was formed at God's command, so that what is seen was not made out of what was visible" (Hebrews 11:3). As Longman articulates in his commentary on Psalm 8, "What is marvelous is the Great King's revelation of his glory in, and thereby his self-involvement with, his creation."[87]

A unique and awe-inspiring quality of God as the creator is identified in the verse, "When I consider your heavens, the work of your fingers" (Psalm 8:3). The psalmist's use of the anthropomorphism "work of your fingers" points to the intricate care and sensitive manner in which God "sculpted" all of His creation. The psalmist then contrasts the glory of the celestial bodies of the heavens and sky with the earthly body of humankind. Through the use of two complementary rhetorical questions placed as poetic devices, "What is mankind that you are mindful of them, human beings that you care for them? (Psalm 8:4), the psalmist invokes a sense of amazement for God's intended intrinsic value of human beings.

Answering the question, "What is mankind?" the psalmist seems to establish a chain of command and suzerain relationship between God and His creation. Being made in the image of God, human beings are divinely endowed with the "likeness" of God and are granted authority over "everything put under their

---

86   Longman, p.137.
87   Ibid., p. 138.

feet" (Psalm 8:6). God is presented as absolutely sovereign and independently responsible for His creation of mankind. As creator of mankind and through divine decree, God "crowns" mankind with "glory and honor" (Psalm 8:5). Therefore, in God's creation of nature and the establishment of His covenantal relationship with the vassal kings of the earth, everything originates and flows from the Creator to the creation. "The LORD who stretches out the heavens, lays the foundation of the earth, and forms the spirit of man within him" (Zechariah 12:1).

In this context, the psalmist encourages the reader to understand that God remains above the foundations of the earth and is therefore independently responsible for holding His creation in place. The verses, "He set the earth on its foundations; it can never be moved" (Psalm 104:5) and "He who looks at the earth, and it trembles, who touches mountains, and they smoke" (Psalm 104:32), encourage the reader to meditate on the eternal and sovereign rule of the Creator God. Furthermore, the psalmist seems to warn the reader of the temporal aspect of what has *already been created* and to turn their attention instead to what will *always remain the same*. "They will perish, but you remain; they will all wear out like a garment. Like clothing you will change them and they will be discarded" (Psalm 102:26).

By continually reinforcing the eternal aspect and sovereignty of God, the psalmist promotes the praise and worship of the one Creator-God. "In the beginning you laid the foundations of the earth, and the heavens are the work of your hands" (Psalm 102:25).[88] The psalmist conclusively argues that human beings derive their source and substance from God, which therefore requires "a relationship of responsibility as well as a response of praise to the good Creator."[89]

Continuing to both reference and promote awe and wonder of the creation account of Genesis, the psalmist encourages the reader to understand and fully appreciate the scope of appointment mankind has as "rulers over the works of God's hands" (Psalm 8:6). As "God's appointed governors (vassals) over creation," mankind's function is to judicially rule over all that God has created on earth: "The flocks and herds, and the animals of the wild, the birds in the sky, and the fish in the sea" (Psalm 8:7-8).[90] In this context, the psalmist presents mankind

---

88 Psalm 102:25, which builds on the creation account of Genesis and establishes that "In the beginning, God laid the foundations of the earth" is reinforced in Psalm 104:5: "He set the earth on its foundations; it can never be moved."

89 Longman, p. 141.

90 The reference to "God's appointed governors over creation" was cited in Longman, p. 141.

as vassal kings who serve at the discretion of the Great and Sovereign King of the Universe. Having appointed humans' authority over "everything under their feet" (Psalm 8:6), God's intention was for humankind to rule over the earth, while simultaneously remaining subordinate to His authority and rule.[91]

THE WORK OF HIS HANDS

IN PSALM 19, the psalmist continues the theme of presenting the glory of God's creation to the reader, with an initial emphasis on the general revelation of God through "the work of his hands" (Psalm 19:1). The psalmist seems to argue that although the "heavens declare the glory of God; the skies proclaim the work of his hands" (Psalm 19:1), they do so in a manner devoid of words. Nevertheless, mankind is held responsible to the proclamation of God's revelation that "pours forth speech; night after night they reveal knowledge" (Psalm 19:4). Although these words remain "voiceless" they nevertheless "go out into all the earth; their words to the ends of the world" (Psalm 19:4). The revelation of God through His creation makes every creature that is witness to it "without excuse" to God's "eternal power and divine nature" (Romans 1:19-20). In this context, not only did God "pitch a tent for the sun" that could be observed "like a bridegroom coming out of his chamber" (Psalm 19:4-5), God presents Himself as even more majestic than all of creation. As the sun circumnavigates the earth and "nothing is deprived of its warmth" so too does God "set the earth on its foundations" (Psalm 104:5) and "wrap himself in light as with a garment" (Psalm 104:2).

The general revelation of God within nature, being without words, was unrestricted by the division of language.[92] The power and glory of God could therefore be understood by beholding the divine qualities of His creation. The psalmist seems to encourage the reader to not only behold God in nature, but more importantly to "praise the name of the LORD, for at his command they were created" (Psalm 148:5). From this perspective, the psalmist argues that everything created by God is therefore absolutely dependent upon God for substance and life: "All creatures look to you to give them their food at the

---

91   "Setting everything under their feet" is utilized by the psalmist in Psalm 8:6 and was subsequently referenced in Hebrews 2:8.

92   Longman, p. 215.

proper time" (Psalm 104:27). The psalmist uses creation to point the reader to the *cause* of creation that is exalted in radiance above both the earth and even the heavens (Psalm 148:13).

The psalmist argues the brilliance of God's revelation of Himself through nature is that nothing could be hidden from Him. As if contemplating this very phenomenon, the psalmist asks, "Where can I go from your Spirit? Where can I flee from your presence?" (Psalm 139:7). The psalmist points the reader to the knowledge that God is omnipresent and without regard for linguistic barriers, for God reveals Himself everywhere and at all times within the world "He makes the clouds his chariot and rides on the wings of the wind. He makes winds his messengers" (Psalm 104:3-4).

Similar to the proclamation of God's glory set forth in the heavens observed in Psalm 8, in Psalm 19 the psalmist continues to call attention to the word "heavens" and the vastness of space within God's creation. "The heavens declare the glory of God; the skies proclaim the work of his hands" (Psalm 19:1).[93] The psalmist furthermore continues the theme of substantiating the creation account of Genesis by elaborating on "the heavens" and "the skies" to signify the place God set the sun, moon and stars.[94] God's establishment of light was to distinguish "day" from "night" and to ensure that His creation would "day after day pour forth speech" (Psalm 19:2) and "sing praise to God as long as they live" (Psalm 104:33). God's creation of "day" and "night" also served to establish the regularity of the seasons: "He made the moon to mark the seasons, and the sun knows when to go down" (Psalm 104:19).

The psalmist brings to the reader's attention the fact that all of creation remains obedient to God. Furthermore, and perhaps even more awe-inspiring to the psalmist, the reader is encouraged to behold in amazement that even "the land is satisfied by the work of God's hand" (Psalm 104:13). The psalmist seems to intentionally attempt to humble the reader by pointing out that the mightiest animals of prey are obedient and reliant upon God. "The lions roar for their prey and seek their food from God. The sun rises, and they steal away; they return and lie down in their dens" (Psalm 104:21-22). In addition to the revelation that the animals of the "sky, land and sea" find their substance in

---

93   It is interesting to note the differences between the poetic parallelism in the first verses of Psalm 8 and Psalm 19. Psalm 8 first draws attention the proclamation of God's name on the *earth,* and the revelation of God's glory in the *heavens.* Psalm 19, on the other hand, reverses this sequence of events, first attributing God's glory in the *heavens,* then the work of his hand in the *skies (earth).*

94   Longman, p. 215.

God "all creatures look to you" (Psalm 104:27), the psalmist reinforces that God was independently responsible for their creation in the first place: "When you send your Spirit, they are created" (Psalm 104:30).

It is interesting to note the psalmist's use of the phrase "pours forth" in 19:2. The verb "pour forth" is formed from the Hebrew word "bubble forth" and tends to encourage the reader to consider the spontaneity of God's revelation in nature.[95] The psalmist seems to direct the reader to understand God's inherent inclusiveness in both everything that is *seen and unseen.* While much of God's revelation in nature is temporal and subject to change, God is eternal and remains unchanged throughout all time and space "for the things which are seen are temporal, but the things which are not seen are eternal" (2 Corinthians 4:18). Like a spring continually "bubbling forth" the revelation of God "is over all and through all and in all" (Ephesians 4:6). In this context, continuity in the use of "pouring forth" as a wisdom motif in revelation of God is established in Proverbs 1:23 that promises "I will *pour out* my thoughts to you, I will make known to you my teachings."[96]

Psalm 19 verses 7-11 elaborate on the revelation of God both in nature and through God's law. Although a departure from the "pouring forth," "display," and "proclamation" of God inherently made manifest in nature, the psalmist now invokes the reader's heart to create parallelism between the effect of God's revelation in nature and the greater revelation of God in His law. In verse 19:8, "The commands of the LORD are radiant, giving light to the eyes," the psalmist seems to encourage the reader to understand and appreciate the increasing glory of both "the Creator-God" and "Yahweh the LORD." While the Creator-God's "setting of the sun" ensured "nothing was hidden from its heat" (Psalm 19:6), the revelation of the covenantal God through His law served humankind as "a lamp unto our feet and a light on our path" (Psalm 119:105). "Thus Yahweh has made the sun for light in creation and has given his word for light in redemption."[97]

In addition to imagery that reflects the enlightening quality of God's law within the heart of man (Psalm 19:8), the psalmist continues to create parallelism between the beneficial effects of nature and the restorative benefits of God's law. The natural benefits of God's revelation serve mankind on a

---

95   Longman, p. 216.
96   The argument of "pouring forth" was identified in Longman, p. 216. Author's use of italics in Proverbs 1:23 to emphasize continuity of "pour forth."
97   Longman, p. 217.

daily basis. "When you open your hand, they are satisfied with good things" (Psalm 104:28). However, when the faithful turn their attention to the very Word of God, the psalmist promises the reader will discover them to be "more precious than gold, than much pure gold" (Psalm 19:10).[98] By juxtaposing the benefits of God's revelation through creation against the benefits of God's revelation through His Word, the psalmist encourages the reader to understand that "God's self-revelation is perfect in its effects in faithful men."[99] The psalmist seems to encourage the reader to appreciate how the laws, precepts, and statutes of God have the effect of "giving joy to the heart" (Psalm 19:8), resulting in increased inner peace, tranquility, and righteousness.[100]

Reflecting on the glory of both the Creator-God and Yahweh, the psalmist turns the reader's attention inward, forcing a deep sense of introverted self-inspection and examination. In Psalm 8:4, the psalmist presents the question to mankind, "Who are we that God is mindful of us?" Now the psalmist encourages similar self-study, as he asks, "Who can discern his errors? Forgive my hidden faults" (Psalm 19:12). Just as the psalmist provides the example of the sun that provides warmth to everyone, the revelation of God through His law "penetrates and examines humans."[101] Therefore, the psalmist promotes the reader's understanding of the full implications of God's law by examples of similarity between God's revelation in nature and the power of His word in the lives of mankind. In the same fashion that the general revelation of God was made abundantly manifest in nature, God "sent his commands to the earth, his word runs swiftly" (Psalm 147:15) and God "revealed his word to Jacob, his laws and decrees to Israel" (Psalm 147:19).

In the same manner in which no person can claim ignorance of God's revelation through His creation (Rom 1:20), the psalmist now seems to advise the reader to consider the greater sin of denying knowledge of the law, decrees, and word of Yahweh. The theme of pointing the reader to contemplate their "hidden faults" and "willful sins" (Psalm 19:12-13) is also made evident in the declarations of the psalmist in Psalm 139. By drawing further connection between the futile attempts to hide from the warmth of the sun and hiding from God, the psalmist now encourages the reader to understand that God can

---

98   As noted by Longman, the choice of synonyms for God's revelation utilized by the psalmist in Psalm 19 – "law," "statues," (v.7); "precepts," "commands" (v.8); and "fear," "ordinances" (v.9) all direct the reader to the Word of God.

99   Dr. Gary Tuck. *Arguments of the Books of the Old Testament, p. 166.*

100   Longman, p. 217.

101   Ibid., p. 219.

"perceive our thoughts from afar" (Psalm 139:2) and is "familiar with all our ways" (Psalm 139:3). In humble surrender, the psalmist acknowledges there is no place he can hide from Yahweh. "Where can I go from your Spirit? Where can I flee from your presence? If I go up the heavens, you are there; if I make my bed in the depths, you are there" (Psalm 139:7-8).

THE HEAVENS ARE HIS TENT

IN PSALM 104, the psalmist emphasizes the sovereign rule of the Creator-God who is "clothed with splendor and majesty" (Psalm 104:1). The psalmist's inclusion of the verb "clothed with" seems to point the reader to the realization that God is intimately involved in the world and is expectant of recognition by His creation.[102] "He wraps himself in light as with a garment, he stretches out the heavens like a tent, and lays the beams of his upper chambers on their waters" (Psalm 104:2-3). The majesty and glory of God is "stretched out" both through His acts of creation and the revelation of His Word. The reference to God being "wrapped in light" signifies the vital and life-sustaining aspect of God. "Light is vital to life; hence its primary importance places it as the first of the creative acts."[103]

The psalmist encourages the reader to understand that in addition to creating light and thus intimately involving Himself with the sustaining of mankind, God controls everything in the heavens and earth. "The moon marks off the seasons, and the sun knows when to go down" (Psalm 104:19). The psalmist points out that although the Canaanites attributed the sunlight and lunar cycle to specific deities, Yahweh independently and wisely ruled over His creation. "How many are your works, O LORD! In wisdom you made them all; the earth is full of your creatures" (Psalm 104:24).

In Psalm 104:33, "I will sing to the LORD all my life; I will sing praise to my God as long as I live," the psalmist reflects on the wondrous splendor of creation and concludes his response should be one of praise and worship. Fully aware of God's intimate involvement and pure awareness of His creation, the psalmist hopes that his "song of praise" would please Yahweh. The verse "May

---

102   Longman, p. 763.
103   Longman, p. 764.

my meditation be pleasing to him, as I rejoice in the LORD" (Psalm 104:34) complements and reinforces the psalmist's prayer in verse 19:14: "May the words of my mouth and the meditation of my heart be pleasing in your sight, O LORD, my Rock and my Redeemer." In both instances the psalmist prays his expressed and unspoken words (the "meditation of the heart") would be acceptable and pleasing to God. In the decisive conclusion of Psalm 104, "But may sinners vanish from the earth and the wicked be no more" (104:35a), the reader is left with a choice, either to worship God, or to deny God as the true source of creation and all material gifts. For the psalmist, the choice is clear, and they encourage the reader to follow their example: "Praise the LORD, O my soul. Praise the LORD" (Psalm 104:35b).

CONCLUDING THOUGHTS

THROUGHOUT THE BIBLE and particularly in Psalms, the theme of creation focuses on the invocation of praise for the wonderful Creator-God.[104] In Psalms 8, 19 and 104, the psalmist encourages the reader to stare in sheer wonder and amazement through the looking glass of what has been created onto the *Source of the creation*. The psalmist repeatedly directs the reader to meditate on the "work of God's fingers" (Psalm 8:3) by beholding the revelation of God's glory through His creation. The revelation of God is made manifest as the "skies proclaim the work of his hands" (Psalm 19:1) and all of creation "pours forth speech" (Psalm 19:2) of the knowledge of God. In addition to God's revelation through creation, God also revealed Himself through His Word. The combined effect of God's revelation in creation within both Genesis and Psalms calls the faithful to "Praise the LORD" with the humble realization that He is the creator and sustainer of all things.

---

104   Longman, p. 137.

CHAPTER
SIX

UNDERSTANDING THE SABBATH

"In quiet and in trust your strength lies."
– Isaiah 30:15

IN HIS SEVENTH LETTER, the Spanish friar Saint John of the Cross said, "Our greatest need is to be silent before this great God."[105] Throughout the Bible and across the redemptive-historical timeline of God's covenants with creation, we discover a staggering and profound message: The God we seek is simultaneously seeking us. Furthermore, not only does God seek and find us, there has never been a moment in eternity that we have been without God. The Psalmist wrote, "It was you who created my inmost self and put me together in my mother's womb. You know me through and through, from having watched my bones take shape when I was being formed in secret."[106] Created in the image of God, and that image being deemed good,[107] we have been and always will be *known by God.* This eternal knowingness was further affirmed by the Prophet Jeremiah when he wrote, "Before I formed you in the womb, I knew you."[108]

Our souls' search for rest and peaceful abiding in the presence of God was impregnated within us by our Creator.[109] From the first book of Genesis through the entire biblical narrative, the overarching theme of *Sabbath* was central to the ancient Prophet's and New Testament Gospel message. The promise of everlasting peace was at the very heart of Jesus Christ's ministry, who in the moments before his accession comforted his faithful Apostles with the words, "Peace be onto you."[110] In specific relation to the *Sabbath* association with work and rest, Jesus also said, "Come to me all you who labor and are heavy laden, and I will give you rest."[111]

Through investigation, reflection, and integration of the biblical theme

---

105   St. John of the Cross (Author), Kieran Kavanaugh (Translator). Collected Works of Saint John of the Cross (ICS Publications, Revised Edition, October 1, 2010).
106   Psalm 139:13-15.
107   Genesis 1:25.
108   Jeremiah 1:5.
109   John 15:1-5.
110   John 20:19-21.
111   Matthew 11:28.

of *Sabbath* in our lives, we discover ourselves empowered to quench the thirst within our soul, and in the words of the Apostle Luke, "Increase in wisdom, stature and favor, with God and man."[112] By carefully tracing the Old Testament implications of obeying the *Sabbath* by ceasing works, through the New Testament practice of abiding within the true *Sabbath* of Jesus Christ, we come to realize the central assurance of the Bible: Our soul will remain restless until it rests in God.[113]

SABBATH IN THE COVENANTS

IN THE OLD TESTAMENT, the term "covenant" appears on 285 occasions[114] and was utilized by various authors to describe specific commitments, promises, and obligations between two or more parties. Within the scope of the Bible, the term was most importantly used in agreements between God and His creation. God chose to reveal Himself through the biblical narrative within the framework of a covenant to solidify the intimacy of relationship He desired with creation. Through the governing infrastructure of a covenant, the generations of mankind chronicled throughout the Old Testament were able to relate to God in a manner that increased their realization of His presence.

As discussed in Chapter 3, a covenant was historically utilized to govern the international relations between a great king and a vassal king.[115] Therefore, within their historical context, covenants adopted a standardized and structured form in which the promises, stipulations, signs, and witnesses to the agreement were defined and recorded. For our purposes of investigating and integrating observance of the *Sabbath*, it is of immense importance to understand covenants, for God choose to use this unique format and historical framework to reveal Himself as the Great King and His creation as vassal kings.[116] Furthermore, it was through the context of a covenant with Moses that God commanded *Sabbath* remembrance as a means of remaining faithful to His promises.

---

112   Luke 2:52.
113   *Confessions of Saint Augustine.*
114   *The New Dictionary of Biblical Theology (Downers Grove, IL: InterVarsity Press, 2000). Covenants, p. 420.*
115   Lawrence, Michael. *Biblical Theology in the Life of the Church (Wheaton, IL: Crossway, 2010), p. 55.*
116   Ibid., p. 56.

A covenant began with a preamble, which identified the great king who would author the covenant, and who would be responsible for establishing the scope and framework of the agreement to be reached. Next, the covenant included a historical prologue, which served to justify and substantiate the reasons why the vassal king should be obedient to the great king. Next, and of significant importance to the vassal king, the covenant would establish the stipulations that the vassal king would be obligated to perform and uphold. The covenant also included the blessings and benefits the vassal king would enjoy for keeping the covenant, as well as the curses and punishments they should expect for disobedience and breaking the covenant.[117] Finally, witnesses before the agreeing parties and a specific sign of the covenant were formally established.

SABBATH AND GOD'S CREATION

ALTHOUGH THE SPECIFIC WORD and subsequent commandment to observe the *Sabbath* would not be revealed by God until the establishment of a covenant with Moses, careful study of the Bible reveals the intention of *Sabbath*, namely rest and holiness, was in fact associated with God from the inception of His creation.[118] The implications of this interpretation of the Bible are of immense importance for two significant reasons. First, we note that as beings made in the image of God, we associate our likeness to God within the context of our mind, not our physical being. Our experience of *Sabbath*, in particular through the Gospel of Jesus Christ, may thus be associated as a withdrawal from the physical senses of the world, into a soul-experience of the peace of God's presence. This claim is substantiated in Genesis 2:2-3: "And He rested on the seventh day from all his work which He had made. And God blessed it, and sanctified it, because on that day He rested from all His work which God created and made." This verse may be best understood by reflecting on what preceded its revelation.

Genesis commenced with a description of God's work through the establishment of creation. God's creative work was then immediately contrasted with an equal and opposite cessation of work. One must consider, however, the

---

117   This paragraph was largely taken from the section "What is a Covenant" in the book *Biblical Theology in the Life of the Church, p. 56.*
118   Genesis 2:1-3.

ratio of work to rest, and the fact God sanctified only the Seventh day, and associated that specific day with rest, and deemed it a holy day. Therefore, as noted in *The New Dictionary of Biblical Theology*, "The end of God's creative work brought about a new type of time, blessed and set aside, presumably in order that what was already created could now *be*. The Seventh day was to be a day for fruitfulness, for dominion, and relationship."[119]

Secondly, as beings made in the image of God, we turn to the staggering words of Jesus Christ, "Be ye perfect, even as your Father in heaven is perfect."[120] Reflecting on the words of Jesus, and unifying their implications throughout the entire biblical narrative, we discover that our perfection can only be complete by abiding within Jesus. As fruitfulness and dominion are expressions and components of what it means to *be made in the image of God,* the significance and close association between abiding in Jesus, fruitfulness, and restfulness may be faithfully understood.

OLD TESTAMENT SABBATH

THE SPECIFIC USAGE AND APPEARANCE of the word *Sabbath* was first noted in Exodus 16:23: "Tomorrow is the rest of the holy *Sabbath* onto the LORD." This one verse is of immense importance to our investigation, for we immediately observe the relationship between three distinct yet simultaneously integrated qualities of the *Sabbath*:

1. The *Sabbath* was deemed a day of rest,
2. The *Sabbath* was deemed holy,
3. The *Sabbath* was performed *onto the LORD*.

Exodus 20:8-11 further elaborates on the commandment of *Sabbath* remembrance, and strongly associates the cessation of work as necessary for the achievement of rest. It is interesting to note that throughout the Old Testament, the *Sabbath* was specifically intended to be observed on the Seventh day. This practice can be traced to Exodus verse 20:11 and the manner in which the substitution of the word "Seven" for "Sabbath" effectively grafted the two

---

119   R. T. Beckwith and W. Stott. *This is the Day: The Biblical Doctrine of the Christian Sunday (*London, 1978) in *The New Dictionary of Biblical Theology, page 746.*

120   Matthew 5:48

together: "The LORD rested the *Seventh* day: wherefore the LORD blessed the *Sabbath* day, and hallowed it."[121] The word "hallowed," utilized within the verse, reinforced the sacred and blessed nature of the Sabbath, and was the identical descriptive word Jesus taught his disciples through the Lord's Prayer: "Our Father, who art in heaven, Hallowed be thy name."[122]

Further interpretation of Exodus 20:8-11 reveals three additional qualities of immense significance. We begin with the realization that *Sabbath* observance was not merely advice nor a recommendation, but rather a commandment, and a sign of the covenant between God and his chosen people.[123] Therefore, with this perspective guiding our investigation and biblical interpretation, the following conclusions may be reached.

We begin by noting the *Sabbath* was not intended as a relief or break from work. Furthermore, *Sabbath* was not a means to ensure the intervals of work were more productive.[124] While in many physical pursuits, rest was a direct correlate to more productivity, this was not the intention of the *Sabbath*. Rather, the *Sabbath* reinforced the idea there was more to life than work, creation, and productivity. Finally, we note the *Sabbath* was not inactivity, stagnation, or idleness. Rather, the word "observance" introduced another type of activity, far more important than the physical activity associated with labor, work, and production. The new type of *"Sabbath activity"* was meant to be experienced through worship and communion with God.

When we allow the principle of *"Sabbath activity"* to guide our investigation, the ministry of Jesus Christ becomes rich with encouragement for the spiritual devotee. Throughout the Old Testament, the *Sabbath* was associated with a specific day of observance. However, in the case of Jesus, we see something quite different unfold in the true measure of *Sabbath* observance. In the Gospel of Mark, the Pharisees had accused Jesus and his disciples of breaking the *Sabbath* law. Jesus' rebuke of their accusation was astounding, for he declared Lordship over the *Sabbath*, and that "the *Sabbath* was made for man, and not man for the *Sabbath*."[125] In this respect, we see the conclusion of *Sabbath* observance within the context of historical Old Testament law, and the authority

---

121   Authors italic emphasis on the word "Seventh" and "Sabbath"

122   Matthew 6:9

123   The Fourth Commandment was not a mandate for all humanity, but was rather originally intended for the Israelite people, as an extension of their covenant remembrance with God.

124   *The New Dictionary of Biblical Theology, Sabbath, page 747.*

125   Mark 2:27-28.

of *Sabbath* observation delivered into the hands of Jesus Christ. By declaring Lordship over the *Sabbath*, Jesus effectively removed the legal framework associated with *Sabbath*, and instead provided God's people true and lasting rest through a relationship with Him.

Traditionally throughout the Old Testament, the Promised Land and temple were associated with the physical place and location of God's rest.[126] However, in Hebrews, we observe the author now encouraging believers in Jesus Christ to experience true *Sabbath* in heavenly realities, rather than in traditional artifacts.[127] This transition was of immense importance, for just as Jesus ultimately ceased his physical work and entered into rest, through Him the believer may now enter a similar degree of rest and union with God. In Hebrews 4:11, we read, "Let us labor therefore to enter into that rest." By use of the word-phrase, "*That rest,*" the author referred less to the fourth commandment association of *Sabbath* and more to the "Law of Christ," which Jesus invites us to actively experience on a daily basis through a love relationship with Him.

TRUE SABBATH – INVESTIGATIVE SUMMARY

THROUGHOUT THE OLD TESTAMENT, the emphasis, framework, and application of the *Sabbath* was delivered through the fourth commandment. By "taking rest" one was able to observe the *Sabbath*, obey traditional Jewish law, and remain faithful to God's covenant by keeping His commandment. However, as Lord over the *Sabbath*, Jesus reprioritized the focal point for the believer from traditional *Sabbath* law, to a more intimate and permanently abiding relationship with God. Through Jesus' encouragement to "seek first the kingdom of God,"[128] he effectively issued a new law of daily *Sabbath*, with a promise of astounding proportion: By seeking God first and on a continual basis, all other matters of the world would be provided. Returning to the words of Jesus, he said, "Therefore, take no thought of tomorrow, for tomorrow shall

---

126 Psalm 95 is an example of the traditional artifacts and association of the Temple and Promised Land as the physical location of God's rest.

127 Hebrews 9:11 described the *Sabbath* experience within: "A tabernacle not made with hands, that is to say, not of this building." This new "Heavenly and Supernatural" *Sabbath* would be ultimately entered into through a relationship with Jesus Christ.

128 Matthew 6:33.

take thought of the things of itself." The emphasis, rather than waiting for a specific day of *Sabbath* observance, was placed once again on the importance of entering into God's rest on a daily basis.

Through a relationship with Jesus Christ, a believer therefore no longer needs to toil or wait upon the *Sabbath* to experience the blessedness of God's embrace. Rather, Jesus Christ offers believers a "much more excellent ministry, through a better covenant, established upon better promises."[129] The new covenant described by the author of Hebrews invites those who believe in Jesus Christ to follow Him into rest—a rest that may be experienced both on a daily basis, and throughout all eternity.

---

129 Hebrews 8:6.

CHAPTER
SEVEN

THE REVELATION OF GOD
WITHIN PSALM 2

REBILLION AGAINST GOD was first recorded in the book of Genesis, which introduced the great error of human thinking and reasoning.[130] Succumbing to temptation, God's creation decided to rebel against God, rather than trust God and live in cooperation with Him. In the graphic and intricately structured poetry of Psalm 2, the psalmist illustrates God's ultimate plan for the salvation of His creation from the evil plotting of those who have set their minds on rebellion. As the Psalm unfolds, the psalmist reveals the miraculous coming of God's Anointed One who will become His son and rule the earth. Only by serving God and His son, and through the admonishment of their rebellious plans, can the kings and inhabitants of the nations avoid God's wrath and enjoy His eternal blessing.

A LITERARY PERSPECTIVE

PSALM 2 IS COMPOSED of four stanzas, each containing three verses, and is concluded with a bookending monocolon. The psalmist's creative use of rich imagery and metaphor juxtaposes the nations' rage and desire for independence, against God's decree of wrath for their disobedience. In addition, the psalmist's careful placing of various forms of parallelism, including ladder, progressive, and antithetic, are structured in such a manner as to provide contrast between the individual pieces of each stanza and the stanzas themselves. Finally, by proposing a rhetorical question in the opening verse of Psalm 2, the psalmist prepares the reader for a journey of two possible outcomes: The sorrowful fate of the nations who set themselves against God and the joyful blessing for those who serve the Lord and His son.

---

130   *The New King James Version* (Nashville: Thomas Nelson, 1982), Genesis 2:16-17 – 3:6. This edition of the Holy Bible is referenced throughout.

THE NATIONS RAGE

AS PSALM 2 BEGINS, the psalmist introduces the rhetorical question, "Why do the nations rage, and the people plot a vain thing?"[131] The use of the word "vain" conveys the psalmist's utter amazement that nations would conceive of a plan ultimately destined to failure.[132] Through the use of the wording, "The kings of the earth set themselves,"[133] the psalmist illustrates the intensity of the plotting that was taking place. A visually illustrative term consistent with military action, to "set themselves," the nations were preparing for war with God.

In the first stanza, the psalmist introduces God's "Anointed One" and subsequently utilizes *a fortiori* statement throughout the remaining Psalm to gradually increase the revelation of how God's Anointed One will redeem and rule the world. In the first stanza, the psalmist also introduces the literary characters plotting against God. Specifically, verses 1 and 2 use a bicolon to draw the reader's attention to the totality of the rebellion that was underway. The "nations," as a collection of geographic territories, in addition to the individual people within their borders, are unified in their rage against God. Furthermore, those people in positions of leadership and influence, described by the psalmist as "rulers" and " kings of the earth," have banded together in a collective effort to rise up against God.

Through the use of ladder parallelism in verse 3, the psalmist describes the magnitude of the nations' rebellious plans. Not merely a departure from God, the nations are intent on absolutely destroying any control or reign that God has over them. The psalmist's specific use of the word "break" in verse 3 reveals insight into the aggression the nations are preparing to use against God. The nations are not merely expressing their intention to "remove" their bonds, but rather to "break their bonds into pieces."[134]

---

131   Psalm 2:1.
132   Ross, Allen P. "Psalms," in *The Bible Knowledge Commentary: An Exposition of the Scriptures,* ed. J. F. Walvoord and R. B. Zuck, vol. 1 (Wheaton, IL: Victor Books, 1985), 791-793. Ross observed in his *Exposition* the psalmist's "amazement in the form of a rhetorical question."
133   Psalm 2:2.
134   Psalm 2:3.

THE RESPONSE OF THE LORD

IN VERSE FOUR, the psalmist uses antithetic parallelism to sharply contrast the Lord's *laughter* at the nations' futile plans with the Lord's *anger* at the nations for their rebellion. To aid the reader in noticing the antithetic parallelism of verse 4, the psalmist ends the contrasting sentences with distinctly opposite descriptive words. The first line of verse 4 concludes with the word "laughs" while the second line of verse 4 ends with the word "derision."[135]

It is interesting to note the psalmist's sharp contrast between the first stanzas (vv.1-3) and the second stanzas (vv. 4-6) in relation to the description of the entities rising up against God. In the first stanza, the psalmist went to great length to specifically list the antagonists: the nations, the people, the kings of the earth, and the rulers who take counsel together. This level of detail draws the reader's attention to the magnitude of the rebellion against God. However, in the second stanza, the Lord simply refers to and addresses the rebellion with the word "them."[136]

The psalmist describes the reaction of the Lord to the nations' rebellion using anthropomorphism. This technique ascribes the human quality of both laughter and anger to the Lord, and draws further awareness to how futile and vain any plot against the Lord will be. In verse 5, the psalmist uses a bicolon to describe the Lord's response against the nations' rebellion. Furthermore, in verse 4 and verse 5, the psalmist differentiates between the natural and supernatural presence of the Lord. In verse 4, the psalmist assigns the Lord to Heaven, where He observes and laughs at the vain attempt of the nations to rise against Him. However, in verse 5, the psalmist describes the reaction of the Lord as "distressing them in his deep displeasure"[137] and by this description, assigns the effect of the Lord's displeasure to the natural world. Thus verse 4 is seen as taking place in heavenly realms, and verse 5 in earthly realms.

In verse 6, the psalmist continues the theme of moving the presence of the Lord throughout the world. The psalmist describes the Lord bestowing His rule onto "My king on My holy hill of Zion."[138] In verse 6, the psalmist also clearly distinguishes the Lord in Heaven from the embodiment of the Lord's

---

135   Psalm 2:4. *New Kings James Bible.*
136   Psalm 2:4-5.
137   Psalm 2:5.
138   Psalm 2:6.

presence on earth as King. Verse 6 further reveals the Lord's Anointed One establishing dominion and kingly rule over the nations. The response of the Lord in verse 6, "I have set My King," is a form of antithetic parallelism to the kings of the earth who set themselves against God.

THE DECLARATION OF THE LORD

IN THE FIRST TWO lines of verse 7, the psalmist uses staircase parallelism to build momentum towards the decree of the Lord. Furthermore, verse 7 continues the psalmist's theme of delegating the presence of the Lord from Heaven onto the earth through the rule of an anointed king. Once again, the psalmist uses anthropomorphism to draw attention to an aspect of God that takes human form. The concluding line of verse 7 complements verse 6, as the psalmist assigns the rule of God onto an earthly king, who is in fact the son of the Lord.[139] The combined effect of the third stanza (vv. 7-9) suggests the psalmist was describing a permanent and lasting rule the "son of God" would establish over "the ends of the earth."[140] [141]

In verse 8, the psalmist returns to words used in the first stanza to describe the characters involved in the rebellion against God. However, in verse 8, the words "nations" and "earth" are now used in relation to the extent of the rule of the Lord's King, as opposed to the extent of the rebellion against the Lord. In verse 9, the psalmist uses ladder parallelism and imagery to describe the power of the Lord's delegated rule on earth. In verse 9, the psalmist uses the word "break" to describe the harshness of God's response against the rebellious nations. By returning to the use of the word "break," which was previously ascribed to the nations' declaration against God (verse 3), the third stanza acts as a graphic foretelling for the nations' future should they pursue a rebellion.

---

139   Psalm 2:7.
140   Psalm 2:8.
141   2 Samuel 7:16 substantiates the psalmists' reference to a "Kingdom" and "Throne" that would endure forever.

ADVICE TO THE NATIONS

IN THE FINAL STANZA, the psalmist returns to the specific description of the rebellious characters introduced in the first stanza. In this manner, the psalmist structures the argument of the nations expressed in the first stanza (vv. 1-3) as rebutted by the Lord in the fourth stanza (vv. 10-12). The psalmist makes clear to the nations that the rule of the Lord and His son are inseparable; by serving the Lord, the nations serve His son.[142] The psalmist exhorts the nations that unless they surrender to the rule of the Lord's son, they will surely perish. The psalmist reiterates the word "wrath," last seen in verse 5 in relation to "God's wrath," and now assigns God's wrath to His son. Through the concluding use of a monocolon, the psalmist leaves hope and the promise of blessedness for all those who put their trust in the son of God.

CONCLUDING THOUGHTS

PSALM 2 REVEALS GOD'S ultimate plan for the salvation of His creation from the evil plans of those who have set their minds on rebellion. The psalmist explains redemption can be found by serving God and His son. Any plotting against God, according to Psalm 2, is laughable and destined for failure. However, when the nations trust God and are agreeable to His plan, they will experience blessedness through the sovereign rule of His son.

---

142   Ross, Allen P. The Exhortation of the Psalmist *(2:10-12)*.

CHAPTER
EIGHT

KING OF KINGS

Monarchy in Samuel: Davidic,
Messianic, and Divine

MONARCHY AND THE ESTABLISHMENT of an earthly vassal king anointed as a representative of the heavenly Suzerain king was a major turning point in the outworking of God's purposes for salvation. The book of Samuel illustrates the full implications of the rise of monarchy in Israel, and reveals the progressive stages of transition from judges to kings. Although Samuel was serving the people of Israel as both a prophet and judge, he was decisively not a king. Therefore, as Samuel grew old, the elders of Israel gathered together and demanded, "Now appoint a king to lead us, such as all the other nations have" (1 Samuel 8:5). The change of government structure from judges to kings begins at this point in the biblical narrative and subsequently reveals three key distinguishing factors of great importance:

1. The rejection of Samuel and demand for an earthly king was in fact a rejection of God as the king of Israel (1 Samuel 8:7),
2. The human vassal king would only succeed when faithfully representing God and following His decrees, mandates, and law,
3. The people misunderstood their oppression as lacking a king to lead them in battle, when in fact they were oppressed due to their sin and rejection of God (1 Samuel 8:20).[143]

The progressive transition of monarchy in Samuel from Davidic to Messianic to Divine reveals that no matter how well intentioned, an earthly vassal king would not be sufficient to successfully lead the people of Israel. This realization was certainly in the mind of Samuel, who warned the people of Israel about the king they requested: "If you fear the LORD and serve and obey him and do not rebel against his commands, and if both you and the king who reigns over you follow the LORD your God—good! But if you do not obey the LORD, and if you rebel against his commands, his hand will be against you, as it was against your ancestors" (1 Samuel 12:14-15). Although God's plan for salvation did include the transition from judges to kings, the book of Samuel reveals that only God could provide the security and divine rule the people of Israel so desperately needed.

---

143   Hill, Walton. *A Survey of the Old Testament, Third edition (Zondervan, 2009),* p. 262.

THE IMPLICATIONS OF THE DAVIDIC MONARCHY

THE DAVIDIC COVENANT STATEMENT is revealed in 2 Samuel 7:12-16 and presents a promise of a bright future for Israel and the line of David. In addition to the covenant promise, God had previously made several additional promises to David of immense importance for understanding the implications of Davidic Monarchy. In 2 Samuel 7:9, God promised to make David's name great and to include his name along with the greatest men on earth. This promise echoes God's promise to Abraham in Genesis: "I will make your name great, and you will be a blessing" (Genesis 12:2), and thus a parallel is recognized between the covenant with Abraham and the covenant with David.[144]

Furthermore, God promised through the kingship of David to "provide a place for my people Israel and will plant them so that they can have a home of their own and no longer be disturbed" (2 Samuel 7:10). In addition to the promise of a place (a kingdom) for the people of Israel, God further declared that through the establishment of the Davidic covenant, "Wicked people will not oppress them (Israel) anymore" (2 Samuel 7:10), and that Israel would achieve rest from their enemies (2 Samuel 7:10-11). The promise of both land and security draws further parallel between the Davidic and Abrahamic covenants and reveals that David was placed in the line of Abraham.

These conditions and inclusions within the Abrahamic covenant reveal that the earthly vassal king would rule under the authority of God, the ultimate Suzerain king. It is also interesting to note that in 2 Samuel 7:11, God declared that the people of Israel would cease to experience oppression as they did ever since the rule of judges over them. This statement therefore serves to progress in a positive light the authority and rule the transition in government from judges to kings would entail. However, a positive outcome for Israel would only be possible when the vassal king obeyed God and remained in covenant with Him.

The episode of David and Goliath clearly records the grave misunderstanding the people of Israel were under with regards to their expectations of a king. The people of Israel expressed their desire for a king as a representative who would "go out before us and fight our battles" (1 Samuel 8:19). The error in

---

144   Ibid., p. 270.

thinking was that the vassal king would independently fight the battles of Israel and establish security for the people. This flawed view and expectation for the vassal king was made expressly clear when Saul remained unwilling to fight Goliath. It was David, the true king and retainer of the proper understanding of the relationship between the vassal and Suzerain king, who knew that God alone would secure victory and fight the battles for the people of Israel (1 Samuel 17:47). The Davidic covenant established by no uncertain terms that a proper monarchy would entail the earthly king as a representative and head of God's sovereignty.[145]

The Davidic covenant also reveals the importance of the authority the vassal king would hold. Samuel clearly establishes the fact that God appointed David to rule over the people of Israel (2 Samuel 7:8). This verse alone is sufficient to qualify the argument that David was subordinate to God (as were all vassal kings), for in all instances of the delegation of authority, the lower power (David and all vassal kings) is both set by, and therefore responsible to, the higher power (God). The nature of authority, influence, and power between the vassal king and Suzerain king is further established in the verse, "I will be his father, and he will be my son" (2 Samuel 7:14). As father, God retains the authority to punish the vassal king for insubordination when "he does wrong" by means of "floggings inflicted by human hands" (2 Sam 7:14). Although God set the stipulations for the hierarchy of power clearly in place, God also promised that His love would never be taken away from the line of David, and that David's house and kingdom would endure forever (2 Samuel 15-16). This promise is the stepping-stone in the progression from the Davidic to the Messianic Monarchy.

---

145   Ibid.

THE IMPLICATIONS OF THE MESSIANIC MONARCHY

IN SAMUEL, THE PROMISE OF AN ULTIMATE earthly vassal king succeeding from the line of David provides hope for the future of Israel. The implications of the Messianic Monarchy complement and build upon the foundation established within the Davidic Covenant. This section of the paper will focus upon unique distinctions between the Abrahamic Covenant and the Davidic Covenant, which will in turn illuminate how the author of Samuel seems to promise an ultimate vassal king and kingdom for Israel. As the argument is developed, the ultimate Divine Monarchy and supremacy of the spiritual-heavenly Suzerain upon which both the Davidic and Messianic Monarchies are built will be presented as the true hope for Israel.

In 2 Samuel 7:12, God promises David that "when your days are over and you rest with your ancestors, I will raise up your offspring to succeed you, your own flesh and blood, and I will establish his kingdom." This promise is a definitive turning point between the Abrahamic and Davidic Covenants, for although the it mirrored the promise of descendants witnessed in the Abrahamic Covenant, it now clearly developed in the new theme of a parental relationship between the vassal and Suzerain king.[146] "I will be his father, and he will be my son" (2 Samuel 7:14). The author presents a strong case for a permanent and ultimate king that would succeed through the line of David as noted in the verse, "My love will never be taken away from him, as I took it away from Saul, whom I removed before you. Your house and your kingdom will endure forever before me; your throne will be established forever" (2 Samuel 7:15-16). These two verses are of resounding significance and point the reader to an ultimate earthly king (and line of kings) that would succeed through David. In addition, the author ensures the reader understands the ultimate spiritual-heavenly Suzerain king is solely responsible for setting earthly vassal kings.

Samuel's inclusion of the key statement, "As I took it away from Saul," points to God as the ultimate delegator, equipper, and enabler of earthly kings. God alone would set His vassal king, and therefore God alone would also remove His appointed king for insubordination and failure to obey His decree, mandate, and law. That David was aware of his requirement to remain in covenant with God is

---

146   This observation and argument was discovered in *A Survey of the Old Testament, p. 272.*

evident in his statement of faith, "I have kept the ways of the LORD, and have not acted wickedly against my God. For all His ordinances were before me, and as for His statues, I did not depart from them" (2 Samuel 22:22-23). Furthermore, that David understood his subordinate role as the vassal king before God is made expressly clear when he prayed, "Now be pleased to bless the house of your servant, that it may continue forever in your sight" (2 Samuel 2:29). This verse indicates that David understood the terms of the covenant and the assurance of the continuation of his family's line of kings would be acutely dependent upon observing the "laws and decrees" God set before him.

Perhaps the most compelling argument for David's awareness that the reign of his kingdom (and the reign of an ultimate, earthly king descending from his line) would be dependent upon remaining in covenant with God was written in reflection of David's life: "If you walk before me in integrity of heart and uprightness, as your father David did, and do all I command and observe my decrees and laws, *I will establish your royal throne over Israel forever*, as I promised David your father when I said, 'You shall never fail to have a man on the throne of Israel'" (1 Kings 9:4-5).[147] In this verse, the author presents David and his successive line as acknowledging the ultimate earthly king would be set by God to rule Israel.

For example, David continually makes reference to the assurance that his line would remain the head of nations, while simultaneously basing his faith on remaining in covenant with God. "You have kept me as head of the nations; A people whom I have not known serve me" (2 Samuel 22:44). The specific reference that "a people whom I have not known serve me" seems to point to a future and successive line of kings that would continue through David's descendants. In addition, David had been told by God that his "own flesh and blood" would build a house for the LORD, and that God would establish his kingdom (a descendant of David) forever (2 Samuel 7:12-13). This verse presents a strong argument for the author's intention to present an ultimate earthly king that would reign over an ultimate kingdom on earth. Finally, the author seems to point towards a bright future, when a king from the line of David would arrive who would be sinless and remain in perfect covenant with God, and thus remain on the throne forever: "He is a tower of deliverance to His king, and shows lovingkindness to His anointed, to David, and his descendants forever" (2 Samuel 22:51).

---

147   Author's use of italics to emphasize the ultimate earthly king and successive line of kings established through the Messianic Monarchy. This argument first identified in Survey of the Old Testament, page 271.

IMPLICATIONS OF THE DIVINE MONARCHY

THE PRAYER OF HANNAH sets the stage for the realization of the ultimate supremacy of Israel's spiritual-heavenly Suzerain king. "For the foundations of the earth are the LORD'S; on them he has set the world" (1 Samuel 2:8). Samuel seems to encourage the reader to understand that every degree of hope and expectation Israel placed upon their vassal king would in fact be provided and fulfilled by God. However, as further demonstrated in Samuel, oftentimes the people of Israel put their trust in a source other than God. The grave mistake of associating eternal fulfillment (God's provision) by the means of temporal substitution (a vassal king) is a resounding theme in Samuel.

The establishment of the Divine Monarchy presented in Samuel is substantiated by the contrast and parallelism between two additional verses in Hannah's Prayer: "It is not by strength that one prevails; those who oppose the LORD will be broken" (1 Samuel 2:10). This verse illuminates the futile attempts of a vassal king (or a nation, people, or individual) to act independently of God. As clearly depicted in the battle of David and Goliath, it was not David's individual strength or merit that ensured his success in battle, for even David knew "it is not by sword or spear that the LORD saves; *for the battle is the LORD'S* " (1 Samuel 17:57).[148] Rather, Samuel directs the reader to the ultimate power, sovereignty, and exclusivity of the One true King in the following verse of Hannah's prayer: "He (The LORD) will give strength to his king and exalt the horn of his anointed" (1 Samuel 2:10). To the extent the vassal king remained in covenant with God and obeyed His laws and decrees, then the full power and strength of God would be made available. This truth was certainly known by David, who prayed, "You have also made my enemies turn their back to me, and I destroyed those who hated me" (2 Samuel 22:41).

The supremacy of the Divine Monarchy and of Israel's true Heavenly King is expressed by contrasting the kingship of Saul with the divinely appointed "shepherding" of David: "In the past, while Saul was king over us, you (David) were the one who led Israel on their military campaigns" (2 Samuel 5:2). This verse is of immense significance, for it encourages the reader to understand David's destruction of Israel's enemies was only made possible by his obedience to

---

148   Author's use of italics to emphasize David's realization that it was not material (or temporal) objects of strength (a sword or spear) that ensured victory; David knew the battle belonged to God, and God would therefore bring about his victory.

God. Furthermore, this verse clearly articulates the difference between the limited capacity of a vassal king who refused to obey God (Saul), in comparison to the strength of a vassal king who ruled in accordance with God's Word (David). Samuel seems to encourage the reader to understand and appreciate that only through the faithful rule of God's anointed king would the earthly kingdom of Israel come to experience the full favor and blessedness of God.

Throughout Samuel, God's destruction of His enemies and the enemies of His chosen people reveals the true reign over the earth was from the heavenly realms. That Samuel includes frequent reference to the fact that David "inquired of the LORD" tends to encourage the reader to understand and appreciate the authoritative chain of command God had established for His creation and His delegation of a vassal king. The vassal king was absolutely dependent upon and subordinate to the Suzerain for victory in every foreseeable matter. Therefore, to the extent the vassal king humbled himself before God, success in their kingship would be ensured.

The stark contrast between David's humble confession of sin in his affair with Bathsheba (2 Samuel 12) is juxtaposed against Saul's defense and denial of his failure to obey the Word of God as spoken by Samuel (1 Samuel 15). Saul's "rejection of the word of the LORD" (1 Samuel 15:23) resulted in the kingdom of Israel being "torn from his hands" (1 Samuel 15:28). These episodes of vassal kings either subjecting themselves to God (as David did) or rejecting the Word of God (as Saul did) point the reader to the ultimate supremacy of Israel's true heavenly King.

CONCLUDING THOUGHTS

MONARCHY AND THE ESTABLISHMENT of an earthly vassal king anointed as a representative of the heavenly Suzerain king was a major turning point in the outworking of God's purposes for salvation. Samuel illustrates the full implications of the rise of monarchy in Israel, and reveals the progressive stages of transition from judges to kings. The transition of monarchy in Samuel from Davidic to Messianic to Divine revealed that no matter how well intentioned, an earthly vassal king would never be sufficient to successfully lead the people of Israel. Samuel reveals that only God could provide the security and divine rule the people of Israel so desperately needed.

CHAPTER
NINE

YAHWEH IS MY GOD WHO SAVES
The Role Of Elijah And Elisha In Kings

IN THE BOOK OF KINGS, Elijah and Elisha are presented as key characters directly responsible for confronting Baalism and the covenant unfaithfulness of King Ahab. Throughout Kings, the author presents the collective verdict on the causes of the fall of the Israelite kingdom, while simultaneously providing the hope of salvation and the restoration of a Davidic-Messianic monarchy. Although Kings initially portrays a picture of Israelite prosperity, peace, glory, and splendor as ushered in through the kingship of Solomon, an equal and opposite decline at the end of Solomon's rule ultimately led to religious idolatry and moral decay.[149] This downfall into sin and disobedience to God provides the sharp contrast and positive expectancy at the sudden arrival of Elijah (1 Kings 17:1).

Kings attributes the division of Israel's united monarchy to the sin of idolatry. "I will do this [tear the kingdom out of Solomon's hand] because they have forsaken me and worshiped Ashtoreth the goddess of the Sidonians, Chemosh the god of the Moabites, and Molek the god of the Ammonites" (1 Kings 11:33). The sin of idolatry was further exacerbated by the fact Solomon and the people of Israel did not walk in obedience to God and violated the established law of Sinai (1 Kings 11:33). As the momentum of increasing sin is traced throughout Kings, a tipping point comes when King Ahab institutes Baalism as the official religion of the northern kingdom. The magnitude of disgust and anger this caused God is clearly articulated in the verse, "There was never anyone like Ahab, who sold himself to do evil in the eyes of the LORD, urged on by Jezebel his wife. He behaved in the vilest manner by going after idols" (1 Kings 21:25-26).

The progressive increase of sinful behavior ranging from worship of false idols to human sacrifice "aroused the anger of the LORD" and caused the LORD to "remove the Israelites from his presence, as he had warned through all his servants the prophets" (2 Kings 17:23). Against this backdrop of decline into sin and despair, the prophets Elijah and Elisha unite in an effort to bring the people of Israel back into covenant relationship with God. Elijah and Elisha

149   Hill, Walton. *A Survey of the Old Testament, Third edition (Zondervan, 2009), p. 294.*

stand as pillars of faith and served to demonstrate God's covenant faithfulness to Israel and His supremacy over Baal.[150] Furthermore, through the prophets Elijah and Elisha, the author demonstrates the grace and mercy of God, and encourages the reader to retain hope that the line of David would "never fail to have a successor on the throne of Israel" (1 Kings 9:5).

It is interesting to note the Hebrew meaning of the name Elijah was "Yahweh is my God," and the meaning of Elisha was "God saves."[151] When combined together, the united significance of the great prophets' names becomes "Yahweh is my God who saves," and serves to unify their mission of confronting Baal with the superiority of God. The author of Kings seems to promise that if the Israelite people would only affirm for themselves that "Yahweh is my God who saves" then they would experience a prosperous covenant relationship with Him. In this manner, the author of Kings continues the biblical theme that only by obedience to God's mandates, laws, and decrees would the vassal kings and people of Israel experience the blessedness they so desperately needed.

THE FOUR CONFRONTATIONS OF ELIJAH AND ELISHA AGAINST BAAL

AGAINST THE BACKDROP OF FAILED vassal leadership and the establishment of Baalism within the northern kingdom, the role of Elijah and Elisha is portrayed as a mission to eradicate the false god Baal by demonstrating the power of Yahweh. The author of Kings presents four specific episodes with Elijah and Elisha in direct confrontation with the popular understanding of Baal's basic character and false beliefs.[152] In each instance, the author demonstrates the sovereign power of Yahweh as superior to any false god, and encourages the reader to trust solely in Yahweh. Within these demonstrations of the power of Yahweh, the theme of faithful obedience to God is emphasized through the repeated sequence in which Elijah hears and immediately obeys the Word of God.[153] The author of Kings highlights the obedience of Elijah and

150   Ibid., p. 293.
151   *The New Dictionary of Biblical Theology (Downers Grove, IL: InterVarsity Press, 2000). Covenants, pp. 456-457.*
152   Hill, p. 292.
153   The seven accounts in which the word of the Lord comes to Elijah and is obeyed by Elijah were observed in

Elisha to inspire the reader to model their behavior and faithfulness after these two great prophets.

The Canaanite god Baal was believed to control the rains, bring agricultural fertility, control fire and lightning, and life and death.[154] The first false belief Elijah confronts is the perceived control Baal had over rain. Elijah achieves his purpose through the duality of positioning himself as the deliverer of both blessing and curse. "As the LORD, the God of Israel, lives, whom I serve, there will be neither dew nor rain in the next few years except at my word" (1 Kings 17:1). Immediately following Elijah's prophetic declaration of drought, the Word of the LORD came to him and instructed Elijah to hide near the Kerith Ravine, east of the Jordan. While in hiding, the LORD promised that despite the drought, Elijah would have water from the brook, and would receive a miraculous distribution of food from ravens (1 Kings 17:1-5). The author of Kings parallels the drought in the land stemming from the covenant curse of idolatry, with the supply of water Elijah would enjoy stemming from covenant faithfulness. Furthermore, the close proximity of blessing and curse (drought and water) concisely and immediately point the reader to understand the superiority of God over Baal.

In 1 Kings 18, the author demonstrates for a second time the power of God over Baal in relation to famine and drought. Although belief in Baal was thought to ensure agricultural fertility, the author points out that "the famine was severe in Samaria" and King Ahab was on a desperate quest to find grass to keep the horses and mules alive (1 Kings 18:3-6). Capitalizing on the dire situation of King Ahab and the Israelites, the Word of the LORD came to Elijah to present himself to Ahab. When Ahab saw Elijah, he said, "Is that you, you troubler of Israel?" (1 Kings 18:17). The following exchange between Elijah and Ahab beautifully illustrates the illusion that Ahab and the Israelites were under in relation to the curse of famine and drought they were experiencing.

The author of Kings points the reader to the common mistake of blaming other people or circumstances (as Ahab blamed Elijah) as the cause of a curse, when in fact the cause resided within the individual sin of idolatry. Furthermore, the author encourages the reader to understand only through a faithful covenant relationship with God would the vassal kings of the earth and the people of God experience blessedness and fulfillment. The great failure

---

Dr. Gary Tuck's "Notes on Elijah – Elisha."
154   Hill, p. 292.

repeated throughout Samuel and Kings was directly associated with failure to obey the Sinai covenant. Specifically, both vassal kings and the Israelites repeatedly violated the Sinai covenant through the sin of idolatry and the mistaken belief that something other than God would fulfill their needs.

Immediately after Elijah is blamed for the "trouble he caused Israel," the author of Kings beautifully illustrates the *true cause* of the trouble: "I have not made trouble for Israel (replied Elijah) but you and your father's family have. You have abandoned the LORD'S commands and have followed the Baals" (1 Kings 18:18). This exchange between Elijah and Ahab is extremely important, and concisely articulates the author's verdict that the fall of the Israelite kingdom was due to covenant unfaithfulness and the corresponding sin of idolatry. As the momentum builds, the author uses this opportunity to demonstrate the superiority of God by eradicating another false belief the people held regarding Baal.

Baal was believed to control lightning and fire.[155] Capitalizing on this false belief, Elijah proposed a test to determine the superiority of the God in which the people of Israel would put their faith. "How long will you waver between two opinions? If the LORD is God, follow him; but if Baal is God, follow him" (1 Kings 18:21). The test devised by Elijah would have seemed to place the odds in favor of Baal, for it was a commonly held belief that Baal controlled fire and lightning. "Then you (the prophets of Baal and Asherah) call on your god, and I will call on the name of the LORD. The god who answers by fire — he is God" (1 Kings 18:24).

As the people of Israel stood in observance, the prophets of Baal "called on the name of Baal from morning till noon. 'Baal, answer us!' But there was no response; no one answered" (1 Kings 18:26). The taunting of Elijah that followed served to demonstrate the foolishness of faith in a god other than Yahweh. Furthermore, the author utilizes this episode to inspire the reader to understand that God always remained faithful to His covenant. Unlike Baal, that could "be deep in thought, or busy, or traveling, or asleep" (1 Kings 18:27), the one true God was always present and available to the faithful. Any lack of demonstration of the power of God the Israelites may have experienced was due to their own sin. The author seems to encourage the reader to understand that the experience of blessing or curse was the independent will of the people. If they followed God, they would experience His covenant blessing. However,

---

155   *A Survey of the Old Testament*, p. 292.

if they chose to follow Baal, they would incur His covenant curse. In order to return into the covenant blessing of God, the people of Israel only needed to "turn from their wicked ways in order to live" (Ezekiel 33:11).

After the prophets of Ball experienced repeated failure, Elijah prepared the people to witness the power of God. Following the construction of the altar and preparation of the sacrifice, Elijah ordered the people to "fill four large jars with water and pour it on the offering and on the wood" (1 Kings 18:33). Once the wood and altar were completely drenched with water, Elijah stepped forward and prayed that God would turn the people's hearts back to Him by a demonstration of His sovereign power (1 Kings 18:36-37). As the "fire of the LORD fell and burned up the sacrifice, the wood, the stones and the soil" the people fell prostrate and cried, "The LORD — he is God!" (1 Kings 18:38-29). Having captured the hearts and minds of the people of Israel, Elijah then ordered them to seize and slaughter all the prophets of Baal.

Finally, the author confronts the false belief the people of Israel held regarding Baal's ability to control life and death by demonstrating the true power of Yahweh to raise the dead back to life. Having requested a "double portion of Elijah's spirit" (2 Kings 2:9), Elisha continues the mission of eradicating the worship of Baal from the Israelites by confronting the final popular belief that Baal controlled life and death. In 2 Kings 4:8-36, the author presents additional evidence for the fact that only when the Israelites turned to "their God who saves" would they experience covenant blessing. Within the episode of Elisha first prophesying the birth of the Shunammite's child, and then returning the child to life after he had died, the author concisely demonstrates the sovereign power God retained over life and death.

The author of Kings seems to present Elisha's leadership role as a continuation of the mission initiated by Elijah. In this respect, Elisha is presented as a successor to Elijah as Joshua was a successor to Moses.[156] As representatives of God in the unified destruction of Baalism, the process initiated by Elijah was brought to final completion through Elisha. "That for which Elijah had prepared the way was, in Elisha's time, made a reality."[157]

---

156   *The New Dictionary of Biblical Theology, p. 456.*
157   Ibid., p. 457.

CONCLUDING THOUGHTS

IN THE BOOK OF KINGS, Elijah and Elisha are presented as key characters directly responsible for confronting Baalism and the covenant unfaithfulness of King Ahab. In 1 Kings 9:1-9, the author clearly presents the crossroads the people of Israel stood at. If King Solomon continued to walk in the ways of his father David, and maintained covenant faithfulness with God, then God promised to "establish His royal throne over Israel forever" (1 Kings 9:5). Only covenant faithfulness would ensure the vassal king and people of Israel would experience blessedness and the favor of God. God warns Solomon that if he or his descendants did not maintain Sinaitic faithfulness and "go off and serve other gods and worship them," then Israel will experience covenant curse and would be cut off from the land God had given them (1 Kings 9:6-7).

Throughout Kings, the author presents the collective verdict on the causes of the fall of the Israelite kingdom, while simultaneously providing the hope of salvation and the restoration of a Davidic-Messianic monarchy. Kings attributes the division of Israel's united monarchy to the sin of idolatry. "I will do this (tear the kingdom out of Solomon's hand) because they have forsaken me and worshiped Ashtoreth the goddess of the Sidonians, Chemosh the god of the Moabites, and Molek the god of the Ammonites" (1 Kings 11:33). The progressive sinful behavior of the Israelites ranging from worship of false idols to human sacrifice "aroused the anger of the LORD" and caused the LORD to "remove the Israelites from his presence, as he had warned through all his servants the prophets" (2 Kings 17:23).

Against this backdrop of decline into sin and despair, the prophets Elijah and Elisha unite in an effort to bring the people of Israel back into covenant relationship with God. As Kings comes to a close, the author leaves hope for the Israelite kingdom and the return of the Davidic-Messianic monarchy. By including the unexpected release of Jehoiachin from prison and his subsequent "seat of honor higher than those of the other kings who were with him in Babylon," the author demonstrates the grace and mercy of God, and seems to inspire the reader to retain hope that the line of David would "never fail to have a successor on the throne of Israel" (1 Kings 9:5).

CHAPTER
TEN

A DIVINE PROMISE
The Significance Of Blessing, Land, And Seed In Genesis

BLESSING, LAND, AND SEED are concepts within the Bible of immense importance. First introduced in Genesis, and then continuing to weave their way through the entire biblical narrative, these three central categories are each a critical aspect of God's revelation of Himself. In many respects, the governing category of "blessing" subsequently results in the outpouring of "land" on which "seed" will flourish, as depicted in the diagram below:

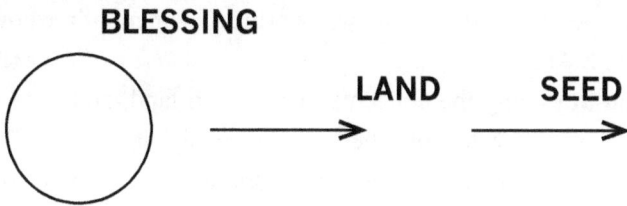

BLESSING

LAND   **SEED**

Therefore, this chapter will work sequentially through the categories in this order, developing each theme individually, while simultaneously identifying their relationship to each other. Specifically, this chapter will seek to identify the correlation of God's promises to Abraham, Isaac, and Jacob, with a faithful understanding of the ultimate Salvation that would be provided by Jesus Christ. Furthermore, this chapter will make reference to the implications of an "anti-seed," and the importance of understanding the natural and supernatural quality of the promised "seed" God would provide for His creation.

GOD'S BLESSING ONTO CREATION

BLESSING IS A KEY CONCEPT in Scripture, and the image of God as one who blesses His creation with land and seed is presented at the start of the Old Testament. God, as the creator of everything, inherently infused His creation with goodness and blessedness. God specifically blessed animal life (Genesis 1:22-25), human life (Genesis 1:27-28), and the seventh day (Genesis 2:3), thus firmly implanting the theme of blessing in Genesis, and as a foundational aspect of His ultimate intention for the world.[158]

In Genesis 1:26-28, God blessed His creation by assigning dominion over the earth, with the specific task to "Be fruitful, multiply, fill the earth, and subdue it" (Genesis 1:28). God, as the creator and owner of the whole earth, retained the authority to give creation land as an outpouring of His blessing onto them (Exodus 19:5). Furthermore, the Hebrew word for "land" and "world" (*eres)* is the same, thus firmly and nearly immediately establishing the connection between blessing and the occupation of land for God's creation.[159] Finally, Genesis introduces God's promise of land and seed as an expression of His blessing to the Israelites, and was a critical element of the covenant God established with Abraham.

In addition to tracing the concepts of blessing, land, and seed throughout Genesis, it is important to note the simultaneously developing theme of an "anti-seed" and subsequent manifesting of curse and sin within God's creation. Following the serpent's deceit of Eve in the temptation to eat from the tree of knowledge, God forewarned creation of the "anti-seed" and resulting enmity that would take place: "I will put enmity between you (the serpent) and the woman, and between your *offspring* and hers."[160] Furthermore, the theme of deceit and the "selling" of birthright (God's blessing and inheritance) for a meal (in the case of Eve "fruit" and in the case of Esau "Red stew") are intricately woven throughout Genesis.

GOD'S PROMISES TO ABRAHAM

GOD'S FIRST CALL TO ABRAM (who subsequently became known as Abraham) is recorded in Genesis 12:1. Following the fall and scattering of the nations at Babylon, the Lord told Abraham to go to the land He would show him. The initial establishment of promises between God and Abraham thus begins at this part in the biblical narrative. Of paramount importance for understanding the implications of "blessing" and the manner in which

---

158   Tuck, Dr. Gary. *The ARGUMENTS of the Books of THE OLD TESTAMENT (Dr. Gary Tuck, 1993). Genesis, 3.*

159   *The New Dictionary of Biblical Theology (Downers Grove, IL: InterVarsity Press, 2000). Land, 623.*

160   Genesis 3:15. Authors use of italics within the verse; The word "offspring" in many translations is "seed."

"blessing" extends through land and seed, is expressed in Genesis 12:1-3. In many respects, Genesis 12:1-3 is a summation of the relationship between the three concepts. God emphasized the blessing He would bestow upon Abraham through the promise that Abraham would become a great nation, and that all the people of the *earth* (land) would ultimately be *blessed through him* (his seed).

In Genesis 12, although the word "trust" is not used in the text, the stipulation made upon Abraham by God was to trust His leadership and direction. The theme of trusting God in order to receive His blessing in the outpouring of land and seed is intimately woven into the book of Genesis. In Genesis 12.1, God told Abraham to "Go out from your land" and to leave his relatives and his father's house. (Genesis 12:1) Immediately after telling Abraham to go to the land He would show him, God made several promises to Abraham. The specific promises God made to Abraham in the first call were:

1. Making Abraham into a great nation,
2. Making Abraham's name great,
3. Abraham would be a blessing,
4. God would bless those who blessed Abraham,
5. God would curse those who cursed Abraham,
6. God would bless all the peoples on earth through Abraham.[161]

Although not an explicit blessing of land or seed, it is important to note the encounter between Abraham and Melchizedek in Genesis 14:19. It is also important to understand that a divine blessing pours from "the greater to the lesser."[162] In this context, God revealed Melchizedek as greater than Abraham. In the specific prayer Melchizedek spoke over Abraham, a close connection is made between the blessing of God onto Abraham ("Blessed be Abram by God Most High") and God's creation of heaven and earth. (Genesis 14:19) This connection further substantiates the observation that God's blessing onto Abraham would be experienced by the inheritance of land, on which Abraham's seed would multiply and expand.

In Genesis 15:1, God promised Abraham that his reward would be very great. Telling Abraham to look at all the stars in the sky, the Lord promised Abraham that his offspring would be equally numerous. (Genesis 15:5) In addition to promising Abraham an extensive offspring, the Lord also promised

---

161   Promises 1 – 6 identified in Genesis 12:1-3.
162   Tuck, Dr. Gary. Lecture on "Genesis and Blessing, Land and Seed." Western Seminary, January 22, 2018.

to give Abraham "this land that he possessed" (Genesis 15:7). In Genesis 15:18, the explicit recording of the dimension of land Abraham's descendants would inherit was also recorded.[163]

In regard to the blessing of land, it is significant to note the manner in which the initial promises God made to Abraham were expanded throughout Genesis. For example, in Genesis 15, the promises God made in regard to Abraham's possession of land were restricted to specific geographic territories (Genesis 15:18-21). However, in Genesis 17, God was much more expansive and unrestrictive in His promises. In Genesis 17:5, when God changed Abram's name to "Abraham," God bestowed the title "Father of all nations" onto him. Furthermore, in 17:6-7, God extended the territory of Abraham's rule to "many nations," and promised that "nations and kings will come through you." God's promise as defined in Genesis 17:8 was also noted as being an "eternal possession." This particular promise points the reader forward to the true eternal and everlasting blessing of Jesus Christ.

In Genesis 18:19, God explained that in order for blessing to extend through Abraham to all the nations (Abraham's seed) of the earth (land), Abraham must "teach his children and his house after him to keep the way of the Lord by doing what is right and just" (Genesis 18:19). The requirement of obedience and trust in God was put to the ultimate test in Genesis 22. Because Abraham completely trusted God and remained obedient to Him, the Lord declared, "Because you have done this thing" Abraham would be blessed (Genesis 22:16). Following Abraham's confirmation of trust and obedience, God revealed the extent to which Abraham's seed would be blessed in the promise, "Through your offspring all the nations of the earth will be blessed, because you have obeyed me." (Genesis 22:18)

THE PROMISES TO ISAAC

GENESIS 25:5 INTRODUCED a key concept in understanding God's blessing of land and seed: A blessing from God can be transferred from one person to another. When "Abraham left everything he owned to Isaac" (Genesis 25:5) then God's promise, "Through your offspring all the nations

---

163   Genesis 15:18 further substantiates the connection between land and seed; it was Abraham's descendants' (seed) that would inherit the land.

of the earth being blessed," (Genesis 15:19) was essentially transferred from Abraham to Isaac. At this point in the biblical narrative, the theme of blessing, land, and seed is thus continued through Isaac and his family line. The verse, "After Abraham's death, God blessed his son Isaac" (Genesis 25:11), further solidifies the transference and continuance of blessing from Abraham onto Isaac. In verse 26:24, God appeared to Isaac and further solidified the continued blessing that Isaac would receive on behalf of Abraham. God promised Isaac "I will bless you and will increase the number of your descendants for the sake of my servant Abraham." (Genesis 26:24) This particular promise continued to build the theme of closely unifying the association of blessing occurring through an increase of seed (descendants).

THE PROMISES TO JACOB
A Theme of Brotherhood and Birthright

ALTHOUGH ISAAC HAD TWO SONS, the oldest being Esau, who was by birthright entitled to Isaac's blessing, Isaac's blessing was ultimately bestowed and thus transferred onto the younger son Jacob. The foretelling of this episode was introduced in Genesis 25:23, when the LORD appeared to Isaac's wife Rebekah and told her that of the two children within her womb that "the older will serve the younger." Furthermore, although by deceit and trickery, the oldest son Esau sold his birthright to his younger brother Jacob.

The incident of transference of birthright between brothers indicates God's blessing is not restricted to custom or cultural mandate. Although Esau was entitled by birth to receive Jacob's blessing, he chose not to realize the immense value of the anticipated blessing, and rather sold his birthright (and future eternal inheritance) for a simple meal (temporal gratification) of "Red stew" (Genesis 25:30). God revealed through this episode the contrast between the sin of Jacob's deceit of his brother and Esau's disparagement of birthright, pointing the reader to the more severe sin committed by Esau.[164]

In addition to Jacob receiving (although through deceit) a claim to birthright, he also (again through deceit) received the blessing of Isaac, and thus the

---

164   This observation was discovered in Dr. Gary Tuck's *"The ARGUMENTS Of the Books of THE OLD TESTAMENT," p. 5.*

continuance of inheritance that had initially been bestowed upon Abraham. It is especially important to note the totality of Isaac's blessing onto Jacob included reference to the three categories of God's promises for blessing, land, and seed: "May God give you heaven's dew and earth's richness *(land)*—and abundance of grain and new wine *(seed)*. May nations serve you *(land)* and peoples *(seed)* bow down to you."[165]

Genesis 28:13-14 revealed God's ultimate promise of blessing, land, and seed onto Jacob, which is clearly established through the continuance of promises initially bestowed upon Abraham. This particular verse depicts the inherited line of blessing from God onto Abraham, to Isaac, and finally placed upon Jacob. The magnitude of the promise of descendants (seed) is visually described as being immensely plentiful: "Your descendants will be like the dust of the earth" (Genesis 28:14). This particular promise echoes the visual representation provided to Abraham ("I will bless you and make your descendants as numerous as the stars in the sky and as sand on the seashore"[166]), and further substantiates the manner in which Jacob's seed will spread across the four corners of the earth.

CONCLUDING THOUGHTS

BLESSING IS A KEY CONCEPT in Scripture, and the image of God as one who promises blessing, land, and seed is a significant component of understanding His Word. God, as the creator of everything, inherently infuses His creation with goodness and blessedness. However, as a result of creation's succumbing to temptation, the theme of an "anti-seed" and sin is equally important to understand in order to faithfully appreciate and embrace God's redeeming plan of salvation.

Through carefully tracing the concepts of blessing, land, and seed through the promises made to Abraham, Isaac, and Jacob, a correlation is discovered: The governing category of "blessing" is manifested in the acquisition of "land" on which God's chosen "seed" would flourish. As the Divine Author beautifully outstretches His hand in continual redeeming grace, the faithful reader of

---

165   Genesis 27:28-29. (Author's emphasis of "land" and "seed" within parentheses of the verse).
166   Ibid., 22:17.

Scripture is presented with the awesome reality that God's creation would be saved through the very seed of His own Son, Jesus Christ. Therefore, those who submit in faith to Jesus Christ resemble Abraham, and in effect become his "spiritual seed," which is distinguished and separate from the seed belonging to the serpent (evil one).[167] Through the outpouring of the Holy Spirit, the fulfillment of God's promise of blessing, land, and seed can now be experienced through all those who embrace Jesus Christ as their Lord and Savior.

---

167   This observation and insight was discovered in *The New Dictionary of Biblical Theology (Downers Grove, IL: InterVarsity Press, 2000). Seed, p. 772.*

CHAPTER
ELEVEN

THE REVELATION OF DIVINE WISDOM

A Composite Picture of Old Testament Wisdom

IN BIBLICAL AND THEOLOGICAL STUDIES, the term 'wisdom' is used as a literary category for classifying certain books of the Old Testament including Proverbs, Ecclesiastes, and Job. Within these books the pursuit of wisdom focuses on the ability to judge matters rightly, the cultivation of self-understanding, and the increasing revelation and knowledge of God.[168] Although each book offers the reader with an opportunity to "increase in wisdom, stature and favor with God and mankind" (Luke 2:52), none of the books is able to stand alone as the definitive authority on the subject. Rather, all three books serve to provide the reader with a composite picture of wisdom and highlight the conclusive argument that "The fear of Yahweh is the beginning of wisdom" (Proverbs 1:7).[169]

The collective message of the three books effectively positions the reader at the starting point of a life-long journey of divergent destinations. "A wise man's heart directs him toward the right, but the foolish man's heart directs him toward the left" (Ecclesiastes 10:2).[170] The image of "life as a path" is an important image in Proverbs, and seems to set the stage for a journey that results in either fullness of joy or doom and sorrow. "For he guards the course of the just and protects the way of his faithful ones. Then you will understand what is right and just and fair – every good path" (Proverbs 2:8-9). The author of Proverbs therefore presents the stark contrast between the path of wisdom and the path of foolishness. The truly wise seek their wisdom from God, while the foolish believe they do not need instruction and advice. "The wise in heart accept commands, but a chattering fool comes to ruin" (Proverbs 10:8).

Although the author of Proverbs encourages the reader to understand that the pursuit of wisdom "adds length to one's life" (Proverbs 10:27), they also acknowledge that in God's absolute sovereignty, He retains the authority to overrule even the most prudently laid plans. "All our steps are ordered by the Lord; how then can we understand our own way?" (Proverbs 20:24). The

---

168   *The New Dictionary of Biblical Theology (Downers Grove, IL: InterVarsity Press, 2000), p. 844.*

169   The expression, "The fear of the LORD" occurs 14 times in Proverbs. The command to "Fear God" is also expressed by the authors of Ecclesiastes (Eccl. 12:13) and Job (Job 28:28).

170   The author's interpretation of Ecclesiastes 10:2 is that the "path toward the right" is the pursuit of *divine wisdom resulting in fear and reliance on God,* and the *"path toward the left"* is the pursuit *of worldly wisdom and independence from God.*

author of Ecclesiastes further illustrates the complexity of life, and encourages the reader to understand the human tendency to trust in their own instincts and self-assuredness may be counterproductive to harmony and good order. In fact, many scholars argue the ability to abide within the natural fundamental order of God's creation was paramount in the pursuit of divine wisdom.[171]

It is important to note the author of Ecclesiastes brackets the entire speech of the Teacher with a summary of the message, "Meaningless! Meaningless! Utterly meaningless! Everything is meaningless" (Ecclesiastes 1:2, 12:8). The author purposely positions the opening proposition and concluding reinforcement of the *meaningless of life* to draw the reader's attention to the *purpose of life*, which is fear of God. Although some people may go through life with a happy-go-lucky mindset, the author of Ecclesiastes seems to argue, "God has set eternity in the human heart" (Ecclesiastes 3:10) a result of which compels mankind to seek more than temporal objects of desire.

The author of Ecclesiastes encourages the reader to understand that all toil in the world is ultimately for nothing: "And the dust returns to the ground it came from, and the spirit returns to God who gave it" (Ecclesiastes 12:7). This sentiment is also reinforced in Job, as the author initially portrays the wealth and material possessions of Job and then immediately demonstrates their fragility and temporal nature by describing their destruction.[172] Therefore, the authors of Proverbs, Ecclesiastes, and Job seem to agree the ultimate source of everything good comes from God alone: "The blessing of the LORD brings wealth, without having to toil for it" (Proverbs 10:22).

Israel's sages believed every quality of God's creation was determined by a fundamental order, and to act in harmony with the universal order that sustained creation was the supreme goal.[173] Therefore, a great deal of the wisdom literature, in particular within Proverbs, seems to paint the picture of a universe that operates in a very mechanical way. This view tends to present wisdom as the ability to discern between a good deed that would produce a good result and a bad deed that would produce a bad result. However, this somewhat simplistic view of wisdom is contrasted with the books of Job that account for the mystery and uncertainty of God's creation, and encourage the reader to remain humble to Yahweh's

---

171   *New Dictionary of Biblical Theology, p. 844.*

172   In Job 1:1-3 the author describes the wealth and prosperity of Job: "He had seven sons and three daughters, and he owned seven thousand sheep, three thousand camels, five hundred yoke of oxen and five hundred donkeys, and had a large number of servants. He was the greatest man among all the people of the East."

173   *The New Dictionary of Biblical Theology, p. 844.*

involvement in everything that happens. "Can you fathom the mysteries of God? Can you probe the limits of the Almighty? They are higher than the heavens above – what can you do? They are deeper than the depths below – what can you know?" (Job 11:7-8). Within this verse, the author of Job encourages the reader to embrace the fundamental principle that true wisdom begins with reverence and fear of God.

The authors of Proverbs, Ecclesiastes, and Job seem to encourage a life in the pursuit of wisdom and righteousness that is pleasing to God. "Crooked minds are an abomination to the Lord, but those of blameless ways are his delight" (Proverbs 11:20). However, the authors also acknowledge that although living wisely is pleasing to God, wisdom does not necessarily shelter one from the experience of suffering and calamity. "Better a little with righteousness than much gain with injustice" (Proverbs 16:8). This sentiment is also made evident in Ecclesiastes, as the author encourages the reader to understand that although wisdom is not an assurance of wealth, the goal for the prudent should always be the path of knowledge: "Better a poor but wise youth than an old but foolish king who no longer knows how to heed a warning" (Ecclesiastes 4:13).

It is important to note the authors of Proverbs, Ecclesiastes, and Job collectively encourage the reader to understand *divine wisdom* is distinctly different than *worldly wisdom*. "Trust in the LORD with all your heart and lean not on your own understanding; in all your ways submit to him, and he will make your paths straight" (Proverbs 3:5-6). Divine wisdom focuses on God's involvement with His creation, and conclusively points to the fact that wisdom is the firstborn of creation: "The LORD brought me forth as the first of his works" (Proverbs 8:22), and that wisdom was present when God first made the world: "I was there when he set the heavens in place" (Proverbs 8:27).

The author of Job further encourages the reader to understand that the faithful pursuit of wisdom is in fact a pursuit of knowing God. "For he views the ends of the earth and sees everything under the heavens" (Job 28:24). Continuing to reinforce the Proverbs authors' definitive argument that "the fear of the LORD is the beginning of wisdom" (Proverbs 1:7), the author of Job similarly directs the reader to understand true wisdom begins with fearing God. "And he said to the human race, 'The fear of the Lord—that is wisdom" (Job 28:28). Strategically placing his conclusive argument at the end of the book, the author of Ecclesiastes seems to summarize for the reader the unified message in the pursuit of wisdom: "Here is the conclusion of the matter: Fear God and keep his commandments, for this is the duty of all mankind" (Ecclesiastes 12:13).

CONCLUDING THOUGHTS

THE COLLECTIVE MESSAGE OF Proverbs, Ecclesiastes, and Job encourages the reader to understand and cherish the fact that true wisdom comes from God. The authors are united in their metaphor of mankind born at the inception of a life-long journey along a path of divergent destinations. Successful navigation of life therefore requires the reader to "watch the path of your feet, and your ways will be established" (Proverbs 4:26). The critical warning to be wary of false promises of worldly wisdom is reinforced by the author of Ecclesiastes, "A wise man's heart directs him toward the right, but the foolish man's heart directs him toward the left" (Ecclesiastes 10:2).

Within the books of Proverbs, Ecclesiastes, and Job, the image of "life as a path" sets the stage for a journey that results in either fullness of joy, or doom and sorrow. "Ponder the path of thy feet, and let all your ways be established" (Prov 4:26). The authors of the three books present the difference between the path of wisdom and the path of foolishness, and encourage the reader to ensure the "path of their feet" is established in divine wisdom. A truly wise person fears God and seeks their wisdom from Him. The strict adherence to fearing God and the "path of the righteous" is therefore "like the first gleam of dawn, shining ever brighter till the full light of day" (Proverbs 4:18).

CHAPTER
TWELVE

THE GOSPEL OF MATTHEW AND THE PRIMARY TEACHINGS OF JESUS CHRIST

THE GOSPEL ACCORDING TO Matthew provides an account of the primary teachings of our Lord Jesus Christ. As a whole, the gospel is divided into five distinct discourses, with each discourse intended to provide the reader with specific and actionable knowledge on the life of Jesus Christ, and the furtherance of the Kingdom of God. Each of the five discourses is pronounced with a concluding statement similar or exact in nature to: "And it came to pass, when Jesus had ended these sayings."[174] The five discourses are a combination of narrative on the life and activities of Jesus in addition to Matthew's recollection of Jesus' teachings. Furthermore, the five discourses are grouped in such a manner as to accomplish three primary goals.

First, Matthew confirms that Jesus was the prophesied King of Israel. Second, Matthew addresses the question of why Jesus, if he was the King, did not rule the Kingdom in accordance with traditional Jewish expectations. Finally, Matthew provides the reader with explicit instructions on how to advance the Kingdom of God.[175] This paper is specifically concerned with Jesus' second discourse, in which Jesus instructs his 12 disciples on matters including by what means and to whom they were to preach, their behavior, the likelihood of their suffering and expected faithful response, and finally encouragement for their future endeavors.

In addition to addressing the content of Jesus' second discourse in relation to the audience at the time, namely his 12 disciples, this paper will also investigate the unique hermeneutical challenge of understanding the relevance of Matthew's text in regard to today's reader. By understanding the relevance of both the historical event in addition to Matthew's text, the reader of the Gospel of Matthew is better equipped for a richer and more meaningful spiritual life.

---

174   Dr. Tuck, Argument on Matthew, p. 2; further referencing New King James Bible. Matthew 7:29, 11:1, 13:53, 19:1, 26:1.
175   Dr. Tuck, Argument on Matthew, p. 2.

THE ORIGINAL DISCOURSE

AS WE BEGIN OUR observation and interpretation of Matthew 10, we reflect on the concluding narrative and text of Jesus' first discourse.[176] Following a season of Jesus' preaching and healing sickness throughout all the cities, villages, and synagogues, we discover that our Lord was "moved with compassion" because the people were "sheep without a shepherd."[177] According to Matthew, Jesus observed the vast multitudes of "lost sheep," and then said to his disciples, "The harvest truly is plenteous, but the laborers are few."[178] Matthew described through this narrative account the building of momentum towards our Lord's instruction to his 12 disciples provided in the second discourse.

Matthew 10 begins with a profound statement of delegated power, in addition to a key statement that progresses Jesus' original twelve from *disciples* to *apostles* with an appointed mission to perform on his behalf. Matthew 10:1 describes this opening sequence of events, and the reader is immediately compelled to observe two key facts: The first being that Jesus called His 12 disciples onto Him; the second that Jesus bestowed power upon them that enabled their subsequently appointed mission. Therefore, in one single verse, we discover the original context of Jesus' discourse was between Himself and his appointed twelve. Furthermore, we observe the manner in which Jesus empowered those whom he called.

From a hermeneutical perspective, the verse 10:1 is of immense importance, for the reader is introduced to the original sender (S1 = Jesus Christ) and the original receiver (R1 = 12 Disciples). Therefore, the first context we bring our attention to is the historical event in which Jesus instructed his twelve. The second context, of significant importance for our purposes today, is Matthew's text (Matthew = S2), which was intended for the "Lost Sheep of Israel" in addition to future generations of readers (Future Oral Recipient, i.e., "Lost Sheep" and Textual Reader = R2).

As noted above, the historical context of Matthew 10 and the relationship between Jesus (S1) and his twelve (R1) was greatly influenced by the words "disciple" and "apostle." In 10:1, when Jesus first called his twelve onto Him, Matthew used the word "disciple." However, in Matthew 10:2, following Jesus' appointment and delegation of power, Matthew used the word "apostle."

---

176   Matthew 5:1 – 7:29.
177   Ibid., 9: 35-36.
178   Ibid., 9:37.

The implication of this subtle progression of terminology is significant for understanding the original context of the discourse (S1 – R1). Rather than being mainly observers of Jesus' life and ministry, his 12 apostles were now being instructed, empowered, and sent forth to take specific actions to advance the Kingdom of God. In this context, verse 10:1 was strategically placed by the author to provide historical relevance (Event = S1 – R1) in addition to providing a source of encouragement for all future recipients of Matthew's gospel (Text = S2 – R2).

Observing the manner in which our Lord *empowered* his original twelve (S1 – R1) is of immense importance both in the historical context and for readers today (S2 – R2). In verse 10:19-20, Matthew further elaborates on the power bestowed on the original twelve (S1 – R1). The careful interpreter of text realizes the dual implications of our Lord's discourse in the historical context (S1 – R1) and Matthew's subsequent reframing of Jesus' words for all future generations (S2 – R2). The key understanding and insight is the progressive manner and sequential steps our Lord took in furthering the Kingdom of God. Jesus called his faithful to Him and empowered them (S1 – R1 / v. 10:1) then commanded them to preach (S1 – R1 / v. 10:7), all of which would be accomplished not by their own means, but through the Holy Spirit (S1 – R1 / v. 10:20). By reframing our Lord's words, Matthew encourages future generations of readers (S2- R2) to boldly preach the Kingdom of God, not by our own means, but through the empowering of the Holy Spirit. In this respect, Matthew makes brilliant use of both the original context and his subsequent text to provide a *doxological* aspect (namely the R1 and R2 furtherance of the Kingdom of God that would ultimately be accomplished by God) for today's reader.[179]

A PROGRESSIVE UNFOLDING

IN MATTHEW 10:5-6, we notice the first command of Jesus to the twelve. This original command, notably between S1 and R1, is important for our investigation into the discourse, for we discover this was a clear delineation between the grouping of S1 – R1 and S2 – R2 text and message. In other words, the original command was in relation to S1 – R1, and provided them direction to "go not into the way of the Gentiles, and into any city of the Samaritans enter

179   Kostenberger, Andreas J. and Richard D. Patterson. *For The Love of God's Word* (Grand Rapids, MI. Kregel Publications, 2015), p. 107.

ye not: But go rather to the lost sheep of the house of Israel."[180] The boundaries and geographic restrictions observed between S1 – R1 were provided for two reasons, one of which retained significance in relation to the specific S1 – R1 relationship, and one which retains relevance to the reader of today.

The original intention of the command and communication between S1 – R1 may have been based on two key facts, observed in earlier and later parts of Matthew. First, we return our attention to Matthew 9:36-37, in which Jesus (in the context of S1 – R1 communication) was moved with compassion for the "lost sheep of Israel." The "plenteous harvest" that Matthew draws the reader's attention to was contrasted with the "few laborers" who would be sent forth to gather. Therefore, in the manner of interpretation, Jesus knew the "lost sheep of the house of Israel" would be adequate "harvest" to occupy his 12 apostles during their immediate mission. Second, Jesus was still alive with his apostles, and therefore the great commission had not yet been bestowed upon them.

Next, we turn our attention to the S2 – R2 context for the originally imposed geographic restriction on the twelve, which prohibited their preaching to Gentiles or entrance into a city of the Samaritans. In Matthew 28:18-19, we discover that following the death and resurrection of Jesus, Jesus further empowered the apostles to teach "all the nations." Therefore, the S1 – R1 context is expanded from Matthew (S2) through the apostles (R1) to all recipients of the message (R2). In this context, Matthew provided all future generations of reader (R2) a *didactic* dimension trough the text (S2 – R2), encouraging proper conduct and response to anticipated hardship and rejection of the Kingdom of God.[181]

In Matthew 10:27-28, the historical event and foretelling of our Lord's death and the subsequent persecution of his faithful apostles has dual implications for both S1 – R1 and S2 – R2 purposes. In the historical context, Jesus explained in 10:27 (S1 – R1) the private conversation "heard in the ear" by the apostles would ultimately need to be "preached on the rooftops." Of specific relevance to the original receiver (R1), our Lord also encouraged a *didactic* response to the anticipated hardship his apostles would experience. By reframing the context through his text, Matthew was able to encourage the reader (S2 – R2) to relate to the original apostles and to boldly profess the Kingdom of God

---

180   Matthew 10:5-6.
181   Kostenberger and Patterson. *For The Love of God's Word,* p. 107.

without fear of persecution. The emphasis for both R1 and R2, therefore, was to focus on the eternal Kingdom of God, and to dismiss the transient nature of the world.

In addition to the specific discourse presented in Matthew 10, it is important to understand the author's strategic placement of this discourse between the first and third discourses of the gospel. The building of momentum towards our Lord's observance of the "plenteous harvest" resulted in the apostles being commanded to preach the Kingdom of God. However, as previously articulated, the apostles were restrained geographically to the "Lost Sheep." In the discourse between our Lord and the apostles (S1 – R1), specific guidance was provided in regard to their behavior in the face of persecution and rejection. This careful placement of text by the author receives due regard in the subsequent discourse and narrative in which Jesus was in fact rejected. In this manner, we are able to interpret the theme of the first three sections or discourses in the following manner: The observation of lost souls, the command to preach the Kingdom of God, and the likelihood of rejection and opposition we should expect to face.

CONCLUDING THOUGHTS

THE GOSPEL ACCORDING to Matthew provides an account of the primary teachings of our Lord Jesus Christ. Of the five discourses within the gospel, the second discourse presented in Matthew 10 is unique in nature. From a hermeneutical perspective, the original context was the historical event between our Lord and his appointed 12 apostles, in which Jesus provided them with directions on furthering the Kingdom of God. The second context is the actual text of Matthew 10, in which Matthew reframes our Lord's words for the benefit and application of all future generations of readers. Our ability to understand the relevance of both the historical event and Matthew's subsequent reframing of our Lord's words through his text allows for a richer and more meaningful spiritual life.

CHAPTER
THIRTEEN

THE TRUE VINE OF JOHN 15

JESUS CHRIST WAS THE MASTER TEACHER who frequently utilized his surroundings, figurative language, and analogy in order to illustrate spiritual truths. Through the example of a vine and the viticulture application of producing fruit, Jesus lifted up the minds of his 11 disciples to help them understand their relationship to God, each other, and most importantly, to Himself. John 15 was the author's written account of the "vine and branches" discourse Jesus provided to the disciples, which included several key lessons of relevance to both the disciples and Christians today. Understanding Christ's foundational analogy and the unique qualities of the vine, the branches, the husbandman,[182] and fruit bearing was critical for the disciples to achieve compliance with Christ's command to *abide in Him*.[183]

This chapter will focus on the essential nature of the vine analogy and critically examine the implications of interpreting the Greek word *airei* found in verse 15:2 as either "lifts up" or "takes away." Through a careful analysis of commentary on John 15, an exposition of the original Greek word *airei*, and by investigating ancient and modern viticulture practices, this chapter will weigh and contrast the evidence supporting both cases. Furthermore, I will present the relevance of overlaying the author's phrase "abide in" in order to discern the intended meaning *airei* was meant to achieve. Ultimately, this chapter will present an argument for only one valid interpretation of *airei* that must be appreciated and understood through the practice of discerning the author's intended meaning. Although I present my interpretation, I encourage you to weigh the arguments carefully, and see where the Holy Spirit leads you.

THE CASE FOR "LIFT UP"

BY ESTABLISHING A FAITHFUL understanding and appreciation for John 15, and specifically the author's intended meaning of verse 15:2, the reader is set in a superior position to embrace their true identification with

---

182   *Husbandman* in this paper is also referred to as a *vinedresser, vine tender* or *gardener* and is a viticulture term for one who tends and cares for a vineyard.

183   New King James Bible, John 15:1-10.

Jesus Christ. In order to discern the author's intended meaning and substantiate the case for interpreting the use of the word *airei* to mean "lift up," we identify elements of literary context, semantic domain, support from the specific text of John 15, and historical agricultural practices to demonstrate beyond a reasonable doubt the unequivocal interpretation for *airei*.

First, we note that proper understanding for the totality of Christ's analogy of the vine, branches, and vinedresser was dependent upon familiarity with the historical aspects of agricultural and viticulture practices of the biblical era.[184] Jesus utilized the teaching techniques of metaphor, analogy, and figurative speech to help people understand and relate to spiritual truths. Oftentimes, as in the case of John 15, Christ's use of an analogy was in "real time" to ensure his followers were able to fully engage their visual and auditory senses simultaneously. The practice of providing for one's multiple learning styles ensured the vast multitude of Christ's disciples and general populace would be able to relate to his teaching.[185] Therefore, to further substantiate the significance of both the literary and historical context, we overlay Christ's analogy onto the immediacy of his teaching and the original audience present with Christ at the time of the discourse.

In Verse 13:10, we discover a key insight into the moral state of the disciples who would remain present with Christ during the vine discourse. Christ told his disciples, "He that is washed needeth not save to wash his feet, but is clean every whit: and ye are clean, but not all." The relevance of being "clean" was of immense importance, for Judas, the only disciple who was therefore unclean, ultimately removed himself from the company of those who were clean. It is interesting to observe that in the Gospel of John, when the phrase "take away" or "take up" was used, the context was often in relation to the actions or anticipated behavior of a third party. The individual retained dominion over their choice to remove or "take away" their property, person, or behavior. In the case of Judas, we note that *he removed himself* from the company of Christ and the disciples. Even our Lord made reference to the autonomy of the individual when he said, "No one takes it from me, but I lay it down of myself." (John 10:15) Therefore, in the literary context of the Gospel of John, we see no evidence from the author to discern that God retained or partook in the role of "taking away."

---

184 *The Disciplemaker: What Matters Most to Jesus (2001), p. 3.*
185 Ibid., p. 26.

In the concluding verse of John 14, we note the key passage, "Arise, let us go hence" (John 14:31). This verse substantiates the departure from the walls within the residence of the last supper to the garden, and identifies Christ's 11 disciples as being in his company.[186] Furthermore, the time of year and season, since Passover had occurred in the early spring, is important for understanding the immediacy of the analogy and likelihood that Christ's 11 disciples had actually visually witnessed his use of a vine during the discourse.[187] By understanding the historical context and interpreting the author's intended meaning within an agricultural frame, the reader is able to faithfully understand Christ's message through the analogy, and to see within their mind what the disciples observed through their eyes.

Christ, as the master teacher, did not randomly select the vine out of the multitude of objects he could have used to draw the illustration of fruitfulness and the importance of abiding in Him.[188] Rather, Christ likely chose the vine because of its spiritual context within the Old Testament. The analogy of the vine, and Christ's specific declaration that he was the *true vine*, substantiated God's abiding love, protection, and care for God's people. For example, in Psalm 80:9, we read, "Thou has brought a vine out of Egypt: Thou has cast out the heathen, and planted it. Thou prepared room for it, and caused it to take deep root, and filled the land." Nevertheless, although the vine may have been understood by the disciples in the context of a blessing, there were other Old Testament passages that painted a less desirable picture. As noted by D.A. Carson, "Most of these [Old Testament] passages stress how favored and privileged the vine is, but also how corrupt."[189] Therefore, by juxtaposing Himself with the Old Testament reference to the vine, Christ ensured his disciples understood he was the *true vine*, uncorrupted and beyond reproach, and that abiding in Him was essential to fruitfulness.[190]

The viticulture practice of the biblical era portrayed a very special relationship between the vinedresser and the vine. Understanding this relationship encourages the correct understanding of Christ's analogy, and provides greater discernment for the author's intended meaning of the word

---

186   Judas had recently departed from the company of Christ and the other disciples with the intention of betraying him.

187   *The Disciplemaker: What Matters Most to Jesus* (2001), p. 4.

188   Ibid., p. 4.

189   Carson, D. A. *The Farewell Discourse and Final Prayer of Jesus* (*Grand Rapids, Michigan: Baker Book House, 1980), p. 15.*

190   This reference was identified in Exposition of the Gospel of John, p. 6.

airei. Furthermore, the purpose of Christ's analogy can then be fully embraced, for the loving care the vinedresser provided the vine was the very loving care the Father provided the Son and those who abided in Him.

In biblical era Israel, the natural contours of the regional hill country, in addition to constructed terraces labored upon by the vinedressers, were intended to keep the majority of vines off the ground. However, due to the delicate structure of the vine, damage caused by storms, animals, or vineyard pillagers, oftentimes the vine would fall onto the ground and thus be more susceptible to further damage. Therefore, the vinedresser would meticulously walk through the vineyard, and *airei or lift up* the fallen vines, carefully cleaning them and affixing them to the terrace or tying them to a stronger branch already off the ground.[191] As noted in *The International Standard Bible Encyclopedia*, "Fallen vines were lifted (John 15:2, *airei*, from *aireo,* 'To lift,' *not* from *aireo,* 'To catch, to take away,' as in all English versions) into position with meticulous care and allowed to heal."[192] For our purposes of literary context and word study, it is of immense importance and enhances our argument to note the Encyclopedia's definition of the term in question.

Due to the fact the purpose of a vine, in both biblical era Israel and modern viticulture practice, was to produce fruit, then eliminating or cutting off a branch would be counterproductive.[193] Instead of eliminating a damaged or non-fruit-bearing branch, vinedressers would carefully clean the branch to ensure its future fruitfulness. This understanding and context is substantiated in John 15:2, where the author wrote, "Every branch that beareth fruit, he *purgeth* it, that it may bring forth more fruit." To *purgeth* meant to clean, which Christ explained happened spiritually through the Word of God.[194] In addition, Christ's claim to his eleven disciples, "Now you are clean through the word which I have spoken to you" (John 15:3), sheds further light onto the literary context. Due to the fact Christ was specifically addressing his faithful 11 disciples,[195] the literary context was such that his disciples were clean and "fruit bearing." In order to retain their fruit bearing capacity, they needed to remain "in the vine" with Jesus Christ. By remaining in Christ, which they

---

191 *The Disciplemaker: What Matters Most to Jesus, page 14.*

192 In God's Vineyard, the author's counter argument is that God, as the faithful vinedresser, in fact removes from the vine any branch not producing fruit.

193 A counter argument was that *through removal* of a non-fruit-bearing branch, greater growth would take place on those bearing fruit.

194 Pink, Arthur W. *Exposition of the Gospel of John (1945), p. 10.*

195 As noted earlier, Judas was not present with the 11 disciples.

understood through the analogy of remaining connected to the vine, the disciples would bring glory to totality of the vineyard and the vinedresser, namely the Father and Kingdom of God.[196]

Although the approach of many exegetes was to view Christ's analogy in the context of the vinedresser picking only the most fruitful branches and cutting off the non-fruit bearing, we now understand the actual viticulture practice of the biblical era was to preserve, nurture, and "lift up" both types of branches.[197] Therefore, to attach a negative connotation to the word *airei* would be to violate the reality of what Christ actually referred to, and what the disciples had likely observed as the context for which the description arose.[198]

It is helpful to once again recall the literary context we are attempting to interpret. The reader of today is essentially "listening in" on a conversation that took place between Jesus and his faithful 11 disciples.[199] However, although faithful, and according to Christ, also "clean" and therefore fruit bearing, we note even his beloved disciple Peter still failed to abide in Christ during the tragic events that transpired that night, and ultimately denied he knew Christ on three occasions. Yet despite Peter's shortcoming, he was not "cut off" from Christ. Rather, Peter and the other disciples were continually lifted up, nurtured, and empowered. Therefore, the essence of Christ's analogy must be understood through the controlling command to "abide in Christ." And furthermore, given the purpose of a branch was to bear fruit, the significance of Christ's command was to ensure the believer's fruitfulness, which can only be assured by those who "abide in Christ" and invite "Christ to abide" within them. Given Christ's command to his disciples to abide in Him for the intention of fruitfulness, we may conclude "lift up" is the most accurate and applicable meaning of *airei.*

THE CASE FOR "TAKE AWAY"

BY ESTABLISHING A FAITHFUL UNDERSTANDING and appreciation for John 15, and specifically the author's intended meaning of verse 15:2, we set ourselves in a superior position to embrace our true identification with Jesus

---

196 Oftentimes a counter argument is substantiated by making verse six an exposition of verse two.

197 *The Disciplemaker: What Matters Most to Jesus, pp. 14 & 15.*

198 Ibid., p. 18.

199 Ibid., p. 25.

Christ. In order to discern the author's intended meaning and substantiate the case for interpreting the use of the word *airei* to mean "take away," we identify elements of literary context, semantic domain, support from the specific text of John 15, and historical agricultural practices to demonstrate beyond a reasonable doubt the unequivocal interpretation for *airei*.

At the conclusion of chapter 14 of the Gospel of John, we observe Christ told his disciples, "Rise, let us go hence." Because Judas had already departed from the company of Christ and the disciples, we may discern the literary context of this passage was between Christ and his eleven faithful disciples. As they departed the upper room and discourse of the Last Supper and made their way to the garden, Christ expertly used the surrounding vineyards to formulate an analogy to help the disciples understand the relationship between believers, non-believers, Christ, and God. Each component of Christ's analogy, ranging from the branch, to the vine, to the vinedresser, and the overall theme of producing fruit was meant to convey the spiritual implications of a non-believer (or in the context of the analogy, a non-fruit-bearing branch) being subsequently removed or "taken away."

The semantic domain of the analogy Christ used to educate the 11 disciples was viticulture, and thus, the individual literary context must be understood within this framework. Therefore, when Christ referenced the actual vine within the vineyard, he referred to Himself as "the true vine" (John 15:1). This distinction was important, for the 11 disciples were likely familiar with Old Testament references to Israel's relationship as a vine connected with God. In the analogy provided by Christ, the vine and its branches represented "oneness."[200] Without the vine, the branch was without life, and could therefore not bring forth fruit. A branch that willfully removed itself from the vine, and thus experienced the associated negative repercussions, were images and associations the disciples understood within the context Jeremiah 2:21: "I had planted thee a noble vine, wholly a right seed: how then art thou turned into the degenerate plant of a strange vine onto me?" The other Old Testament example of importance for our position of "take away" may be found in Hosea 10:1, "Israel is an empty vine, he bringeth forth fruit onto himself."

When Christ referred to Himself as the "true vine" he made the distinction between the Old Testament vine, which could be "degenerate" and not

---

200   The distinction, "oneness" and vine reference was observed in *Secrets of the Spirit*. Stedman, Ray. Expository Studies in John 13—17: *Secrets of the Spirit (1975)*, pp. 4 & 75.

produce fruit, and the realization that he was therefore not a mere copy, but the genuine, real, and "true vine." As noted by Ray Stedman, "Christ was the vine from which true life is received."[201] Furthermore, as Christ continued to elaborate on the nature of the vine, he explained to his disciples God was the vinedresser, who was responsible for ensuring the fruitfulness of the branches. As the vinedresser within the analogy, and was customary during the biblical era practice of viticulture, their role was two-part: First, to remove branches that were not producing fruit, and second, to prune fruit producing branches to allow for additional fruit bearing.[202]

In order to fully understand the significance of Christ's analogy, and to further substantiate our case for "take away," we now turn our attention to common viticulture practices of the biblical era. During the fruit-bearing season, a vine would produce "shoots" (commonly referred to as "sucker shoots"). These shoots would distract and dissipate the life-giving nutrients of the vine and minimize the capacity for the individual branches to produce fruit. Therefore, a vinedresser would prune away the shoots to ensure the relationship between the vine and the branch would result in fruit bearing. In the context of both the analogy and the actual viticulture practice, the process of pruning and taking away the sucker shoots resulted in a cleaning process that ensured the fruitfulness of the vine, and removal of any part of the vine that hindered prosperity. Therefore, through the analogy, Christ instructed the 11 disciples that God's work as the vinedresser was to prune or take away "shoots" or distractions from the believer's life that prevented their ability to produce fruit.[203]

After Christ explained the nature of the relationship between Himself, the 11 disciples, and God, he encouraged them in the statement, "Now you are clean through the word which I have spoken to you" (John 15:3). Therefore, we discover the tool employed in the pruning and cleansing process was the Word of God, and as long as the Word remained within the disciples, they would "abide in Christ" and remain fruitful. The significance of remaining in Christ, or "abiding in Him," was of immense importance for the disciples, in addition to the modern-day Christians, to understand. As noted by Stedman, to "abide in Christ" is the essence of 'the Law of Fruitfulness' and was central

201 Ibid., p. 4.
202 A counter argument to the practice of pruning was identified in *Secrets of the Vine in which pruning was understood to mean "cleaning" not "cutting away."*
203 Stedman, Ray. Expository Studies in John 13—17: *Secrets of the Spirit (1975), p. 75.*

to Christ's analogy and discourse to the 11 disciples.[204] The role of abiding had dual implication: There was an activity for the disciple in relation to Christ ("Abide in me"), and for Christ in relationship to the disciple ("And I in you.") The notion of an active and passive role in abiding further supports the argument for "take away." In the context of the analogy, those branches that were not actively remaining part of the vine would be removed, and similarly those "branches" that choose not to remain in Christ, would be "taken away."

Perhaps the most significant scripture to solidify the argument for "take away" may be found in John 15:6. As noted earlier, one aspect of the vinedresser's work was the removal of "shoots" or non-fruit-bearing branches that could distract from the life of the vine. John 15:6 expands upon the role of the vinedresser in the removal process, and we discover that a branch removed from the vine was "thrown into the fire and burned." This verse substantiates the author's intended meaning in John 15:2 in relation to the vinedresser "taking away" every branch not producing fruit. Once non-fruit-bearing branches had been removed from the vine, they were collected and burned. In this manner, we may interpret the author's intention to utilize *progressive parallelism* to unite the theme of verse 15:2 and 15:6.

It is very important to note the subtle transition in John 15:6 between the relationship between a non-believer and Christ, and the branch and the vine. The text of John 15:6 is first noted to be in relationship between a man abiding in Christ,[205] then immediately transitions to the relationship between the branch and the vine.[206] The implications of willfully choosing to be removed from the vine of Christ are evident in the actions of Judas. Although he shared in the ministry of Christ with the other disciples, he ultimately decided not to abide in Christ. In the case of Judas, the "withering" process described in John 15:6 was very short; he committed suicide within a few days of his betrayal.[207]

Finally, it is important to observe and take note of the specific usage and number of times the author utilized the phrase "take away" within the gospel. The author's intended meaning of "take away," to be arguably self-evident in the manner in which the phrase was consistently used, may therefore attest to similar use and meaning in John 15:2. Perhaps the best example of this

---

204 Expository Studies in John 13—17: *Secrets of the Spirit (1975)*, p. 77.

205 "If a man does not abide in me," from John 15:6.

206 "He is cast forth as a branch and withers," from John 15:6.

207 Judas as an example of "withering" due to being "taken away" was noted in Expository Studies in John 13—17: *Secrets of the Spirit*, p. 80.

claim may be found in John 1:29, when we read, "The next day John saw Jesus coming toward Him, and said, 'Behold! The Lamb of God who *takes away* the sin of the world.'" In the author's first use of the phrase "take away" we note only one plausible means of interpretation, which was in fact to "take away" or "remove" our sins. It would be difficult if not impossible to interpret the author's intended meaning was that Christ would "lift up" the sins of the world. Therefore, we may conclude, based on the totality of the presented arguments herein, the most appropriate understanding of *airei* would be "take away."

CONCLUDING THOUGHTS

JESUS CHRIST WAS THE MASTER TEACHER who frequently utilized his surroundings, figurative language, and analogy in order to illustrate spiritual truths. Through the example of a vine and the viticulture application of producing fruit, Jesus lifted up the minds of the disciples to help them understand their relationship to God, each other, and most importantly, to himself. By building and then contrasting two arguments for the interpretation of the Greek word *airei* found in verse 15:2 as either "takes away" or "lifts up," we are now able to best discern the author's intended meaning. Through careful analysis of commentary on John 15, an exposition of the original Greek word *airei,* and by fully understanding ancient and modern viticulture practices, we conclude the strongest case for the word *airei* was to "lift up."

FINDING CONGRUENCY
FOR *AIREI* TODAY

ON THE MORNING OF NOVEMBER 17, 2017, at Vintage Faith's "Abby Coffee Shop," over a steaming cup of coffee with Chaplain Johnson of the Santa Cruz County Sheriff's Office, I had the most remarkable and timely conversation. When I brought up the topic of John 15:2, Chaplain Johnson smiled and responded, "Yes of course, what a most precious verse, loaded with significance for the believer." Chaplain Johnson then elaborated on his firsthand knowledge of a gardening and viticulture practice referred to as "grafting." The grafting practice involves taking a withered and dying branch and uniting it ("grafting") into a flourishing vine. Within a few days of this practice, the once withered branch would be vibrant and full of life. Chaplain Johnson explained the spiritual implication in this manner: Whether a branch (a non-fruit-producing believer) falls off the vine of its own accord, or is removed by the gardener ("taken away"), there still remains an opportunity for the branch to find life ("lifted up"). Therefore, in this respect there remains an opportunity for reconciliation and congruence between the dual meanings of the word *airei*.

CHAPTER
FOURTEEN

THE UNITY OF CHRIST IN THE BOOK OF ROMANS

The Preservation of Harmony Between Jewish and Gentile Christians

THE APOSTLE PAUL'S LETTER to "all in Rome who are loved by God" (Romans 1:7) is a masterful exposition on the importance of positive relations between Jewish and Gentile Christians. The underlying context for Paul's letter to the Christian churches in Rome was his keen awareness of the inherent disunity between Jewish and Gentile believers, and the resultant conflict of understanding and application between the Old and New Testaments. In this respect, the backdrop of Paul's plea for unity in Christ between Jew and Gentile was his simultaneous development of an argument for a greater understanding for the purpose of the Law.

Paul seemed to sense the increasing likelihood of discord between Christians living in strict adherence to the Law with others who were living in relative arrogance about their newfound freedom in Christ.[208] In addressing the problem, Paul presents a theology that encourages a new type of obedience of universal application to both the Jew and the Gentile. Rather than reducing his epistle to merely calling for unity on the grounds of his apostleship, Paul strategically capitalizes on the situation to focus both the Jew and the Gentile on Christ and their newfound unified justification by faith.[209] Although the Law provided legalistic grounds for discontinuity between the Jew and Gentile, through Jesus Christ all believers now have "one mind and one voice" (Romans 15:6).

When Paul wrote "that we serve in the newness of the Spirit and not in the oldness of the letter" (Romans 7:6) and then again reiterated, "You did not receive the spirit of bondage again to fear, but you received the Spirit of adoption" (Romans 8:15), Paul pointed to the inherent danger existing among Christians who still acted as if they were under the Law, serving in the "oldness of the letter" and the "spirit of bondage" (Romans 7:6; 8:15). Paul argues that all Christians do in fact have an obligation, but it is not an obligation to the Law of the Old Testament (Romans 8:12). Rather, the Jewish and Gentile believers must now unify themselves under the superior law of grace that is found in Jesus Christ.

---

208   Tuck, Dr. Gary. Class lecture on Romans. Western Seminary. March 10, 2019.
209   Ibid., Class notes on Romans provided by Dr. Gary Tuck.

UNITY IN THE LAW (ROMANS 1 – 8)

THE COMMON DENOMINATOR for both the Jew and the Gentile was the Law, either the Law given to the Israelites or the requirements of the law "written on the hearts" of the Gentiles (Romans 2:15). Although the Law could serve as a point of division and discontinuity, Paul argues that both the Jew and Gentile are now "delivered from the law" and may find common ground and unity in serving "the newness of the Spirit and not the oldness of the letter" (Romans 7:6). Paul adamantly encourages the reader to understand that through faith in Jesus Christ there is "no difference between the Jew and the Gentile" (Romans 3:22) and that all believers now form one unified body in Christ.

Paul demonstrates that the purpose of the Law was to convince the Jews of their collective sinfulness (Romans 3:23).[210] On the other hand, Paul seems to categorically reduce the Gentiles to a single "godless and wicked people" (Romans 1:18) who are helplessly plagued by sin. Although the Christian Jew may seek to find grounds for elevated position or "advantage" based on the Law (Romans 3:1), Paul argues that in fact "none have an advantage" (Romans 3:9) and that "no one is righteous, not even one" (Romans 3:11). Paul points out that rather than providing advantage or elevated position, the purpose of the Law was to convict the totality of the human race of their sinful nature and need of a savior (Romans 3:20-22).

Paul advances his argument to demonstrate that because the Law served the purpose of convicting the human race of their sinfulness, it could not simultaneously provide justification for the Jewish people. Paul exhorts the reader to understand that God equally justifies the Jew and the Gentile apart from any "works of the Law" (Romans 3:20, 28). Rather than justification through the Law, Paul developed a theology that encourages both the Jew and Gentile to embrace a newfound unity in their collective justification through faith (Romans 1:16-17; 3:27-30).

Critical to Paul's argument on the unity of the Jews and Gentiles is his demonstration of righteousness by faith in the life and model of Abraham (Genesis 15:6).[211] Paul had already established that if justification was based on the Law, then both the Jew and the Gentile would be equally dismissed

---

210   K. P. Donfried. "Romans" in *The New Dictionary of Biblical Theology, p. 294.*
211   Ibid., p. 295.

from God's kingdom. However, Paul leads the reader to a new and greater understanding for the purpose of the Law—mainly to convince all people of their need for a savior. Once equally convinced, Paul demonstrates through the example of Abraham's righteousness that God justifies all people by a completely free act of His will (Romans 3:24; 4:3).

Paul unites the Jew and Gentile Christians on the grounds of their newfound righteousness apart from the Law. Rather than struggling fruitlessly to achieve justification by the Law, Paul explains that righteousness is not achieved through works, but rather by believing what God has said (Romans 4:5). Perhaps anticipating the Jewish claim to privilege based on circumcision, Paul points out that Abraham's faith was credited to him as righteousness before he was circumcised (Romans 4:10). Paul then firmly establishes that Abraham is the father of both the Jew and the Gentile (Romans 4:11-12), and that Abraham's model of faith provides unity for all who believe in Jesus Christ (Romans 4:23).

In a brilliant maneuver to once again argue for unity based on the gospel message, Paul exhorts the Jew and Gentile to find common ground in their newfound life in Christ. Any qualified difference between the Jew and Gentile based on the Law is now part of the "old way" from which the believer in Christ has been released (Romans 7:1-2). Using the illustration of a married woman bound to her husband for the duration of their life on earth, Paul explains that both spiritually and legalistically the woman is released from the law that binds them upon the death of her husband. Continuing the illustration, Paul points out that both the Jew and Gentile have collectively "died to the law through the body of Christ" (Romans 7:4) and now live as one unified body "in the new way of the Spirit" (Romans 7:6).

Perhaps one of Paul's strongest arguments for unity between the Jew and the Gentile was his contention that any grounds for division would keep the believer's mind "set on what the flesh desires" (Romans 8:5). Having established the purpose of the Law was to make "man conscious of their sin" (Romans 3:20), Paul exhorts the Jew and Gentile believer to collectively set their mind on Christ. The Law was a faculty of the "old way" and belonged to the "realm of the flesh" (Romans 8:9). However, Paul argues that through the power of God's Spirit, the believer is now free from the flesh. All who believe in Christ are akin to becoming one unified body and are spiritually "children of God" (Romans 8:14).

THE PLAN FOR ISRAEL (ROMANS 9 – 11)

ONCE HAVING ESTABLISHED the collective unity in Christ the Jew and Gentile may now enjoy, Paul next seeks to address any rivalry among the groups that should arise as a result of "not all the Israelites accepting the good news" (Romans 10:16).[212] Paul seems to foresee the potential for Gentile frustration over the Jews' failure to recognize the gospel message despite their receipt of "the covenants, the law, the temple worship and the promises" (Romans 9:4). It would be easy for the Gentile believer to elevate their place in the church based on the Jews' failure to recognize and receive Christ. Therefore, Paul must explain the continued purpose for "the people of Israel" (Romans 9:31).

Paul asks the rhetorical question of whether the Gentile, who did not overtly pursue righteousness yet nevertheless obtained it through faith, is situated higher than the Jew, who pursued righteousness through the law and utterly failed (Romans 9:30-31). Paul answers that although the Jew did in fact stumble, they did not entirely fall (Romans 9:32; 11:11). Returning to his argument on the grounds for unity between the Jew and Gentile through righteousness achieved by faith in Christ, Paul explains that moving forward the Jew must learn to submit to God's righteousness, as opposed to a creation of their own (Romans 10:3). Through faith in Christ, both the Jew and Gentile may now collectively and equally enjoy "the righteousness for everyone who believes" (Romans 10:4).

Paul reiterates that although Israel did stumble they did not fall beyond recovery (Romans 11:11). In an interesting argument, Paul explains that the Gentiles' salvation served the purpose of making Israel envious and furthered their understanding of the purpose of righteousness by faith. In addition, Paul strongly warns the Gentile believer against any arrogance or superiority against the Jew (Romans 11:18). Paul's concern and admonition of Gentile arrogance further reflects the reality of the tensions between the Jews and Gentiles that existed in the Christian churches in Rome.[213]

Perhaps in an attempt to mitigate the Gentile arrogance, Paul explains through a beautiful illustration that Israel is the "natural branch" of God, and that through their enduring faith they will be "grafted into their own olive tree" (Romans 11:24). Paul levels the playing field by contending that the Gentile should be wary

---

212   Tuck, Dr. Gary. "Romans" in *The Arguments of the Books of the New Testament. pp. 83–84.*
213   Ibid.

of any arrogance given the fact that Israel is the established "root" that supports the Gentile (Romans 11:18). Paul contends that rather than arrogance or conceit, the attitude of the Gentile should be one of "trembling and fear" (Romans 11:20) knowing that if God did not spare the "natural branches" God would certainly not spare the "wild branches" either (Romans 11:21).

APPLIED THEOLOGY (ROMANS 12 – 16)

PAUL THEN SHIFTS HIS argument to the practical application of the theology and calls for unity he had previously outlined in his epistle. Rather than differentiating between the Jew and Gentile, Paul now collectively unites all believers together as "brothers and sisters" and urges them to "offer your bodies as a living sacrifice" (Romans 12:1). Utilizing the illustration of the human body with its various parts, Paul now encourages all believers to "form one body in Christ" (Romans 12:5). In the same fashion that each "member" of the human body serves the collective functionality of the body, so does each individual "member" of the church serve the collective body of the church.

Paul continues to exhort the believer to remain united in their faith in Christ (Romans 13:14). Rather than attempting to maintain their newfound righteousness through the Law, Paul focuses readers' attention on the importance of "doing everything onto the Lord" (Romans 14:8). Paul stresses the importance of "not putting a stumbling block in the way of a brother or sister" (Romans 14:13), and instead to "do whatever leads to peace and mutual edification" (Romans 14:19). Continuing to reiterate the gospel message, Paul contends that all believers should now have the same attitude towards each other that Christ had so that "with one voice you may glorify the God and Father of our Lord Jesus Christ" (Romans 15:5-6).

CONCLUDING THOUGHTS

THE UNDERLYING CONTEXT for Paul's letter to the Christian churches in Rome was his keen awareness of the inherent disunity between Jewish and Gentile believers, and the resulting conflict of understanding and application between the Old and New Testaments. In addressing the problem, Paul presents a theology that encourages a new type of obedience of universal application to both the Jew and Gentile. Paul strategically capitalized on Jewish and Gentile tensions to focus all believers on Christ and their newfound collective justification by faith. Paul's hope is that as one unified body of believers, both the Jewish and Gentile Christians would accept each other in order to bring praise to God (Romans 15:7).

CHAPTER
FIFTEEN

PAUL AND THE CORINTHIANS
Developing a Pauline Theology on Spirituality

UNDERSTANDING THE CULTURAL and philosophic background of Corinth in the time of Paul is fundamental to grasping Paul's theology of spirituality. Paul's letters to the churches in Corinth were significantly influenced by an array of existing problematic conditions within the church and an abundance of cultural secular practices and ideologies that were in stark contrast to the gospel message. By first outlining the sociological characteristics of Corinth, in addition to the religious and philosophical practices of the region, the study of 1 and 2 Corinthians comes alive with actionable principles of decision-making on issues that still challenge God's people today.

The city of Corinth was a great commercial center strategically situated on the isthmus that linked the Peloponnesus with mainland Greece. Mariners frequenting the two ports of Corinth, Cenchreae on the Aegean Sea to the east, and Lechaeum on the Adriatic Sea to the west moved their ships on rollers across the narrow isthmus on a stone-paved road. This narrow passageway served as a central artery into Corinth, and contributed to the overt heartbeat of the city that became known for its wealth, indulgence, and sexual immorality.[214]

Paul faced an uphill struggle against a city populace overly concerned with reputation and social status, self-promotion to gain recognition over others, ambition to succeed at all costs, and an interest in Greek philosophy and wisdom over the Christian message.[215] To make matters even more challenging, Paul's message proved to be against the current of a city with an established international reputation for trade, vice, and promiscuity.[216]

Against the backdrop of Paul's teaching on the sacredness of the human body (1 Corinthians 3:16; 6:19) was the fact that Corinth was plagued by immoral sexual behavior including the worship of the goddess Aphrodite that resulted in prostitution in the name of religion (1 Corinthians 6:9-20).[217] The awareness in Paul's mind of the immense challenges he faced in Corinth were evident in the self-

---

214   Laney, Dr. Carl. "First Corinthians" in *Essential Bible Background. p. 191. The first century geographer Strabo recorded that there were 1,000 temple prostitutes who served in the temple of Aphrodite within the city of Corinth.*

215   A. C. Thiselton. "1 Corinthians" in *The New Dictionary of Biblical Theology. p. 297.*

216   Tuck, Dr. Gary. "First Corinthians" in *The Arguments of the Books of the New Testament. p. 96.*

217   In addition to the accepted practice of prostitution in the name of religion, Paul wrote in 1 Corinthians 5:1-2 of a "sexual immorality of a kind even the pagans do not tolerate: A man is sleeping with his father's wife."

admitted "fear and trembling" (1 Corinthians 2:3) he experienced in his missionary work within the city. So difficult and complex were the issues that Paul faced in Corinth that the Lord appeared to him in a vision and said, "Do not be afraid; keep on speaking, do not be silent. For I am with you, and no one is going to attack and harm you, because I have many people in this city" (Acts 18:9-10).

In addition to understanding the cultural and philosophic background of Corinth, it is important to appreciate Paul's general strategic approach to ministry in the context of his arrival at Corinth in the first place. Paul seemed to sense that the key to rapidly spreading the gospel message was establishing churches in major cities whose trade and commerce increased the likelihood that a large demographic of people would take it back to their villages and start smaller churches by proclaiming the "word of the Lord" (Acts 19:9-10).[218] Having made little headway on his missionary journey in Athens (Acts 17:13-15), Paul set his sights on the next largest city, Corinth (Acts 18:1).

THE BODY AND SPIRIT IN PAULINE THEOLOGY

PERHAPS IT WAS THE severity of the challenges facing Christians living in the city of Corinth, combined with the contrast between their proclaimed faith in Jesus as Messiah (1 Corinthians 2-3; 18) and the simultaneous retention of worldly lifestyle choices, that prompted Paul to ask on two occasions, "Don't you know that you yourselves are God's temple and that God's Spirit dwells in your midst?" (1 Corinthians 3:16; 6:19).[219] Paul illustrates that when the Corinthians received Jesus as their King (1 Corinthians 1:23), a transformation was initiated that advanced the believer into a state of "righteousness, holiness and redemption" (1 Corinthians 1:30). For Paul, this state of holiness was even more precious than purity, and therefore necessitated that the Corinthians' abstain from practices that would defile their body (2 Corinthians 7:1).

Paul stresses that purification, cleansing the body, and ceasing practices that defile the temple of God within the believer was essential to being filled with the

---

218   Longman, Temper III and David E. Garland. *The Expositors Bible Commentary on Galatians, p. 242.*

219   This insight was developed in my mind by Dr. Tuck's class notes on Corinthians. As pointed out by Dr. Tuck, although the Corinthians professed with their mouths faith in Christ, their actions remained world-bound and not Spirit-focused: They were concerned with matters of the world (2 Corinthians 4:16-18); they were walking by sight and not by faith (2 Corinthians 5:7); and they were living as people who "were still worldly" (1 Corinthians 3:1).

character and holiness of Jesus (2 Corinthians 7:1). The life and Spirit of Christ within the believer resulted in their "sanctification in Christ" and transformation "into his holy people" (1 Corinthians 1:2). Paul was certainly aware of the implications for the holiness of the tabernacle in the Old Testament, and seemed to draw a correlation between the holiness of the tabernacle when filled with God's presence (Exodus 29:43, 45) and the holiness of the believer when indwelled by the Spirit of God.

By asking a series of five rhetorical and increasingly pointed questions (2 Corinthians 6:14-16), Paul confronts the Corinthians with the ultimate inquiry: "What agreement is there between the temple of God and idols?" (2 Corinthians 6:16). This series of questions illustrates and expounds upon Paul's observation of a divergent gap between the Corinthians' reception of the gospel message (1 Corinthians 1:18) and their insistence on remaining "people who are worldly" (1 Corinthians 3:1-3). For Paul, belief in Christ constitutes a resurrection into a new life (1 Corinthians 5:7), the evidence of which would be a shedding of worldly tendencies and desires (1 Corinthians 3:18; 6:12-20).

Returning to Old Testament reference and correlation, Paul then seems to answer his own questions by explaining that as God's people (2 Corinthians 6:16b), the Corinthians are to separate themselves from "unclean things" and to abstain from practices that would lead to defilement (2 Corinthians 6:17). The body, according to Paul, is daily wasting away (2 Corinthians 4:16), and therefore, to appease the physical desires of a perishable body is antagonistic to, and a distraction from, the Christian message.

However, rather than losing hope or being overly concerned with the "outward body," Paul encourages the Corinthians to see that "the inward body is being renewed day by day" (2 Corinthians 4:16). Paul encourages the Corinthians to turn their attention to the unseen spiritual reality of the indwelling presence of God, and to focus "not on what is seen, but on what is unseen, since what is seen is temporary, but what is unseen is eternal" (2 Corinthians 4:18).

UNITY AND DIVISION IN PAULINE THEOLOGY

A GREAT MAJORITY of the issues that Paul addresses in his letters to the Corinthians can be traced back to the pervasive values of the surrounding culture.[220] The Corinthians' interest in self-promotion to gain recognition over others, ambition to succeed at all costs, and the influence of the Hellenistic culture tended to focus their minds on matters of materialism and "worldly pursuits" (1 Corinthians 3:1-3).[221] Naturally, these concerns served as a means of division within the church and fostered a general sense of jealousy and quarreling (1 Corinthians 3:3). Paul encouraged the Corinthians to understand that the purpose of the gospel message was to create one "church of God" (1 Corinthians 1:1) and one "body of Christ" (1 Corinthians 6:17; 10:17; 11:29; 12:12-16, 27), where a sense of unity, love, and cohesiveness would prevail.

Paul addressed the issue of disunity by declaring the Corinthians were "acting like mere humans" (1 Corinthians 3:3). For Paul, to have received the gospel message (1 Corinthians 1:18) yet to continue to live in a state of "jealousy and quarreling" was simply not compatible and overt evidence of spiritual immaturity (1 Corinthians 3:2-4).[222] Utilizing a brilliant illustration of the individual and corporate body of Christ, Paul demonstrates that if Christians really are the "temple of the living God" (1 Corinthians 3:16, 6:19; 2 Corinthians 6:16), then both individually and collectively they are unified in Christ (2 Corinthians 6:15).

In an interesting metaphor of competitive athletic training and competition, Paul paints a word picture for the Corinthians against the canvas backdrop of the biennial Isthmian Games. Paul points out that when runners participate in a race, only one will achieve the victory, which on face value would seem to create division and a sense of strife between believers (1 Corinthians 9:24). However, Paul then shifts his tactic by illustrating the unity the athletes experienced during the strict training regime that preceded the race (1 Corinthians 9:25). Creating contrast between the temporal and the eternal, and the individual and the collective, Paul emphasized that "everyone who competes in the games goes into strict training" for the purpose of "winning a crown that will not last" (1 Corinthians 9:25a). In the context of Paul's metaphor, the race that Christians compete in is not an individual race where only one person wins and where the prize is temporal. Rather, Christians "go into strict training together" in preparation to collectively run a race while supporting each other in pursuit of a "crown that will last forever" (1 Corinthians 9:25b).

Paul argues that the Corinthians, as believers in Jesus Christ, have a duty to

---

220   Dr. Tuck. Notes on Corinthians.
221   A. C. Thiselton. "1 Corinthians" in *The New Dictionary of Biblical Theology. p. 297.*
222   Dr. Tuck. Class notes on Corinthians.

turn from every source of defilement and thereby "perfect their holiness out of reverence for God" (2 Corinthians 7:1). According to Paul, living for Christ (2 Corinthians 5:15) meant an equal combination of separation from outward evil (2 Corinthians 6:17) and a loving fellowship with other believers. Therefore, the more important issue that Paul addressed was not the isolated problem of being "mere human" (1 Corinthians 3:3), but rather the fact that the outer "flesh" was sin-cursed and fundamentally rebellious against God. Conversely, the inward redeemed spirit is the very Spirit of Christ within the believer, which is fundamentally obedient to God.[223]

One of Paul's key arguments that further illustrates the antagonistic nature of the "flesh" in opposition to the indwelling Spirit of Christ within the believer can be found in 2 Corinthians 4:3-6. Here Paul distinguishes between the effects of idolatry to the "god of this age" and true obedience and faithfulness to Jesus Christ as Lord. Those serving the "flesh" are spiritually blinded by the sin-cursed nature of first creation (2 Corinthians 4:4). However, those indwelt by the power of the Spirit of God receive "the light of the knowledge of God's glory displayed in the face of Christ" (2 Corinthians 4:6).

CONCLUDING THOUGHTS

UNDERSTANDING THE CULTURAL and philosophic background of Corinth in the time of Paul is fundamental to grasping his theology of spirituality. Paul's letters to the churches in Corinth were significantly influenced by an array of existing problematic conditions within the church and an abundance of cultural differences, secular practices, and ideologies that were in stark contrast to the gospel message. Against the backdrop of sexual immorality, disunity, and the behavior of "mere men" (1 Corinthians 3:3), Paul argues that the redeemed believer and follower of Christ should reflect a transformation of values and lifestyle choices that is evident within every area of their life.

---

223   Dr. Tuck. Class notes on Corinthians.

CHAPTER
SIXTEEN

THE SUFFICIENCY OF FAITH IN SALVATION

A Christian's Freedom from the Law in Galatians

PAUL'S LETTER TO the churches of Galatia served the purpose of firmly establishing the doctrine that people are justified by faith in Jesus Christ (Galatians 2:16). Paul insisted that faith in Christ alone was sufficient for receiving righteousness before God, and that demanding legalistic works in addition to faith was in fact a violation of the true gospel message. Reflecting on his own salvation, Paul encouraged the Galatians to understand that people are justified by believing in what God did for them through Jesus Christ, not by what they are capable of doing for themselves (Galatians 2:19-20). Rather than struggling fruitlessly for self-righteousness by legalistic adherence to the Law, Paul explains that when people put their trust and faith in Christ, then what is true of Jesus also becomes true of them.[224]

Paul adamantly exhorts his readers to be firm in their newfound freedom from Jewish regulations, traditions, and Law, and to enjoy the sufficiency of new creation that comes through faith alone (Galatians 6:15). At the heart of Paul's letter to the Galatians is the realization that circumcision and general adherence to Jewish Law were not required of the Gentile believer to enter into God's family. Paul argues that the purpose of the Law was to convince man of his sinful nature and to awaken his confession of powerlessness and need of a savior (Galatians 3:23-24).[225] Through faith in Christ, the Galatians were encouraged by Paul to act on their freedom from the Law, rather than "being burdened by a yoke of slavery" (Galatians 5:1). Instead of regressing to the bondage and curse of the Law (Galatians 3:10), the Gentile believer who will "walk by this rule" (Galatians 6:16) of newfound salvation in Christ will enter into God's family not by works of human flesh but by the grace of God's Spirit.

This chapter will demonstrate the inferiority of the Law in Galatians by arguing for the sufficiency of faith alone. Three specific propositions will prove that the Galatians' faith in Christ Jesus ensured their right to be called children of God, independent of any legalistic adherence to Jewish Law or custom (Galatians 3:26-27).

---

224   Mackie, Timothy. "Galatians" in *Read Scripture: Illustrated Summaries of Biblical Books, p. 110.*
225   Tuck, Dr. Gary. "Galatians" in *The Arguments of the Books of the New Testament, p. 114.*

THE LAW IS INADEQUATE FOR RIGHTEOUSNESS

WITH PAUL'S USE of the rhetorical question, "Did you receive the Spirit by the works of the Law, or by believing what you heard?" (Galatians 3:2), he seems to encourage the reader to witness the self-evident truth of his argument for righteousness by faith and not by works. Paul insists that attempting to achieve righteousness by adherence to the Law is futile, and pointedly states, "No one who relies on the Law is justified before God, because 'the righteous will live by faith'" (Galatians 3:11; cf., Habakkuk 2:4). Furthermore, Paul points out that attempting to achieve righteousness through a system never intended to accomplish such an aim is foolish and equivalent to ensuring both failure and curse (Galatians 5:10).

Paul reminds the Galatians that their experience of God came about by *what they heard, and not by what they did.* In this context, Paul links justification (Galatians 2:16) and righteousness (Galatians 3:2; 3:5-6) as being achieved through faith in Jesus Christ alone. The divine presence and activity of God's Spirit "working miracles among them" (Galatians 3:5) was solely attributed to their belief in Christ. Paul then bridges the Galatians' righteousness by faith to Abraham's righteousness before God as achieved not by his works but because "Abraham believed God, and it was credited to him as righteousness" (Galatians 3:6, cf., Genesis 15:6).

Perhaps Paul's strongest case against any requirement of Law observance for righteousness before God was his confrontation with Peter (Galatians 2:11-21). Through Paul's opposition of Peter "face to face" (Galatians 2:11), Paul demonstrated that Peter had implied, by separating himself from the Gentiles, that some measure of observance of the Law was a requirement for righteousness. Paul insists that the believer's "death to the Law" was settled through "Christ who lives in me" (Galatians 2:19-20).[226] Paul firmly establishes that the Christian life is a life of faith in which one is counted righteous before God based solely on faith in Christ (Galatians 3:11).

---

226   Ibid., p. 113.

THE LAW IS INFERIOR TO THE ABRAHAMIC PROMISE

PAUL ARGUES THAT being justified, receiving the Spirit of God, and becoming children of Abraham and of God are all inseparably related gifts given to those who have faith in Christ. Strict adherence to the Law, in addition to being futile (Galatians 3:10), was now part of an outdated age in which those who believe in Christ have died (Galatians 2:19; 3:13; 3:25).[227] Through faith in Christ, the Gentile believer is now part of a new creation (Galatians 5:15) where the totality of the old Law is fulfilled by "loving your neighbor as yourself" (Galatians 5:14). Rather than relying on mankind's inferior power to uphold the Law, Paul insists that Christ himself becomes the believer's new life, and achieves for the believer that which they could never achieve on their own (Galatians 2:20; 4:6-7).

Paul insists that no amount of adherence to the old Law was sufficient to experience God's promise to bless all nations through Abraham's offspring. To justify his argument, Paul points out that the Abrahamic blessing was based on faith (Genesis 15:6) and not on the works of the Law as demonstrated by the overt act of circumcision. Therefore, according to Paul's logic, attempting to achieve a blessing originally established by faith through the misapplication of the "works of the Law" was futile at best, and subject to curse at worst. The Mosaic Law was never intended to be a means of justification, for as Paul insists, "The only thing that counts is faith expressing itself through love" (Galatians 5:6).

According to Paul, the Law is exceedingly inferior to the ultimate promise of blessing that could only be achieved through faith in Christ. Paul argues that the purpose of the Law was to demonstrate humanity's sinfulness and need of a savior.[228] Paul asserts that if righteousness had been possible through works, then "Christ would have died for nothing" (Galatians 2:21). However, due to the fact that "the whole world is a prisoner to sin" (Galatians 3:22), then no amount of Law can remedy or save man's fallen condition. Paul therefore demonstrates that the true purpose of the Law was not to achieve righteousness, but rather to "lead us to Christ that we might be justified by faith" (Galatians 3:24).

---

227   Ciampa, R. E. "Galatians" in *The New Dictionary of Biblical Theology, p. 313.*
228   Tuck. p. 114.

THE LAW IS THE ANTITHESIS
OF FREEDOM IN CHRIST

PAUL ARGUES THAT there is far more at stake than the Law's adherence to the requirement of circumcision. The believer in Christ has been set free from the totality of the Law (Galatians 5:1). Paul's insistence that "every man who lets himself be circumcised is obligated to obey the whole Law" (Galatians 5:3) aligns with James' contention that "whoever keeps the whole Law and yet stumbles at just one point is guilty of breaking it all" (James 2:10). It is not necessarily the specific act of circumcision that Paul argued against, "but rather the ritual act of circumcision as a means to righteousness as a Law observance, that he fervently opposes."[229] Paul's adamant opposition against the legalistic requirement of circumcision as a requirement for faith is witnessed in his declaration that such an action would mean that "Christ will be of no value at all" (Galatians 5:2).

Paul argues that the freedom found in Christ and the "custody under the Law" (Galatians 3:21) are mutually exclusive. To attempt to achieve righteousness by works of the Law is impossible and equivalent to subjecting oneself to bondage. On the other hand, freedom from the Law gained through faith in Christ leads the Galatians to righteousness, which Paul demonstrated to be based solely on the effects of faith (Galatians 3:6, cf. Genesis 15:6). Paul insists that justification by faith in Christ and justification by adherence to the Law are inherently in opposition to each other.[230] In harsh terms, Paul warns the Galatians that attempting to "obtain the goal by human effort" (Galatians 3:3) through the works of the Law will ultimately lead to "alienation from Christ" (Galatians 5:4). Paul encourages the churches in Galatia to realize that freedom, life, and righteousness come through faith in Christ, and enslavement through observance to the Law (Galatians 5:5-6).

---

229   Longman, Tremper III and David E. Garland. *The Expositors Bible Commentary on Galatians*, p. 621.
230   Tuck. p. 114.

CONCLUSION

PAUL'S LETTER TO THE churches of Galatia firmly established the doctrine that people are justified by faith in Jesus Christ (Galatians 2:16). Paul insisted that faith in Christ alone was sufficient for receiving righteousness before God, and that demanding any additional legalistic works in order to achieve righteousness was antagonistic to his gospel message. Reflecting on his own salvation, Paul encouraged the Galatians to understand that people are justified by believing in what God did for them through Jesus Christ, not by what they are capable of doing for themselves (Galatians 2:19-20). Rather than struggling fruitlessly for self-righteousness by adherence to the Law, Paul explains that when people put their faith in Christ, then "by faith they will receive the promise of the Spirit" (Galatians 3:14).

CHAPTER
SEVENTEEN

ON THE BATTLEFIELD OF LIFE

An Exposition of Paul's Letter to the Ephesians

EARLY IN MY MILITARY CAREER, a longtime mentor of mine pulled me aside and said, "Greg, good leaders are able to reveal things to subordinates they could otherwise never see on their own." His words resonated deep within my soul, and I was held captive by the idea that something obvious to me could be seemingly invisible to someone else. The implications on the battlefield were immense: Unless I opened the eyes of my soldiers and helped them see potential dangers within their midst, catastrophic injury would surely be their end. However, once the danger was revealed to them, their "battlefield knowledge" increased, and they would be more likely to navigate risk independent of my supervision. And perhaps even more encouraging, with their newfound wisdom, the subordinate soldier would be in a position to help reveal to their peers what they would never see on their own.

In many respects and to varying degrees, we are all soldiers on the battlefield of life. Twists, turns, peaks, and valleys are part of the terrain we need to successfully navigate in order to reach our final destination. However, in addition to dangerous valleys, there are also magnificent mountaintops that our soul longs to summit. Yet, unless revealed to us by a trusted source of wisdom and knowledge much greater than ourselves, the tendency is to rely on our independent understanding, which often leads to a closed loop of crisscrossing back and forth across the dark valleys of life.

I recall learning the fundamentals of land navigation during U.S. Army Basic Officer Leadership Training in the hills of North Dakota. During daylight hours, the task was fairly simple. Given a compass and map, I navigated across open terrain to specific points or "plots" that my instructor had assigned me. However, in the pitch-black night, not being able to see the tips of my fingers with outstretched arm, the task became altogether impossible. On one particular night, and very characteristic of North Dakota summers, there was a great lightning storm. Although startling and a bit nerve-racking, I soon discovered the lightning was a blessing in disguise. When the lightning struck, the terrain all around me was instantly illuminated, much like a flare bursting in the night. For a few seconds, the imprint of my surroundings made an impression on my mind. I could essentially "see in the dark." Although brief, those momentary intervals of revelation of my surroundings were enough to allow me to successfully complete the navigation course.

THE POWER OF VISION

IN THE BOOK OF Proverbs, it says, "Where there is no vision, the people perish."[231] In order to navigate the battlefield of life, we need to clearly identify the obstacles before us. However, as my mentor counseled me years ago, we also need a trusted source to reveal to us what we could otherwise not see on our own. This idea of "not being able to see on our own" is further expressed in Proverbs: "Be not wise in thy own eyes."[232] In other words, if we rely on our own understanding, knowledge, and worldly acquired wisdom we will not be able to see clearly.

The potential pitfall and shortcoming of limited understanding and "battlefield blindness" was certainly at the heart of the Apostle Paul in his letter to the Ephesians. In Ephesians 1:17, we read, "I pray that the God of our Lord Jesus Christ, the Father of glory, might give you spiritual wisdom and revelation in the knowledge of Him." In other words, Paul's prayer was that God would grant us a specific type of spiritual wisdom we could otherwise never arrive at on our own.

We may interpret through verse 17 that Paul was specifically describing a type of wisdom that could only be achieved through the power and working of the Holy Spirit. Paul specifically prayed the Ephesians would experience a supernatural endowment of wisdom that would be achieved through God's revelation of Himself. Paul's contention, therefore, was to ensure the believer understood that worldly wisdom, gained through the intellect of humanity, would never be enough to truly know the "surpassing greatness"[233] of God. Paul's use of the term "revelation" referred to God's own self-disclosure, which would be experienced supernaturally by the believer.

In the New Testament Epistle of James, the author made clear the distinction between wisdom of the world, and wisdom revealed by God. James describes worldly wisdom as "earthly, unspiritual and demonic."[234] In the context of navigating the battlefield of life, the result of following and "seeing" through the eyes of our own wisdom is like a landmine waiting to be stepped upon. A torrential explosion of "envy, selfish ambition, disorder and evil"[235] is

---

231 Proverbs 29:18.
232 Proverbs 3:7.
233 Ephesians 1:19.
234 James 3:15-16.
235 Ibid.

dangerously underfoot. The Apostle Paul foresaw the treacherous terrain the Ephesians, in addition to future believers, would need to safely transverse, and through his prayer, Paul's hope was that God would reveal Himself to us. Through this supernatural revelation, our wisdom and knowledge would be increased to heavenly proportion, which is distinctly different and abundantly more important than worldly wisdom.

James articulated this difference in verse 3:17: "Wisdom that comes from heaven is first of all pure; then peace-loving, considerate, submissive, full of mercy and good fruit, impartial and sincere." With this newfound perspective of "Heavenly wisdom" held in mind, we turn once again to the beauty and magnitude of the opening line of Paul's prayer. With gratitude in our heart, we discover that Paul prayed you and I would have a direct experience of the power and glory of God. Like a flash of lightning in the middle of a dark night, Paul's prayer was such that we would experience an imprint of God on our minds and hearts, and that through this divine revelation, our spiritual wisdom would be increased.

THE EYES OF THE HEART

THE SECOND COMPONENT of Paul's prayer for the Ephesians was equally inspiring and complemented the revelation of God invoked in verse 17. Paul prayed, "Since the eyes of your heart have been enlightened, that you would know what is the hope of His calling, what are the riches of the glory of His inheritance in the saints."[236] By focusing on Paul's use of the word "heart" in this verse, and through an understanding of the bodily function of the heart, we can truly appreciate the magnitude of Paul's prayer.

Being made in the image of God,[237] we have an ordained birthright and divine capacity to know and *experience* the presence of God. Before going any further, let us turn our attention to the words of Jesus, who said, "This is eternal life, *that they may know you*, the one true God, and Jesus Christ, whom you have sent."[238] Oftentimes when reading the Bible and the words of Jesus, it is equally important to note what Jesus said, in addition to what *Jesus did not say*. Therefore, take special consideration that Jesus' prayer was for you and me to *know God*. He did not say,

---

236   Ephesians 1:18.
237   Genesis 1:27.
238   John 17:3 – Use of italics are the author's emphasis.

"Know *about* God." In other words, Jesus' prayer and hope was that you and I would have a direct experience and firsthand knowledge of God. And now, through the words of Paul in Ephesians verse 1:17, we arrive at the understanding this knowledge of God will not be possible through our own understanding or human intellect. Knowing God is a supernatural experience, which is the direct result of God revealing Himself to us.

In the context of any personal relationship, this makes total and complete sense. No matter how hard we might try, in order to really know someone, they ultimately need to reveal their mind and soul to us. This specific type of "revelation," understood through verse 18 of Paul's prayer, was experienced within the "eyes of our heart" that were enlightened through the revelation of God. In the same manner in which our mind has thinking, reasoning, and intellectual capacities, Paul understood our heart shared these capacities on an even deeper and more spiritually significant level. In fact, according to Paul, the mind may have even blunted the true spiritual wisdom of the heart.

In Corinthians, Paul wrote, "Their minds are made dull because a veil covers their hearts."[239] We can interpret through Ephesians 1:17-18 that Paul's prayer for the believer was to "see" that if truth, wisdom, and knowledge about God were to be faithfully grasped, then the heart must be enlightened. Furthermore, as the heart is a central and life-sustaining organ of the body, it is responsible for circulating both blood and oxygen throughout the entire cellular system. Thus, when Paul prays for the "eyes of our heart to be enlightened," he is praying that in addition to knowing *about* God at the intellectual level of our mind, that through the circulation of God's love throughout every cell of our body, we would be "enlightened" to truly *know God* by the revelation of His presence. Finally, it is important to note that in the Bible, the word "heart" often referred to the genuine self as distinguished from appearance, identification with the mind, and physical presence.[240] And this "heart-self" had its own nature, character, and disposition, which ultimately affected the thoughts, words and actions of the believer.[241] Therefore, a believer whose "heart" was illuminated by the revelation of God would radically change the entire makeup of their life, and would never be the same again.

Due to the tendency of our human intellect to attach through the senses to

---

239 2 Corinthians 3:14-15.
240 Elwell, Walter A. and Barry J. Beitzel. "Wisdom, Wisdom Literature," *Baker Encyclopedia of the Bible* (Grand Rapids, MI: Baker Book House, 1988), p. 2149.
241 *Baker Encyclopedia of the Bible*, p. 2149.

material objects and "desires of the flesh,"[242] Paul's prayer centered on *spiritual* acquisition. For example, we observed that in verse 17, Paul's hope was that we would acquire *spiritual wisdom* in the knowledge of God. Through the revelation of God in our lives, the eyes of our heart would be enlightened, allowing us to faithfully see what truly mattered most. Therefore, as we continue to journey though the totality of Paul's prayer, we observe the "riches" Paul is desirous of us both seeing and inheriting are meant to be enjoyed spiritually and not worldly.

We take note that verse 18 concluded with Paul's use of the word "inheritance." This word is of immense importance, and is best understood through the context of the Old Testament. Time and time again, we note that God referred to His creation as His own inheritance. In Deuteronomy, we read that God took His creation, "As the people of His inheritance"[243] and that God's people were "His own inheritance, redeemed by His great power."[244] As sons and daughters of God, our relationship with Him is similar to that of Father and child. The intimacy of this relationship is absolutely vital for us to comprehend, and was at the heart of Jesus' ministry. In the first two words of the "Lord's Prayer," Jesus explained the nature of our relationship with God by the declaration, "Our Father."[245] In this manner, Jesus invoked our understanding of the divine connection to our "Father of glory."[246] Jesus embraced and perfectly articulated the magnitude of this relationship and his divine right to the inheritance of his Father when he declared, "All I have is yours, and all you have is mine."[247]

Paul's prayer as expressed in verse 18 is therefore twofold. First, his hope is that we would embrace our relationship with God as that of Father and child. Second, through the context of this Fatherly relationship and through spiritual revelation, Paul prayed that we would embrace our true inheritance as sons and daughters of God. It is exceedingly important to take note of Paul's use of the word "glory," which is evident in both verse 17 and 18. In verse 17, God was declared to be the "Father of glory." Throughout the Old Testament, the glory of God was oftentimes so bright and of such overwhelming power that it was shrouded in a cloud.[248] In verse 18, we discover the brilliance and intensity of God's glory is to be shared with us as a component of our inheritance as children of God.

---

242   Galatians 5:17.
243   Deuteronomy 4:20.
244   Deuteronomy 9:26.
245   Matthew 6:9.
246   Ephesians 1:17.
247   John 17:10.
248   Exodus 16:10.

THE SURPASSING GREATNESS OF GOD

IN VERSE NINETEEN OF Paul's prayer, we take special note of the connection between the "surpassing greatness" and power of God, in direct proportion toward those who believe in Him, and "what is the surpassing greatness of His power towards us who believe, in accordance with the working of the strength of His might." As described by Paul, it was according to one's level of belief, which was furthermore achieved only through God's revelation of Himself, that a believer could fully experience the "strength of His might."[249] Paul's use of the word-phrase, "Surpassing greatness," when understood within the context of navigating the battlefield of life, is worthy of our thankfulness and delight. "Surpassing" can best be understood as "superior" or ranking higher than any other type of power, regardless of how immense our intellect may attempt to convince us it is. The magnificent, supreme, and nearly incomprehensible power of God's greatness is directed with love towards those who believe in Him. Through God's own revelation of Himself, we may thus be faithfully "inherited" into His enduring love and embrace.

CONCLUDING THOUGHTS

NAVIGATING THE BATTLEFIELD of life can be a treacherous task, full of unsuspecting danger. However, this same battlefield, when faithfully illuminated, can become a place of beauty and spiritual splendor. In order for the terrain around us to become visible, a transformation will need to take place within both our mind and our heart. The biblical word "grace" was described to me once as the "effect of God giving us what we do not deserve," and "mercy" taking place when "God *does not give us* what we do deserve." Paul's prayer invokes this very measure of grace, in his hope that you and I would experience the revelation of God, and through this supernatural opening and enlightenment of the "eyes of our heart" we would fully embrace our right to an inheritance of epic proportion.

---

249 Ephesians 1:19.

CHAPTER
EIGHTEEN

THE SUFFICIENCY OF JESUS CHRIST: EXEGESIS OF COLOSSIANS 2:20 – 3:4

OFTENTIMES IN THE SPORT of professional boxing, the trainer's primary function is to encourage their fighter to believe that their training, experience, and talent is entirely sufficient to defeat their next opponent. This encouragement is absolutely essential for the boxer; in contrast to their trainer's encouragement for sufficiency, the tendency of the boxer's mind is to entertain thoughts of needing something more in order to be complete, ready, and prepared for their opponent. In this context, the relationship between the trainer and the boxer is one of developing faith in the absolute sufficiency of the fighter's current ability to defeat their opponent.

In contrast to the *temporal reality* provided in the illustration of a boxer and trainer, Paul's letter to "God's holy people in Colossae" (Colossians 1:2) serves the even more important illustration of an *eternal reality* that firmly establishes the absolute sufficiency of faith in Christ. Paul exhorts the believer to understand that "Christ is all—and all you need!"[250] According to Paul, you do not need Christ plus philosophy, human wisdom, or tradition (Colossians 2:22-23). You do not need Christ plus strict adherence to Mosaic custom or bodily restriction (Colossians 2:21). In essence, Paul firmly and encouragingly establishes the truth of the Gospel message: Through the redemptive work of Christ, the believer has been made complete (Colossians 2:20a; 3:1). There is nothing that human effort can do that could even remotely contribute to our salvation and standing before God. In essence, "Christ is all—and all you need!"

SETTING

THE HISTORICAL AND GEOGRAPHICAL SETTING for the Apostle Paul's letter to "God's holy people in Colossae" (Colossians 1:2) was the town of Colossae located on the Lycus River along the great east-west trade route leading from Ephesus on the Aegean Sea to the Euphrates River.[251] The Gospel

---

250   The phrase "Christ is all—and all you need" is from Dr. Carl Laney's book, *Essential Bible Background*, p. 212.
251   O'Brien, P. T. "Colossians." In *The Dictionary of Paul and His Letters, p. 147.*

was first introduced to the city of Colossae during Paul's ministry at Ephesus (Acts 19:10, 26), although Paul himself did not convert the faithful believers in the city (Colossians 1:4, 2:1). Rather, the Christian community and church in Colossae came into existence during Paul's Ephesian ministry (recorded in Acts 19) and was likely established by Epaphras.[252]

Paul described Epaphras as "a fellow servant, who is a faithful minister of Christ on our behalf" (Colossians 1:7). Paul's confidence in Epaphras seems to indicate that Paul had personally sent him to Colossae, and thus retained a vested interest in the progress of the church.[253] The occasion for Paul's letter was the arrival of Epaphras from Colossae (Colossians 1:7-9, 4:12) who reported to Paul news of a theological error circulating and being taught within the church. Having learned of the false teachers and tarnished doctrine that had come to Colossae, Paul subsequently wrote a letter to refute their errors and restore sound theology to the church.[254]

PURPOSE AND THEME

PAUL WROTE THE LETTER to the faithful believers in Colossae to refute false teaching that could potentially circumvent the true Gospel message and bring the Colossians into spiritual bondage.[255] Although some of Epaphras' report to Paul included encouraging news (Colossians 1:8; 2:5), the specific matter of a "Colossian Heresy" alarmed Paul and necessitated that he send Tychicus back to Colossae with a letter to the church.[256]

The Colossian error in doctrine and false teaching circulating within the church is a key to understanding the interpretation of Paul's letter.[257] The Colossian error contained a combined emphasis on Mosaic ordinances (Colossians 2:8,11,16), the cancellation of "legal indebtedness" (Colossians 2:14), strict adherence to ceremonialism including religious festivals (Colossians 2:16-17), and circumcision (Colossians 2:11; 3:11). The false teachers seem to have preached an inadequate and incomplete Christ (Colossians 1:15-19; 2:9) and

---

252   Ibid.
253   Longman, Tremper III and David E. Garland. *The Expositors Bible Commentary on Colossians, p. 266.*
254   Carson, D. A. and Douglas Moo. "Colossians." In *An Introduction to the New Testament, p. 523.*
255   O'Brien, P. T. "Colossians." In *The Dictionary of Paul and His Letters, p. 148.*
256   Ibid., p. 148.
257   Dr. Gary Tuck. "Colossians." In *The Arguments of the Books of the New Testament, p. 134.*

placed a special emphasis on wisdom and knowledge (Colossians 2:3), angel worship (Colossians 2:18), and asceticism (Colossians 2:18, 20-23).[258]

The primary purpose and theme of Paul's letter was to refute the Colossian heresy and false teaching and to simultaneously build up sound doctrine within the church that would result in proper behavior, church unity, and adherence to the true Gospel of Christ.[259] To accomplish his goal, Paul exalts Christ as the "very image of the invisible God" (Colossians 1:15), the Creator of all things (Colossians 1:16), and the "head of the church" (Colossians 1:18). Paul exhorts the reader to understand that Jesus embodied the fullness of deity in bodily form (Colossians 1:19; 2:10) and that only through Christ could one be reconciled to God (Colossians 1:20).

Perhaps refuting the false teaching that suggested the inadequacy of Christ alone, Paul argues that Christ is in fact completely adequate and entirely sufficient. Paul encouraged the believer to understand that through Christ "they had been brought to fullness" (Colossians 2:10). Paul warns the faithful believers in Colossae to be wary of "hollow and deceptive philosophy" (Colossians 2:8) that had no ability whatsoever to restrain the flesh (Colossians 2:23).

Rather than relying on "human tradition and elemental spiritual forces of the world" (Colossians 2:8), Paul exhorts the reader to fully identify with Christ both in his death (Colossians 2:20) and in his resurrection (Colossians 3:1). The identification with Christ in his death served the purpose of refuting the false teachers' emphasis on asceticism (Colossians 2:21; 23). Conversely, Paul's insistence that the faithful believer had been "raised with Christ" (Colossians 3:1) served the purpose of calling the believer to "set their minds on things above" (Colossians 3:2) and to become entirely absorbed with their new life with Christ in heaven.[260]

EXPOSITIONAL SUMMARY

THE PRIMARY PURPOSE of Paul's letter was to refute the Colossian heresy and false teaching that was circulating within the church. In addition

---

258   My argument for the "Colossian Heresy" was identified and developed through the work of Dr. Tuck in *The Arguments of the Books of the New Testament, p. 133.*

259   Ibid., p. 134.

260   Ibid.

to quelling the false teaching, Paul sought to simultaneously reinforce sound doctrine within the church that would result in proper behavior, church unity, and adherence to the true Gospel of Christ.[261] From this perspective, the text of Colossians 2:20 – 3:4 is rich with meaning and significance, and achieves the goal of advancing the totality of the book's argument.

Paul himself seems to set the stage for his admonishment of false teaching by pointing to the true purpose of his letter, namely to encourage faithful believers to be "full of the riches of complete understanding, in order that they may know the mystery of God, namely, Christ, in whom are hidden all the treasures of wisdom and knowledge" (Colossians 2:2-3). In this context, Paul's rebuke of the false teaching simultaneously served the purpose of firmly establishing the true Gospel message.

Paul's brilliant use of an interrogative series of questions forces the Colossians to self-identify with the incompatibility of their unity in Christ and lifestyle choices (Colossians 2:20-21). Following Paul's line of logic, he reasons that if the Colossians had indeed died with Christ (Colossians 2:20), then why had they adopted lifestyle choices that in fact "led them to betray who they were in Christ?"[262] Paul seems to argue that it makes absolutely no sense for the Colossians to proclaim faith and unity in Christ while simultaneously regressing to the submission to regulations that in essence return them to spiritual bondage. Paul establishes a clear delineation between the true Gospel message (Colossians 2:6-7) and "the rules that are destined to perish with use, and are based merely on human commands and teachings" (Colossians 2:22).

Paul further establishes the critical argument that no amount of external regulation or bodily mortification (Colossians 2:23) are sufficient to restrain the sinful nature of the flesh. Rather than focusing on *what not to do* (Colossians 2:21, 23) Paul encourages the faithful believer to *focus on Christ*. In opposition to external regulations and vain ascetic attempts to control the "unspiritual or fleshly mind" (Colossians 2:18), the true Christian will orient their behavior and direct their thinking to the things of Christ (Colossians 3:1-4).

The historical and geographical setting for the Apostle Paul's letter to "God's holy people in Colossae" (Colossians 1:2) was the town of Colossae located on the Lycus River along the great east-west trade route leading from Ephesus

---

261   Ibid., p. 134.
262   Longman, Tremper III and David E. Garland. *The Expositors Bible Commentary on Colossians, p. 320.*

on the Aegean Sea to the Euphrates River.[263] The occasion for Paul's letter was the arrival of Epaphras from Colossae (Colossians 1:7-9, 4:12) who reported to Paul news of a theological error circulating and being taught within the church. Having learned of the false teachers that had come to Colossae, Paul subsequently wrote a letter to refute their errors and restore sound doctrine to the church.[264] The critical text of Colossians 2:20 – 3:4 serves the purpose of juxtaposing two opposing realities: the believer's position in their death with Christ (Colossians 2:20-23) and subsequent resurrection with Christ (Colossians 3:1-4).

Utilizing the brilliant tactic of an interrogative mode of questioning, Paul asks why the Colossians were allowing themselves to be governed by the "spiritual forces of the world" (Colossians 2:20). Paul asserts that the believer's position should be one of death to the world. Any of the former rules, regulations, or Mosaic tendencies of the former life were now part of an old system no longer applicable to the believer in Christ. According to Paul, claiming faith in Christ while simultaneously maintaining allegiance and submission to the false teachers' rules and regulations was incompatible and akin to spiritual regression.[265]

Paul asserts that the rules and regulations mandated by the false teachers focused on *what the believer ought not to do* (Colossians 2:21). These ascetic restrictions were part of the false teachers' emphasis on restricting the flesh and focused on material and worldly matters. It seemed Paul was more concerned with focusing the believers' minds on *what they should do* rather than on the negative injunction of *what they should not do.* It is also important to note that the three prohibitions that Paul speaks ("Do not handle! Do not taste! Do not touch!") each focused on matters of the flesh (Colossians 2:21). Paul's broadly cast net served the purpose of essentially combining the totality of the false teachers' philosophical restrictions of the body into one category. This is important to note, for rather than an objective rebuttal of the false teachers' mandates, Paul asserts that any attempt to regulate or restrain the body for purposes of godliness is futile (Colossians 2:22-23).[266]

Rather than focusing on restraining the body and submitting to "human commands and teachings" (Colossians 2:22), Paul asserts that the true Christian will elevate their thinking and orient their lives in the heavenly direction of their new position with Christ (Colossians 3:1-2). Clearly juxtaposing his illustration

---

263   O'Brien, P. T. "Colossians." In *The Dictionary of Paul and His Letters, p. 147.*
264   Carson, D. A. and Douglas Moo. "Colossians." In *An Introduction to the New Testament, p. 523.*
265   Longman, Tremper III and David E. Garland. *The Expositors Bible Commentary on Colossians, p. 320.*
266   Ibid., p. 320.

of the believer's death with Christ that he established in Colossians 2:20-23, Paul now turns his attention to the reality of the believer's new life with Christ. The new life the believer enters into is experienced both as a present reality (Colossians 3:3) and in the life to come (Colossians 3:4). This is important to note, for although the believer has not yet been raised bodily, Paul asserts they have been raised spiritually and are therefore "spiritually seated with Christ" (Colossians 3:1-2).[267]

Because the believers have been spiritually raised with Christ, Paul encourages them to "set your minds on things above" (Colossians 3:2) and to spiritually reside with "Christ who is with God" (Colossians 3:3). The phrase "set your mind" (Colossians 3:2) is critically important to Paul's argument and seems to require an element of diligence on the part of the believer to maintain spiritual residence with Christ in Heaven. Whereas the tendency of the mind is to regress to temporal matters and "earthly things" (Colossians 3:2b), Paul exhorts the believer to continually realign their minds to "things that are above" (Colossians 3:2a). The elevated position of the believer is possible through God and a spiritual "renewing of their mind" (Romans 12:2). In opposition to thoughts focused on matters of the flesh and world, Paul contends that spiritual thoughts are focused on Christ and his superiority over all matters of the earth.[268]

In Colossians 3:3-4, Paul offers the believer two foundational reasons why they should "set their minds on things above" (Colossians 3:2). The first reason has to do with the believer's past and their death with Christ. The juxtaposition between the death of the believer—"since you died with Christ" (Colossians 2:20)—and their subsequent "resurrection with Christ" (Colossians 3:1), is critical to understanding the progression of Paul's logic. Because the "old self" is now dead, Paul contends the "new self" is no longer regulated by "merely human commands and teachings" (Colossians 2:22) but is rather "hidden with Christ" (Colossians 3:3a) and therefore ruled by "Christ in God" (Colossians 3:3b). The resurrected life is not "worldly" but is in fact "heavenly" and "hidden with Christ" (Colossians 3:3b) and is therefore an eternal and spiritual life. The new life with Christ should therefore motivate the believer to enjoy a resurrected spiritual life while still on earth, while positively anticipating their physical resurrected life "with Christ in glory" (Colossians 3:4).

---

267   Ibid., p. 322.

268   The reference to Romans 12:2 and the contrast between "worldly thoughts" and "spiritual thoughts" were identified in *The Expositor's Bible Commentary on Colossians*, p. 322.

THEOLOGY

ONE OF THE MAIN THEOLOGICAL points that Paul beautifully makes in his letter to the faithful believers in Colossae is their "new life in Christ" (Colossians 3:1-4). By firmly establishing the supremacy of Christ (Colossians 3:1), Paul advances the Gospel by dispelling the heresy circulating within the church that "Christ plus works" (Colossians 2:20-23) was needed to enjoy a relationship with God. In opposition to the false teachers' denial of Christ's proper place (Colossians 2:8, 19), their requirement for ritualistic observances (Colossians 2:16-17), and ascetic practices (Colossians 2:21), Paul exhorts that the person and work of Christ is entirely sufficient (Colossians 1:15-23). Paul presents Christ as the Lord of creation, head of the church, and reconciler of believers to God. Paul asserts that "Christ is the image of the invisible God" (Colossians 1:15) and that through death and resurrection with Christ (Colossians 2:20; 3:1), the believer can be reconciled to God (Colossians 1:20).

The specific text of Colossians 2:20 – 3:4 is a significant contribution to our understanding of the Gospel. By illustrating the death and subsequent resurrection the believer experienced through faith in Christ, Paul asserts that their new life with Christ is not dependent upon human tradition (Colossians 2:8) or human rules and regulations (Colossians 2:20-23). Rather, since the believer "has been raised with Christ" their new life is entirely based on faith and their new spiritual residence "with Christ in God" (Colossians 3:3). According to Paul, the believer has died with Christ (Colossians 2:20), been buried with Christ (Colossians 2:12), and raised with Christ (Colossians 2:12; 3:1)—a sequence that requires the believer to maintain proper allegiance to their new spiritual life with Christ in Heaven (Colossians 3:1-2).

In the text of Colossians 2:20 – 3:4, Jesus is revealed directly by his redemptive work on the cross (Colossians 2:20). Through Christ's death, God has forgiven our sins and "canceled the charge of our legal indebtedness" (Colossians 2:14) that stood against mankind. Through the death, resurrection, and eternal reign of Christ (Colossians 3:1), the "elemental spiritual forces of the world" (Colossians 2:20) no longer hold mankind captive and enslaved. Through faith in Christ, the believer is now spiritually raised with him and "hidden with Christ in God" (Colossians 3:3) until the time they are identified with him in bodily resurrection and eternal glory (Colossians 3:4).

CONCLUSION

OFTENTIMES IN LIFE the tendency of the mind is to think: "I'll be happy, satisfied, and complete when ...." and then the mind directs the anticipated source of "completeness" out into the world. In many respects, this was exactly what threatened the church in Colossae—false teaching that suggested Christ was not independently and entirely sufficient. Thankfully, Paul provided encouragement and sound doctrine for both the historical church in Colossae and for the modern-day, faithful believer to understand that Christ is entirely, absolutely, and independently sufficient. Simply put, when we have Christ, we have all we need! Through faith in Christ, the believer experiences a spiritual death to the world (Colossians 2:20-23) and a subsequent resurrection into the very place where Christ is seated—at the glorious right hand of God (Colossians 3:1).

CHAPTER
NINETEEN

THE PURPOSE AND POWER OF FAITH IN HEBREWS

THE EPISTLE TO THE HEBREWS is a magnificent exhortation that serves the threefold purpose of teaching the superiority of Jesus, warning against backsliding into sin and disobedience, and encouraging the readers to advance into spiritual maturity and unequivocal faith in God.[269] In this context, the author first substantiates the supremacy of Jesus in order to justify steadfast and enduring faith in his redemptive work. The superior and exalted person of Jesus Christ (Hebrews 1 – 7) is made manifest and demonstrated in the superiority of his work (Hebrews 8:1 – 10:18), which justifies and encourages the believer's superior life of faith (Hebrews 10:19 – 13:24).[270]

The elevation and superiority of Jesus begins immediately in the opening sentence of the book's introduction: "In the past God spoke to our ancestors through the prophets at many times and in various ways, but in these last days he has spoken to us by his Son, whom he appointed heir of all things, and through whom he also made the universe" (Hebrews 1:1-2). In a tightly constructed, single sentence, the author makes the authoritative claim that Jesus is the "radiance of God's glory and the exact representation of his being" (Hebrews 1:3a). The metaphor of "radiance" illustrates that just as the radiance of light rays are inseparable from the sun, so is Jesus' radiance inseparable from God.[271] Furthermore, as the "exact representation" of God, Jesus is not merely an image or reflection of God but is rather the true and authentic depiction of God's essential being.[272] For the author, there is no God apart from Jesus who is the one true creator God who became human as the Son (Hebrews 1:3b).

The author's strategy of immediately elevating the position of Jesus (Hebrews 1:1-3) served the purpose of capturing the attention of a community of believers who were facing persecution and imprisonment (Hebrews 10:32-34; 13:3). The supremacy of Jesus provided incentive for the believer to "not throw away their confidence" (Hebrews 10:35) and to persevere in their faith in God (Hebrews 10:36). Furthermore, although it appears that persecution had not yet advanced to the level of martyrdom, the author acknowledges the intensity of the struggle the believer was facing (Hebrews 12:4).

It seems that in addition to addressing the issue of persecution, the author

---

269   Laney, Dr. Carl. "Hebrews" in *Essential Bible Background (CreateSpace, 2016), p. 239.*
270   Ibid.
271   Mackie, Dr. Timothy. "Hebrews" in *Read Scripture: Illustrated Summaries of Biblical Books, p. 130.*
272   Longman, Tremper III and David E. Garland. *The Expositors Bible Commentary on Hebrews, p. 37–38.*

also had concern over the believers' slowness to learn (Hebrews 5:11) and spiritual laziness (Hebrews 6:12). In many respects, the author's emphasis on the elevated position of Jesus was to increase the believer's spiritual maturity by advancing beyond the "elementary teachings" of Judaism that they were already familiar with (Hebrews 6:1-3). In a rhetorical sense, the author asks how having once been "so enlightened" (Hebrews 6:4; 10:32) by the initial conversion experience of his readers, could they now "drift away" (Hebrews 2:1) or completely abandon their faith by reverting to Judaism (Hebrews 10:29).

According to the author, if the reader were to lose his hold on Christ (Hebrews 3:14) it would be equated with "falling away from the living God" (Hebrews 3:12). The author described the seriousness and danger of the abandonment of faith in Christ as both a passive occurrence and a deliberate sin. When the author warned against "drifting away" (Hebrews 2:1) and "ignoring such a great salvation" (Hebrews 2:3), the implication was not primarily that the reader was overtly doing something he should not do, but rather failing to take the positive action associated with a full conversion experience.[273] On the other hand, loss of faith in Jesus could also be demonstrated by deliberate sin (Hebrews 10:26) that would result in "a fearful expectation of judgment and of raging fire" (Hebrews 10:27).

Whether turning from Jesus was the result of a passive or deliberate act, the author hopes that by exalting both the position and work of Jesus the reader will find renewed cause for steadfast and enduring faith even in the face of persecution.[274] Furthermore, based on the author's demonstrated superiority of Jesus as God's very Word (Hebrews 1 – 2), his superiority to Moses and eternal hope for new creation (Hebrews 3 – 4), and Jesus as the eternal high priest (Hebrews 5 – 7) and perfect sacrifice (Hebrews 8 – 10), he argues that it only makes sense to follow Jesus who is the "pioneer and perfecter of faith" (Hebrews 12:2).[275] Therefore, the essence and uniqueness of the author's argument for steadfast faith is "sureness of what we hope for" (Hebrews 11:1) however improbable it may seem within the context of the present circumstances.[276]

---

273 Ibid., p. 47.

274 As pointed out in the section of "Hebrews" in *The New Dictionary of Biblical Theology, p. 340, the author's extensive use of the name "Jesus" within the letter illustrates the deity of the human figure of Jesus and further positions Jesus as superior to all the other ways that God had previously revealed Himself to Israel.*

275 Mackie, Dr Timothy. "Hebrews" in *Read Scripture: Illustrated Summaries of Biblical Books, p. 130.*

276 Longman, Tremper III and David E. Garland. *The Expositors Bible Commentary on Hebrews, p. 168.*

FAITH IN ACTION

CHAPTER 11 OF HEBREWS is often referred to as "the great celebration of faith."[277] For the purpose of this chapter, it is critical to my argument that the model of faith presented by the author was first established in the superiority of Jesus. Faith is either strengthened or weakened depending on the thoughts of the one in whom we put our faith. For the author of Hebrews, a call to enduring faith was both established and substantiated by the elevated position of Jesus who was supremely above and beyond "the different times and various ways" (Hebrews 1:1) that God had previously revealed Himself. In other words, before exhorting his readers to *have faith in Jesus*, the author of Hebrews first needed to ensure his audience was *thinking correctly about Jesus*.

The author first introduced the language and context of "faith" through the quotation of Habakkuk: "But my righteous one will live by faith. And I take no pleasure in the one who shrinks back" (Hebrews 10:38; cf. Habakkuk 2:4). This particular quotation seems to perfectly illustrate the duality of the author's position to both encourage his readers to remain steadfast while simultaneously discouraging any possibility of "shrinking back" or "drifting away" (Hebrews 2:1). In this sense, the totality of Chapter 11 serves the purpose of expounding upon the author's definition of what it means to "persevere in faith" and not to "shrink back." Furthermore, as evidenced in Hebrews 10:32-36, the author is not necessarily calling for the establishment of *newfound faith*, but rather reminding the reader of their *past faithfulness* (Hebrews 10:32a) and encouraging "endurance in a great conflict full of suffering" (Hebrews 10:32b).[278]

As pointed out by R.T. France in his commentary on Hebrews, the author's use of the Greek word *pistis* (GK 4411) is not the same as the English understanding of "faith," which commonly refers to the content of belief. Rather, *pistis* calls for an "attitude of commitment and existential trust in God who is real and keeps His word."[279] The "cloud of great witnesses" (Hebrews 12:1) presented in Chapter 11 demonstrates the author's ideal model of what it means not only to trust God but also to prove oneself trustworthy by maintaining loyalty to His will.[280] In this context, the author of Hebrews qualifies faith not just as a feeling

---

277 Ibid., p. 141.
278 The particular insight was brought to my attention in *The Expositors Bible Commentary on Hebrews, p. 142.*
279 Longman, Tremper III and David E. Garland. *The Expositors Bible Commentary on Hebrews, p. 142.*
280 Ibid.

in need of validation from the senses (Hebrews 11:1a), but rather an entire way of life established in absolute belief that God exists and rewards those who seek Him (Hebrews 11:6).

The introductory proposition of Chapter 11 that "faith is confidence in what we hope for and assurance about what we do not see" (Hebrews 11:1) provides the framework within which the author will then draw on examples of the "great cloud of witnesses" (Hebrews 12:1) of the Old Testament. In addition, and of the utmost importance for the author of Hebrews, the heroes and heroines of the past whose faith was attested by God are brought to their climactic and supreme example of faith in Jesus himself (Hebrews 12:2-3).[281] In this respect, the supremacy of Jesus established by the author in previous chapters as the greater Moses, the greater priest, and the greater sacrifice is now also demonstrated as the greatest example of faith. For the author, Jesus is not only a model of faith in line with the "great cloud of witnesses" (Hebrews 12:1), but is also the supreme and perfected example (Hebrews 12:2) and the reason to "not grow weary or lose heart" (Hebrews 12:3).

The common thread and centrality of faith among the heroes and heroines of Hebrews Chapter 11 was demonstrated by their ability to both look forward to the fulfillment of God's Word (Hebrews 11:1a) and spiritual awareness of God's unseen presence (Hebrews 11:1b). According to the author of Hebrews, it was this dual perspective that "the ancients were commended for" (Hebrews 11:2). Furthermore, the various models of faith provide the reader with encouragement to persevere in spite of painful circumstances and hardship. In an effort to radically shift the paradigm of hardship, the author proposes that the reader should in fact "endure hardship as discipline" (Hebrews 12:7) and evidence of God's love (Hebrews 12:9; 11).

The author of Hebrews is concerned with not only a general perspective of those who were "commended for their faith" (Hebrews 11:39), but also with specific examples of faith in action that his readers can model in their behavior.[282] In this context, the author utilizes the story of Abraham and Isaac for the purpose of demonstrating a major theme that runs throughout the chapter: Faith even in the face of certain death.[283] Although faith sometimes resulted in escape from what appeared to be imminent death (Hebrews 11:33-34), at other

---

281 Lane, W. L. "Hebrews." In *Dictionary of the Later New Testament and Its Developments*, p. 453.
282 Tuck, Dr. Gary. "Hebrews." In *The Arguments of the Books of the New Testament*, p. 163.
283 Longman, Tremper III and David E. Garland. *The Expositors Bible Commentary on Hebrews*, p. 142.

times the ultimate sacrifice was made (Hebrews 11:35-37). Therefore, the author's purpose in his illustration of death was to encourage the reader to look *beyond death* to the "gain of an even better resurrection" (Hebrews 11:35b). The author's fundamental point and "most perfect example" (Hebrews 12:2) of faith is that no obstacle is sufficient to thwart God's purposes—a truth that was "supremely exemplified when God gave up his own Son to the cross but then raised him from death."[284]

CONCLUSION

THE EPISTLE TO THE HEBREWS is a magnificent exhortation that serves the purpose of teaching the superiority of Jesus Christ, warning against backsliding into sin and disobedience, and encouraging the reader to advance into spiritual maturity and unequivocal faith in God.[285] In this context, the author first substantiates the supremacy of Jesus in order to justify steadfast and enduring faith in his redemptive work.

The author seemed to intuitively sense that faith is either strengthened or weakened depending on the thoughts of the one in whom we put our faith. For the author of Hebrews, a call to enduring faith was both established and substantiated by the elevated position of Jesus who was supremely above and beyond "the different times and various ways" (Hebrews 1:1) that God had previously revealed Himself. It was critical to the author to both encourage his reader to *have faith in Jesus* in addition to ensuring they were *thinking correctly about Jesus*. Once the supremacy of Jesus was established, the author then exhorted the reader to continue to press forward in their faith as modeled by the "great cloud of witnesses" (Hebrews 12:1) and ultimately perfected in Jesus himself (Hebrews 12:2-3).

284   Ibid., p. 158.
285   Laney, Dr. Carl. "Hebrews" in *Essential Bible Background (CreateSpace, 2016), p. 239.*

CHAPTER
TWENTY

THE CENTRAL TEACHING OF THE BOOK OF REVELATION

Understanding the Themes of Coming,
Kingship, and Worship

THE PRIMARY PURPOSE of the book of Revelation is immediately introduced to the reader as the revelation of Jesus Christ Himself (1:1).[286] In order to understand the greater implications and message of the book of Revelation, it is imperative that above all else, the reader recognizes and responds to the prominence of Jesus within the book.[287] In other words, the book of Revelation is "the revelation of Jesus Christ," which means that Jesus is the central figure of the book and the key to understanding the totality of the book's message.

The book of Revelation is a message to "whoever has ears" (2:7), and in this sense the book contains revelation that everyone needs to know and properly respond to. In the same manner that everyone needs to know "what the Spirit says" (2:7), the book of Revelation is also a call to action and a demand for the world's only appropriate response to Jesus: faithful obedience to His glorious Kingship on Earth. John declares that in addition to hearing the words of the prophecy of Revelation, the expectation is that the message would be "taken to heart and acted upon, because the time is near" (1:3). And what is John's expectation for a faithful response to Jesus? According to, as well as demonstrated by John, the only acceptable posture for the body and heart before Jesus would be "falling at his feet as though dead" (1:17) and worshiping him.[288]

In many respects, the abbreviated and condensed theme of Revelation could be described as the "Soon Coming of King Jesus." In his salutation and twice more in Revelation, John describes Jesus as "the one who is, and who was, and who is to come" (1:4, 8; 4:8). This formula seems to capture the essence of the book and describes Jesus as "the main event not only in history past but history future as well."[289]

---

286   As pointed out by Dr. Tuck in *Revelation Book (A Readers Guide to the Book of Revelation) in 1:1 the author seems to be saying that the book of Revelation is both from Jesus* and *about Jesus.*

287   As the third theme of this chapter will demonstrate, the proper recognition and response to Jesus is *worship.*

288   In this sense, the consolidated message of the book of Revelation declares: "Jesus the King is coming – Worship Him!"

289   Tuck, Dr. Gary. *Revelation Book (A Readers Guide to the Book of Revelation), p. 7.*

The book of Revelation is written with an unmistakably fast tempo, a compelling sense of urgency, and a demand for the preparation for the Second Coming of Jesus. John introduces the idea of "nearness" in the very first verse (1:1) and then with continued tenacity he establishes two of the most significant themes of the book, namely the "nearness" of the Second Coming of Jesus (1:4) and the representation of the Coming One as King (1:5). These two themes are strategically placed as introductory and concluding bookends (1:4,5; 22:20) to Revelation, and are also developed throughout each of the book's major sections.

This paper will expound upon the central teaching of the book of Revelation in addition to tracing and developing the primary themes of Second Coming and Kingship. The natural continuation to Jesus' Second Coming and His Kingship is the appropriate response to the One who is King, and in this respect the theme of worship will also be explored. By identifying and developing these key themes of Revelation, the book comes alive with the reader's awesome awareness that they are experiencing the revelation of God Himself.

THE THEME OF OUR LORD'S COMING

FROM AN INTERPRETATIVE PERSPECTIVE, it is important to consider the book of Revelation through the eyes of its author: the disciple whom Jesus loved, the great apostle John. In order to achieve this perspective, the reader must remember that Revelation is the last book of the Bible, written by the last living apostle. Up to the moment of receiving the vision and revelation contained in the book of Revelation, John had lived with the eager expectation and longing for the return of Jesus, but had not yet seen it.[290]

On the other hand, consider what John *had experienced*: the death and martyrdom of his friends, the destruction of Jerusalem, and the Jewish people driven into exile in addition to his own banishment to the island of Patmos.[291] In this sense, the theme of the "nearness of the Second Coming of Jesus" most certainly brought a combination of joy and comfort to John's heart. For the reader of Revelation today, the "nearness of the Second Coming of Jesus" that

---

290   The idea and content for the "perspective of John" was identified in *Revelation Book, p. 5.*
291   Ibid.

comforted John's heart should bring encouragement to the faithful followers of Jesus, while at the same time result in dread for all those who oppose His reign.

The book of Revelation is about Jesus Christ as King and the dominantly progressive theme of the book is that the Almighty King is returning (His Second Coming). In the context of structure, the theme of Second Coming is prominent throughout what are arguably the three major sections of the book; Verse 1:19 provides the reader with the aerial view and broadest plan, which could be succinctly described as the Lord's direction for John to "write what he had seen, what is now, and what will take place in the future" (my translation of 1:19).[292] This past-present-future outline naturally lends itself to the Kingship of Jesus in all three timeframes, for He is the One "who is, and who was, and who is to come, the Almighty" (1:8; 4:8).

The confession of faith taught by the New Testament authors is that Jesus is "The Christ" and that He reigns. The New Testament author's use of the word "Christ" was not used in the context of a "name" but was rather a "title" and served the purpose of identifying Jesus as the long awaited King.[293] From the moment that Jesus "ascended into the clouds" (Acts 1:9-11) the apostles and all faithful believers have been eagerly awaiting His return "in just the same way" (Acts 1:11).[294]

The "revelation of Jesus Christ" (1:1) and His imminent "coming with the clouds" (1:7) implies that what was once hidden would now be fully exposed. Although spiritually, Jesus is the One "who is, and who was, and who is to come" (1:8), his "coming with the clouds" points the reader to what Jesus will physically do at His return in the future (cf. 22:7, 12, 20). The author's Old Testament references to Jesus Christ's "coming with the clouds" resulting in "all peoples on Earth will mourn because of him" (1:7) serve a dual purpose.

Firstly, the primary message of the Old Testament prophets was their encouragement to eagerly await the coming of a Savior.[295] As beautifully illustrated in the exchange between Jesus and Peter, the long-awaited Savior of the Old Testament was fulfilled in Jesus: "You are the Messiah, the Son of the living God" (Matthew 16:16). Peter's awareness of the true identity of Jesus as

---

292   Tuck, Dr. Gary. "Revelation" in *The Arguments of the Books of the New Testament, p. 199.*

293   Class lecture notes by Dr. Gary Tuck on the book of Revelation, Western Seminary, July 1, 2019

294   Class lecture notes by Dr. Gary Tuck on the book of Revelation, Western Seminary, July 1, 2019. Cf., Dr. Gary Tuck's *"Revelation Book," p. 15.*

295   Dr. Gary Tuck's *"Revelation Book," p. 12.*

King was almost certainly his understanding of Psalm 2:2.[296] Secondly, and in addition to Psalm 2, the prophecy of Daniel 7 was a key focus for John throughout the book of Revelation.[297] The original "son of man" prophecy describes the one who would be crowned King of kings. Therefore, when John "turns around to see the voice" (1:12) that was speaking to him and observes "someone like a son of man" (1:13, cf. 14:14) he is utilizing a direct reference to (and arguably a direct quotation from) the "son of man" prophecy of Daniel 7.[298]

The book of Revelation is about the Second Coming and Kingship of Jesus and the great climax of the book can be found in verse 19:11-21.[299] In many respects, John draws the reader's attention to the teaching tradition (in addition to his own eye-witness recollection) of the Lord's ascension into the clouds in Acts 1:9-11 to describe the Lord's triumphant return "in just the same way" (Acts 1:11). This section of Revelation begins with Jesus in Heaven (19:11) and concludes with Jesus either "capturing" (19:20) or "killing" (19:21) His enemies. Of exceeding importance in this particular section is the self-disclosed name of Jesus being prominently displayed both on His robe and His thigh: "KING OF KINGS AND LORD OF LORDS" (Revelation 19:16). At His Second Coming, Jesus is portrayed as the absolute King "full of divine power and authority."[300]

It is important to note that in the announcement to five of the churches in the province of Asia contained in Chapters 2 and 3, Jesus includes references to both the joyful and fearful results of His Second Coming (2:5, 2:16, 2:25, 3:3, 3:11). In either case, the expectation of the imminence of the Lord's coming would cause one to be faithfully awaiting His arrival, and either maintaining or correcting behavior accordingly. Furthermore, and as will be developed more completely in the third section of this paper, John describes the only proper response to Jesus at His arrival as a posture of worship and "rejoicing with gladness" (19:7).

In the conclusion of the book of Revelation, once again the author turns the reader's attention to the imminence of Jesus' Second Coming (22:7, 12, 20). The first issuance of the "soon coming" of Jesus serves the purpose

---

296   Dr. Gary Tuck, class notes on the book of Revelation, Western Seminary, July 1, 2019.

297   According to Johnson in *The Expositors Bible Commentary of Revelation, there are no fewer than 31 allusions to Daniel 7 in the book of Revelation.*

298   Tuck, Dr. Gary. Class lecture on the book of Revelation, Western Seminary, July 1, 2019. Cf., Dr. Gary Tuck's *Revelation Book footnote 23, p. 14.*

299   Ibid., p. 15.

300   Johnson, *The Expositors Bible Commentary on Revelation, p. 760.*

of encouraging obedience to "the prophecy written in this scroll" (22:7) of the book Revelation. The second announcement of the coming of Jesus is associated with "giving to each person according to what they have done" (22:12). This combination of requiring obedience to Jesus observed in verse 22:7, and the subsequent reward observed in verse 22:12, seems to provide the reader with the much-needed encouragement to remain faithful to the Lord even in the midst of suffering and persecution. Echoing the Lord's announcement of His imminent coming is first the "Spirit and the bride" cry for Jesus to come, followed by "one who hears" the words of the scroll (22:17). Then in a grand conclusive manner, the author himself summarizes the theme of the Lord's Second Coming with the words, "Amen. Come, Lord Jesus" (22:20).

THE THEME OF KINGSHIP

THE BOOK OF REVELATION begins with the glory and Kingship of Jesus, emphasizes and expands upon His glory as the context for the entire book, and then concludes with His glorious judgment of "each person according to what they have done" (22:12). In this respect, the next primary theme in the book of Revelation following Christ's Second Coming is His Kingship. As the theme of Kingship is traced through the book of Revelation, it is of supreme importance to reflect on the teaching of Matthew 6:9-10, specifically the fact that Jesus' prayer focused on God's will and authority as being established "on earth as it is in heaven" (Matthew 6:10). Although Jesus currently sits enthroned at God's right hand in Heaven, the ultimate dominion of His rule will be Earth.[301]

The author almost immediately establishes the theme of Kingship in his opening greetings to the seven churches in the province of Asia in verses 1:4-6. The evidence for this theme can be seen in the author's use of descriptive references to the Kingship of Jesus, including words most commonly associated with a monarchy such as *throne, ruler, kings, kingdom,* and *dominion.* Furthermore, unlike the temporal nature of the types of worldly kingdoms the original reader was familiar with, the Kingdom of Jesus would reign "for ever and ever" (1:6).

---

301   The relationship between Matthew 6:9-10, Kingship and the book of Revelation was brought to my attention during a lecture by Dr. Gary Tuck on Revelation on July 1, 2019, at the Western Seminary San Jose campus.

The author establishes the supremacy of Jesus by describing Him as "the ruler of the kings of the earth" (1:5). This early placement for the theme of the Kingship is meant to clue the reader into the magnitude of its importance. It is also significant that when John was "in the spirit in Heaven" (4:1-2) the first thing he observed was *a throne in heaven with someone sitting on it* (4:2).[302] The fact that Jesus is described as the "Lord of lords and King of kings" (17:14, 19:19) is of immense importance and seems to be further evidence that Jesus will "rule the nations and take possession of the ends of the earth" (Psalm 2:8).

As Jesus makes His triumphant Second Coming to reclaim His rightful kingdom as King of the Earth, He will come into conflict with the "rulers of Earth" (Psalm 2:10) and the anti-kingdom of "Satan who leads the whole world astray" (12:9). In this respect, the theme of Kingship within the book of Revelation now seems to approach finality as the kingdoms of the world come into conflict with the ultimate Kingdom of Heaven. Although Revelation is the final canonical book of the Bible, the depiction of this conflict was forecasted in Psalm 2. The "conspiring of the nations" and "banding together of the kings of the earth" (Psalm 2:1-2) are the same "kings of the whole world" (16:14) portrayed in Revelation who band together at the Armageddon event (16:12, 14). However, similar to the vain conspiring that resulted in "the One enthroned in heaven laughing" (Psalm 2:1, 4), the result of the final conflict depicted in Revelation is that "the kingdom of the world has become the kingdom of our Lord" (11:15).

A critical skill for understanding any particular book of the Bible is the ability to see the big picture that the author is relating to the reader. In this respect, "the big picture is the picture."[303] The complementary themes of Second Coming and Kingship are overarching and dominant in the book of Revelation. They are the primary colors of the tapestry that weave together the "big picture" of the book and form the foundation of the book's message. Although this paper will now turn to the subsidiary theme of worship in Revelation, this theme must been seen and understood as an aspect of Second Coming and Kingship.

---

302   In addition to verse 4:2, there are 26 other references to a throne in the book of Revelation. This figure and observation were brought to my attention in a class lecture by Dr. Gary Tuck on Revelation on July 1, 2019, in addition to Dr. Tuck's book *Revelation Book, p. 20.*

303   Tuck, Dr. Gary. Class lecture on "seeing the big picture" in Hermeneutics, fall 2017, Western Seminary, San Jose campus.

THE THEME OF WORSHIP

IN THE LIGHT OF THE previously developed themes of Second Coming and Kingship, the imminent arrival of Jesus and the establishment of His eternal Kingdom are intended to motivate the proper worship of God. The theme of worship (and specifically *proper worship*) is demonstrated by John himself and serves as a model for all of God's people. When John was in the presence of Jesus, the worship posture of his heart and body displayed a combination of obedience and reverence to the King of Heaven and King of Earth. When John saw Jesus he was so overwhelmed that he "fell at his feet as though dead" (1:17).

It is interesting to note that the passages in Revelation that focus on worship take place where the glory and Kingship of Jesus is highlighted (4:8–11; 5:9–14; 19:3–8). This encourages the reader to connect worship as the only proper response to Jesus' Second Coming and His eternal reign as King. John's description of the four living creatures who perpetually cry out, "Holy, holy, holy, Lord God Almighty," draws the reader's attention to "Him who sits on the throne" (4:8-9). In this sense, the themes of worship and Kingship are intimately connected. Furthermore, the proper hierarchy and chain of command is perfectly illustrated by the 24 elders who "cast their crowns before Him" (4:10; 5:14) and worship at His feet. Although related to the theme of worship, this verse is also evidence of the that fact that at His Second Coming, the kings and rulers of Earth will be subject to the Kingship of Jesus.

Mirroring the same posture as John who "fell down as though dead" (1:17) in the presence of Jesus, all those who gather around the throne of Jesus likewise "fall on their faces before the throne and worshiped God" (7:11; cf. 11:16–18). Once again, the reader is compelled to see the connection between worship and the throne (or Kingship) of Jesus. Further evidence for this observation may be seen in the chapter 19 of Revelation, which depicts Heaven's celebration, and the triumphant victory of Jesus (19:3–8).

CONCLUSION

A CRITICAL SKILL for understanding any particular book of the Bible is the ability to see the big picture, and in this respect "the big picture" in the book of Revelation is the complementary themes of Second Coming and Kingship. They are the primary colors of the tapestry that weave together the entire book and form the foundation of the book's central message. In order to grasp the message of the book of Revelation, it is imperative that above all else, the reader recognizes and responds to the prominence of the "Second Coming of King Jesus." This response should be one of proper worship and obedience to the King of kings. In other words, the book of Revelation is about "the soon coming of Jesus Christ to claim His throne,"[304] which then compels and encourages the reader to take a posture of reverence and worship.

---

304   Tuck, Dr. Gary. *Revelation Book, p. 21.*

CHAPTER
TWENTY ONE

A THEOLOGY OF REVELATION: ESTABLISHING OUR FOUNDATION

REVELATION IS THE DISCLOSURE by God of truths about Himself that people could not arrive at independent of His divine initiative. By God's sovereign decision and enabling, His revelation to humanity is accomplished by both general (Psalm 19:1-3; Romans 1:19-20) and special revelation. The means of special revelation were accomplished by God's manifestation of Himself through historical events (Deuteronomy 26: 5-9; Acts 13:16-41), His divine speech (2 Timothy 3:16-17; 2 Peter 1:20-21), and most importantly through the incarnation of His Word in the person and deity of Jesus Christ (Colossians 1:15-19; Hebrews 1:2-3).

General revelation is God's communication and display of Himself to all persons at all times and places through nature (Psalm 19:1-3), history (Acts 17:26), and mankind (Genesis 1:26-28; Romans 2:11-16).[305] At the most rudimentary level, Jesus taught that evidence of God could be identified through observance of the natural order of agriculture (Matthew 6:28-30). Even the seemingly obvious fact that God had chosen to preserve mankind by providing rain, crops of food for bodily nourishment, and emotional wellbeing (Acts 14:17) points to evidence of His presence within both creation and history (Acts 14:15-18). Although these modes of revelation are clear and leave people without excuse (Romans 1:20), the sinful nature of mankind distorts our thinking, hardens our heart (Romans 1:21, 3:23; 1 Jn. 1:8), and corrupts the truth about God in exchange for a lie (Romans 1:25).

Special revelation differs from general revelation in the sense that God communicates essential qualities of His being that could not be discerned through human reasoning or understanding (1 Corinthians 2:14). God's special revelation has manifested itself through historical events (Job 12:23), divinely inspired speech subsequently recorded in the written Word of God (2 Peter 1:20-21), and the incarnation of the Word in the person and deity of Jesus Christ (John 1:1; 18). Special revelation supremely and uniquely announces God's intention to reconcile mankind onto Himself (John 3:16) by grace through faith in Jesus Christ (Ephesians 2:8). In the life of Christ, mankind is no longer limited to knowing *about God,* but may now *know God* by entering into a personal, saving, and loving relationship with Him (John 17:3).

---

305   Erickson, Millard. *Christian Theology* (Grand Rapids, MI: Baker Academic, 2013), p. 122.

The Christian church holds that the 66 books of the Bible are the *theopneustos* Word of God (2 Tim. 3:16) written by man through the power of the Holy Spirit (2 Peter 1:21) who shaped the thoughts and directed the subsequent written and recorded words of the human authors (1 Corinthians 2:13). The original biblical autographs contain the powerful (Genesis 18:14; 1 Corinthians 2:4-5), authoritative (2 Timothy 3:16-17), clear (Deuteronomy 30:11-14; Romans 10:6-8), sufficient (1 Corinthians 2:9-10), inerrant, (Matthew 19:4-5), and inspired (Acts 1:16; 2 Sam. 23:2) Word of God.

Additionally, the Church has traditionally held that the 66 books of the Bible are the *complete and final canonical revelation* of God to mankind (1 Thessalonians 2:13). Although God chose to speak through human authors at many times and in various ways (Hebrews 1:1), the most complete revelation of His triune nature and program of redemption was made visible through Jesus Christ (John 20:31; Hebrews 1:2-4; Colossians 3:4-7). The canonical books of the Bible have been given authority by Christ himself (Matthew 28:19-20) and are the believer's supreme rule of both doctrine (John 10:35) and behavioral practice (2 Timothy 3:16-17; Titus 1:6-9).

In the Holy Scriptures, the believer encounters the living Word of God and comes to understand it not only says things, but also does things (Psalm 33:6). The interpreter of the biblical text, through the indwelling power of the Holy Spirit, experiences spiritual realities with Spirit-taught words (1 Corinthians 2:10-16) that fundamentally change their entire life (Romans 15:4).

THE BEGINNING OF TIME

SINCE THE BEGINNING OF CREATION at the hand of God (Genesis 1:1; John 1:1-3), revelation about God's nature and Being have been made manifest throughout the universe (Psalm 19:1-3).[306] Through God's sovereign decision and enabling, the gift of His self-disclosure has been accomplished by a variety of means that *can be universally discerned* by all human beings. On one hand, the doctrine of general revelation would suggest that even the seemingly obvious fact that God had chosen to preserve humanity by providing rain, crops of food for bodily nourishment, and emotional wellbeing (Acts 14:17),

306   Yarbrough, R. W. "Revelation" in *The New Dictionary of Biblical Theology* (Downers Grove, IL: InterVarsity Press, 2008), p. 732.

points to evidence of His presence within both creation and history (Acts 14:15-18).[307] General revelation is self-evident, universally clear, and leaves people without excuse (Romans 1:20).

On the other hand, special revelation is unique in the sense that God has also chosen to communicate essential qualities of His being that *could not have been discerned* through human reasoning or understanding (1 Corinthians 2:14). God's special revelation has manifested itself through historical events (Job 12:23), divinely inspired speech subsequently recorded in the sixty-six canonical books of the Holy Bible (2 Peter 1:20-21; 2 Timothy 3:16), and the incarnation of Word of God in the person and deity of Jesus Christ (John. 1:1; 18). Of particular significance for the investigative purposes of this biblical theology, special revelation treats the historical communications and manifestations of God as now uniquely and exclusively available through the consultation of certain sacred texts.[308]

The special revelation contained within the sixty-six books of the Bible supremely and uniquely announces God's intention to reconcile mankind onto Himself (John. 3:16) by grace through faith in Jesus Christ (Ephesians. 2:8). In other words, all Scripture is a unified story that ultimately leads to Jesus (Luke 24:27-45).[309] In the life of Christ, humanity is no longer limited to knowing *about God,* but may now *know God* by entering into a personal, saving, and loving relationship with Him (John. 17:3). In this sense, Jesus is the complete and perfect fulfillment of every conceivable means of God's revelatory self-disclosing communications and manifestations ever made within creation (John 14:6).

INTO THE GREAT UNKNOWN

IS IT POSSIBLE THAT A GLIMMER OF LIGHT—a faint ray of God's glory or a shadowy representation of His Being[310]—could be present within the sacred texts of other world religions? Similar to the uniqueness of a human fingerprint whose impression is retained on everything it touches, is God's

---

307   Erickson, Millard. *Christian Theology* (Grand Rapids, MI: Baker Academic, 2013), p. 125.

308   Erickson, p. 122.

309   The founders of the Bible Project beautifully articulate this position in their doctrinal intention: "To help people see the Bible as a unified story that leads to Jesus."

310   This sentence is an intentional contrast to Jesus Christ's "*full radiance* of God's glory" and "*exact representation* of God's being" described by the author of Hebrews (reference Hebrews 1:1-3).

"fingerprint" within His creation (Psalm 8:3), however dusty or distorted, still faintly visible on the pages of sacred texts outside the Judeo-Christian faith? Within the hearts and minds of the great thinkers and mystics of world religions outside of God's covenant people (Deuteronomy 14:2), might it be the case that the residue of His eternal nature and Devine essence (Ecclesiastes 3:11) was recorded as a forerunner to the arrival of the gospel of Jesus Christ?

What are the implications for sharing the gospel if the sacred texts of all the world's religions recorded *before the birth of Christ* retained varying degrees of the "hidden manna" (Revelation 2:17) that Jesus himself spoke of?[311] Additionally, if *after the birth of Christ* God had continued to clandestinely encode varying degrees of His nature within such texts as the Koran, then much like Nicodemus who timidly sought the Lord in the safety of a dark night, the connective tissue of all spiritual seekers is adequately primed for the arrival of the good news that Jesus ushers in (John 3:1-15).[312] In other words, all the world religions now eagerly await the dawn of a new day and the testimony of the heavenly things our Lord promised that all nations would receive. In the fullness of the gospel, all of God's children can now receive the baptism of the Father, the Son and the Holy Spirit, and the surrendering to the Lordship of Jesus Christ that the first disciples set out to achieve (Matthew 28:19-20).

PREPARING THE HEARTS AND MINDS

MUCH LIKE A SPECIAL OPERATIONS TEAM who deploys in advance of the main element for the purpose of preparing the hearts and minds of the ingenious people, if even a dimly prophetic Word of God was revealed to other world religions for the purpose of preparing them for the arrival of the gospel, then Christian evangelists have much cause to rejoice (Matthew 28:19-20).

The great Christian theologian C.S. Lewis expressed belief that general revelation of God throughout humanity is evidenced within our conscious

---

311   I make a distinction that the *glimmer of light* within the sacred texts of world religions are specific and unique to the historical era before the birth of Christ. Jesus is the fulfillment and final Word of God (John 1:1-3; Hebrews 1:1-3).

312   Needless to say, there seems to be a stronger argument that Divine revelation is the sacred texts of world religions *before* rather than *after* the birth of Christ. Although we can intuitively sense that varying degrees of revelation in such sacred texts as the Vedas served as a cultural "Old Testament" and forerunner for the gospel, once the "Word had become flesh," the necessity for continued revelation outside the gospel would not seem prudent. Additionally, any revelation that contradicted the gospel would, according to the Apostle Paul, "be under God's curse" (Galatians 1:8).

choice between right and wrong, and the long history of all world religions that try (and fail) to obey it.[313] Even the "queer stories scattered all through the heather religions" ultimately and miraculously find their meaning, fulfillment, and explanation in the person of Jesus Christ.[314] Perhaps the mystery of this marvelous Truth about God is best expressed in the words of the Apostle Paul who wrote that God is "over all and through all and in all" (Ephesians 4:6), and proclaimed, "In Him we live and move and have our being" (Acts 17:28).

Throughout the ages, the great prophets, sages, mystics, and gurus of world religions outside of the Judeo-Christian faith have attempted through the constraints of human language to express the inexpressible mystery and Oneness of God (The Bhagavad Gita 4:6; The Tao Te Ching 25:1; The Surangama Sutra[315]). The collective voices of these *rishis* (literally "seers") of ancient India synthesized their understanding of the Divine in a fashion later described as Perennial Philosophy.[316] The universality of mankind's quest for Divine understanding and relationship was consolidated into three truths: (1) There is an infinite and changeless reality that lies behind the world of change; (2) This same reality resides within human consciousness; (3) The purpose of life is to discover this changeless reality: In other words, to realize God while still here on earth.[317] In this sense, the Indian sacred texts including the Upanishads, the Bhagavad Gita, and the Dhammapada were prophetic announcements of a future experience of the Kingdom of God on earth.[318] The dim light of the *rishis* inspired voices were in many respects anticipating a time when a complete, accurate, and fully embodied representation of the Divine would be manifested for the entire world to see.

The Indian Christian Bishop A.J. Appasamy argued in his book, *Temple Bells,* that Indian Christians should become acquainted with the sacred texts of Hinduism.[319] Similarly, those evangelists intent on introducing Christ within

---

313   Lewis, C. S. *Mere Christianity* (New York: Collier Books, 1952), p. 39.

314   Ibid., p. 40.

315   The Buddha is recorded to have said, "One intrinsic Unity enfolds all manifestations." The Surangama Sutra: Identified in the book by Richard Hooper, *Jesus, Buddha, Krishna and Lau Tzu: The Parallel Sayings* (Charlottesville, VA: Hampton Road Publishing, 2007), p. 57.

316   Easwaran, Eknath. *The Bhagavad Gita* (Tomales, CA: Nilgiri Press, 2007), p. 17.

317   Ibid.

318   Easwaran describes the Upanishads as the oldest of the three and functioning much like a roadmap to understanding consciousness. The Dhammapada has traditionally been attributed to sayings of the Buddha. The Bhagavad Gita is considered by scholars both a "map and guidebook" to spirituality. The oldest Hindu scriptures are the Rig Veda, written in a prototype of the Sanskrit language approximately 1500 B.C., and are foundational to the other sacred texts.

319   Tennent, p. 55.

the context of Indian thought must become acquainted with the "storehouse of terms, images, and metaphors" that resonates with the Indian mind.[320] Much of Appasamy's theology rests on his conviction that Jesus "came to fulfill, not to destroy" (cf. Matthew 5:17). Given the magnitude of Hindu spiritual thought that is foundational to Indian culture, Appasamy believed that approaching Christianity through the "impulses, instincts, questions, longings, and aspirations" within his nation's sacred texts was the key to revealing that Christ is the fulfillment to the deepest longings of the Hindu heart.[321]

In the canonical texts of the New Testament, the author of Hebrews summarized the universality of this phenomenon when he wrote, "In the past God spoke to us through the prophets at many times and in various ways" (Hebrews 1:1). Much like the testimony of John the Baptist in explaining the purpose of his authorized bearing of revelation, a liberal position would hold that the purpose of God's prophetic voice throughout the Old Testament, in addition to the sacred texts of other world religions, was "to make straight the way for the Lord" (John 1:23).[322]

The conservative position within the Christian faith would hold that the spoken Word of God has indeed come to human beings at many times and in various ways (Hebrews 1:1). However, God's Divine Word is specifically reserved to the canonical books of the Holy Bible. The Word of God recorded in the pages of the 66 canonical books of the Bible are the expression of God's will to humankind, and they supremely define what we are to believe and how we are to live.[323] Additionally, Scripture itself draws no distinction between the authority and Divine origin of God's oral or written revelation (2 Timothy 3:16; 2 Peter 1:19-21).[324] In this sense, the 66 books of the Bible are the complete and final Word of God to mankind (1 Thess. 2:13). This view holds that the prophets who heard God speak are themselves restricted to the canonical books of the Bible itself. Most supremely, the Bible has been given authority by Christ himself (Matt. 28:19-20) and is the Christians' ultimate rule of both doctrine (John. 10:35) and behavioral practice (2 Timothy 3:16-17; Titus 1:6-9).

---

320   Ibid.
321   Ibid.
322   This view is held by modern spiritual teacher Eckhart Tolle, who has sought to find the similarities between Buddhism, Hinduism, Sufi mysticism, Judaism, and Christianity.
323   Erickson, p. 211.
324   John Frame. *The Doctrine of the Christian Life* (Phillipsburg, NJ: P&R Publishing, 2008), p. 141.

At the other end of the spectrum, certain Indian Christian theologians hold that the sacred texts of their religious history are *their equivalent of the Old Testament*.[325] These theologians look to New Testament passages such as the account of Jesus on the road to Emmaus and his explanation that "all the Scriptures concern himself" (Luke 24:27), and subsequently apply this to Jesus' presence in India today. In their view, "Jesus walks alongside Indian Christians and explains to them how the Indian scriptures point to and bear witness in him."[326] These same theologians note the similarity of the Divine words of Jesus Christ with parallel statements of the Buddha and the spiritual wisdom of Krishna portrayed in The Bhagavad Gita, and then reverse engineer them to a single source, mainly the same One True God. This perspective certainly has merit, and seems to suggest that the commonality and continuity between Jesus' teaching and the teaching of other world religious leaders before Christ's incarnate ministry on earth were a component of God's general revelation to all humanity.[327]

ENLISTING SUPPORT

OBEDIENT OF THE COMMISSION to "make disciples of *all the nations*" (Matthew 28:19 – my use of italics), and aware that the gospel of Jesus Christ must be shared with a sensitivity to the diverse spiritual backgrounds of world religions, I support a position that there may indeed be a *glimmer of light* within the sacred texts outside the Judeo-Christian faith. Perhaps the most intriguing and greatest support for this position, in addition to the integration, interconnectedness, and single-Source of all written revelation about God, comes from the mouth of God Himself (Colossians 2:9). In the company of his apostles, Jesus revealed that everything ever recorded in the Scriptures was ultimately about him and fulfilled in his life (Luke 24:27, 44).

In this sense, all the sacred texts of the world's religions recorded *before the birth of Christ* retain a *glimmer of light* that shines forth most brilliantly and

---

325   Tennant, Timothy. *Theology in the Context of World Christianity*, (Grand Rapids, MI: Zondervan, 2007), p. 53.

326   Ibid., p. 54.

327   As researched by Richard Hooper in his book, *Jesus, Buddha, Krishna & Lao Tzu* (Charlottesville, VA: Hampton Roads, 2007), this was a view held by the Catholic monk and mystic Thomas Merton. Much of Merton's life was spent finding the similarities between Western and Eastern monasticism and mysticism. In his final work, *The Asian Journal*, Merton expounded on the importance of the sacred Hindu text, The Bhagavad Gita.

perfectly in the Divine Light of Jesus Christ (John 1:4-5, 9). In other words, although the sacred texts of world religions may contain revelation about God, the most complete and final revelation is made manifest in Jesus Christ. This position therefore gives final authority to the inspired 66 canonical books of the Holy Bible (2 Timothy 3:16, 2 Peter 1:21).[328] If the words of the great Christian mystic and theologian A.W. Tozer ring true, then the prophetic voices of centuries long ago served the purpose of preparing humanity to *think rightly* about God. Therefore, to achieve the final and supremely right thought about God, one must have an encounter with the person of Jesus Christ (John 14:9) as specifically revealed within the Holy Bible.[329]

Although the sacred texts of ancient world religions may contain a glimmer of light, or in the words of Emil Brunner, "Be God's voice, but scarcely recognizable,"[330] there remains an important distinction between the Judeo-Christian view of a personal and loving God who searches for us (Luke 15:1-32), as opposed to a human seeker in search of God. In this sense, the spiritual seeker of the ancient world religions is finally found by God Himself in the revelation of Jesus Christ. In many respects, the Magi depicted in the gospel of Matthew (Matthew 2:1-12) symbolically represent the embodiment of spiritual seekers in search of God from ancient to modern times.

The gospel of Matthew describes the Magi as "wise men from the East." These wise men are likely a combination of a modern-day astrologer and astronomer. They were part of a stargazing culture that sought to discern the will and nature of God by studying the planets and stars.[331] These wise men represent the spiritual traditions of the human race from ancient to modern times including the Hindu, Buddhist, and Sufi religions. The Magi are the universal embodiment of the spiritual seeker who desires a greater understanding of the nature of God (Reference Acts 8:31). The Magi in the gospel of Matthew and the Ethiopian eunuch in the book of Acts are spiritual seekers in pursuit of Divine explanation and direction. However, they do not know precisely where to go or what to think until they meet representatives of God's covenant people who tell them on the basis of special revelation the gospel of Jesus Christ (Matthew 2:5-6; Acts 8:31-35).

---

328   This view is held by Bishop Robert Barron as discussed in his book, *To Light a Fire on the Earth* (New York: Image Books, 2017), and his Podcast *Word On Fire,* "Following The Star."

329   A. W. Tozer wrote, "What comes into our mind when we think about God is the most important thing about us." *The Knowledge of the Holy* (New York: HarperOne, 1961), p. 1.

330   Erickson, p. 160.

331   The illustration of the Maji and the relationship to the modern-day astrologer was identified in Bishop Robert Barron's Podcast *Word On Fire,* episode titled "Following The Star."

If the dim light of revelation within the sacred texts of the world religions is akin to the star the Magi followed, then evangelists of all Christian denominations have reason to celebrate. Like the mysterious gravitational pull of nature that migrating birds use to navigate across vast oceans, all spiritual seekers are drawn towards the "true light that has come into the world" (1:9). Although the Magi were able to follow the star in the general direction of Christ (Matthew 2:2b), they ultimately inquired and were dependent on the experts of the Torah to tell them precisely where Jesus was to be born (Matthew 2:2a; 5-6, cf. Micah 5:2,4).

The prophet Isaiah foresaw that "Nations will come to your light, and kings to the brightness of your dawn, all assemble and come to you; your sons come from afar. All from Sheba will come, bearing gold and incense, and proclaiming the praise of the LORD" (Isaiah 60:33-4, 6). The great prophetic voices of Israel seemed to sense that something of extraordinary importance was afoot. The spiritual privilege that Israel had long enjoyed was never intended for Israel alone. Rather, Israel's glory was intended to benefit the entire world. This biblical position would seem to suggest that whatever the other nations were looking for would *ultimately* and *only* be found in Israel. In other words, what the spiritual seekers of other nations were pursuing inchoately and without full understanding, Israel had found and was worshiping explicitly.

Although still a mystery shrouded in a fog of revelation, the world religions *outside the covenant people of Israel* were in fact hungry and thirsty *for the God of Israel*. All of their accomplishments and spiritual achievements were in some sense an echo of anticipation for what God would accomplish through Israel. If Isaiah was correct in his prophecy, then the "distant sons from afar" represent all the world's religious, philosophical, artistic, literate, and scientific achievements. The world's deeply encoded desire for eternal light would in fact be discovered in the light already shining on Israel.

THE LIGHT OF THE WORLD

THE CLAIM OF THE CHRISTIAN FAITH is that Jesus is not just another great spiritual teacher, guru, philosopher, radical political figure. Rather, Jesus is the incarnate "Word became flesh" (John 1:14). This means that the Divine mind, the intelligibility through which all things are both created and sustained, was made manifest in the life and person of Jesus. If on one hand Christians affirm this magnificent truth, then on the other we must concede that any attempt to find the good, the true, the beautiful, the transcendent, and the eternal must ultimately lead to and be fulfilled in Christ. Thus, the light shining on Israel is meant to be a light for the entire world to see.

The contrast between the disclosure of Christ's birth to the shepherds and the Magi is meant to represent the contrast between the simple and sophisticated. In this sense, the Magi symbolically portray the cultural, intellectual, scientific, philosophical, and spiritual longings of the human heart. The Magi's studying of the night sky is evocative of the world's collective searching for the good, true, and beautiful. In their attempt to discover a meaningful arrangement of the stars, the Magi are instead brought face to face with the Maker of the stars Himself. Through Divine inspiration, the prophet Isaiah intuitively knew that all spiritual seekers would be drawn towards the light that would illuminate the entire world.

The spiritual seeker depicted in the saga of The Bhagavad Gita is the warrior Arjuna. In the company of his teacher Krishna and through their dialogue together, the path to knowing God is made clear. The attraction to spiritual seekers across the ages has been the promise of following the "spiritual roadmap" of the Gita, and like Arjuna, arriving at the feet of God. However, within the context of the Bible, following the Gita or any other spiritual text will at best only point you in a very vague and general direction of the Divine. Much like the Magi who arrived in a land they did not recognize, specific revelation uniquely given to God's covenant people will always be required before proceeding further. However, in welcoming the fullness of revelation recorded within God's Word by the Divinely inspired authors of the Bible (2 Timothy 3:16), the Magi and all spiritual seekers can finally come to worship at the feet of Jesus (Matthew 2:11).

In the context of this specific example, the Magi did indeed find what they were looking for. However, they would not have found it without the fullness of God's Word as revealed to His covenant people. And in a more general sense, all spiritual seekers who "follow the star" and dim light of revelation within their historical sacred texts may ultimately arrive at the gates of the New Jerusalem (Revelation 3:12, 21:2). However, in order for the seeker to know God in the fullness of His revelation, then like the Magi of centuries long ago, they too must bow down and worship at the feet of Jesus (John 14:6; 2 Peter 2:4).

Jesus Christ is the "fullness of the Deity in bodily form" (Colossians 2:9) and is the "exact representation of God's being" (Hebrews 1:3a). The complete and final revelation of God is "His Word become flesh" (John 1:14) that can only be discovered through the *specific sacred texts* of the Judeo-Christian faith contained in the 66 canonical books of the Bible. In this sense, it is Israel and God's chosen people who announce the coming of Christ and gather together all the spiritual seekers of the human race.

Therefore, the sacred texts of the world religions may indeed contain great wisdom and inspire the "loving, joyful abandon to God" so common within Hindu devotion.[332] This position and view also gives credence to the rich heritage of Indian spirituality and potentially creates greater opportunity for meaningful dialogue across cultural boundaries. However, all the spiritual seeking outside of the Bible will remain largely incomplete unless it draws the archetypal Magi to the God of Israel revealed in the person of Jesus Christ.

ALTERNATIVE POSITIONS AND A UNIFIED SOURCE OF WISDOM

ONE OBJECTION TO OUR PROPOSED position contends that because of the similarity of the teachings of Jesus, the Buddha, and Lau Tzu, the source of their collective wisdom must be from the same God. Therefore, independent of whom the spiritual seeker is choosing to follow or study, the locality of the revelation will ultimately be the same. This position calls into question how two different teachers (in this particular case, Jesus and the Buddha) who lived during different eras, in countries widely separated, and whose religions were quite different, make almost identical statements about spirituality and the meaning of life.[333]

This position looks to the specific words of the great religions and seeks to reduce meaning to statements of universal truth. Because of the unlikelihood these spiritual teachers were influenced by each other, a conclusion is reached that the source of their wisdom was beyond human intellect or understanding. The authors were in touch with the Divine source of all wisdom, and their

---

332   Tennent, p. 54.
333   Hooper, p. 11.

subsequent recording of these great spiritual insights serve as a means of revelation to humanity.

The problem with this position is the authors do not take into consideration that the God of the Bible is more than a mere source of wisdom. In other words, there is no acknowledgement of the degree of revelation that has taken place. For this reason, I contend that although revelation may in fact be present in the sacred texts of other world religions, it is only a *glimmer of light*. The God of the Bible is supremely revealed as relational within Himself, and in His capacity and desire to be a loving Father to His creation (Matthew 6:9-13). The God of the Bible is much more than a mere source of wisdom: He is a personal, individual being, capable of feeling, choosing, and having a reciprocal relationship with other personal and social beings.[334] The spiritual seeker's view of God reduces Him to something to be used to solve problems or meet personal needs. However, the biblical view of God reveals that He is first and foremost relational, and that the only means of establishing relationship between God and mankind is through Jesus Christ himself (1 Timothy 2:5-6).

Another interesting objection to our view asserts the lack of revelation in the sacred texts of other world religions is their inability to prepare the reader to meet the Triune God of the Bible. The Islamic monotheistic view of God leaves no room for biblical themes such as the Trinity, the incarnation of God in Jesus Christ, and the suffering and death of Jesus as an atoning sacrifice for the sins of the world.[335] In the context of the Hindu religion, although particular gods such as Visnu or Shiva may be known for certain deeds or attributes, many scholars believe all the gods may simply be different names for the One Divine Reality.[336] In this sense, the wide arrangement of Hindu gods could potentially still be reduced to One Being, thus posing a complicated monotheistic paradigm quite apart from the Judeo-Christian faith. This would seem to be a hindrance to sharing the Christian faith and evidence of the lack of revelation within the eastern spiritual texts.

However, the Vedic understanding of consciousness and self-realization may in fact provide an evangelistic context for sharing the doctrine of the Trinity. In yogic philosophy, one particular position holds that when the Supreme Being was made aware of himself, it was akin to the *beholder* becoming aware

---

334   Erickson, p. 240.
335   Tennent, p. 37.
336   Ibid., p. 25.

of the *beheld*. This view further holds that the flow of *awareness* between the *beholder* and the *beheld* is fundamental to understanding the essence of the threefold nature of the Supreme Being. In this sense, a bridge is formed between two vastly different worlds of religious thought, and a foundation is established for sharing the full biblical revelation of the Trinity established in the relationship between the Father, His begotten Son, and the Holy Spirit.[337]

TAKING IT TO THE STREET

THE IMPLICATIONS FOR ACKNOWLEDGING a *glimmer of light* within the sacred texts of other world religions is immense and of particular importance for evangelistic purposes. Similar to the approach that the apostle Paul took when he acknowledged that the people of Athens were deeply religious (Acts 17:22), we should make every effort to recognize the rich spiritual heritage of ancient world religions and their respective sacred texts. However, like Paul so wonderfully exemplified, we must then capitalize on every opportunity to share the God they do not yet know (Acts 17:23).

If the "queer stories scattered all through the heathen religions about a god who dies and comes to life again"[338] are the narrative of God's fingerprint within human consciousness (Psalm 8:3), then the advanced element in clandestine preparation for the fullness of God's revelation has long been underway. We must remember that Jesus is not restricted or locked into the tightly bound covers of a book; Jesus Christ is the "true light that gives light to every man" (John 1:9).[339] Evangelists should be sensitive to the possibility that the dim flicker of light within the sacred texts of other world religions is there in anticipation of being completely embraced and brought into the fullness of revelation in the brilliant True Light of Jesus Christ.

Students of theology and missionaries whose hearts are set on sharing the gospel must strive to understand that Jesus Christ does not arrive as a stranger in any culture.[340] However shrouded in darkness a particular sacred text of

---

337   This insight into Vedic philosophy was brought to my attention in an interview with Raja John Bright on November 23, 2019 in Santa Cruz, CA. Bright is a Vedic subject matter expert, teacher of The Bhagavad Gita, and former personal student of the renowned Eastern spiritual teacher Maharishi Mahesh Yogi.
338   Lewis, p. 39.
339   Tennant, p. 69.
340   Ibid.

a world religion might be, there could still remain a small window of God's grace to prepare them for the day they will receive the "radiance of God's glory in the person of Jesus Christ" (Hebrews 1:3a). Much akin to the spiritual seekers described in the gospel of Matthew, the rising star of God's True Light (John 1:9) has come into the world and is drawing all the nations towards Him.

CHAPTER
TWENTY TWO

A THEOLOGY OF HUMANITY

"LET US MAKE MANKIND IN OUR IMAGE, IN OUR LIKENESS" (Gen. 1:26a). With these words, the Bible history of mankind begins. The Word of God reveals both the origin of the human race ("Let us make man") in addition to the eternal purpose to which our race is destined ("In our image, in our likeness"). In the beginning of time, God proposed to make a godlike being, an image bearer that would reflect His image and likeness, and would become a *visible manifestation* of the *invisible One* who brought him to life.[341]

In order for humanity to truly know and image our *essential nature,* we must look to Jesus Christ—Himself the *essential example* of both deity and humanity (Mt. 5:48; Heb. 1:1-3, 4:15).[342] Only from this vantage point can we ever hope to *become like Him* (1Jn. 3:2; 2 Co. 3:18). Because Jesus is the "image of the invisible God" (Col. 1:15) and the "exact representation of God's nature" (Heb 1:3), mankind must arrive at the realization that the image of God *(Imago Dei)* is best exemplified in Jesus' life and teaching.[343] However, far more is needed to image God than to remain satisfied with parroting the teachings of Jesus Christ or modeling his behavior or individualized actions. To actualize the essence of God's image within mankind an entirely new paradigm must be created—the *old man* must pass away in order for the new man to come to life (Ro. 6:6; Eph. 4:22-24).

The disciples were the first to discover that mankind must learn to define humanity by examining the human nature of Jesus, for Jesus alone most fully embodies what humanity was meant to be (Heb. 5:8-9).[344] Yet the disciples and great biblical saints who worshiped Jesus as Lord and God did far more than just contemplate His human nature. Rather, the disciples *rubbed Jesus into their eyes* (Jn. 9:6), they *plugged Him into their ears* (Mk. 7:33), they *submerged themselves in Him* (Jn. 9:7), they *attached themselves to Him* (Jn. 15:1-5), and they *ate His flesh and drank His blood* (Jn. 6:56). In other words,

---

341   The concept of mankind being an *image bearer of God* and a *visible manifestation of the invisible One* was brought to my attention by Michael Heiser in his masterful book, *The Unseen Realm* (Bellingham, WA: Lexham Press, 2015), p. 59, and the chapter *Preaching Christ our Example* in Andrew Murray's book *The Essential Works of Andrew Murray.*

342   Murray, Andrew. *The Essential Works of Andrew Murray* (Uhrichsville, OH: Barbour, 1962), p. 1380.

343   Marc Cortez makes the outstanding argument in his book, *Resourcing Theological Anthropology,* that "the *Imago Dei* has been constricted to such an extent that only one person actually qualifies (Jesus Christ). Cortez, Mark. *Resourcing Theological Anthropology.* (Grand Rapids, MI: Zondervan, 2017), p. 114.

344   Alexander, T. Desmond. *The New Dictionary of Biblical Theology* (Downers Grove, IL: InterVarsity, 2000), p. 566.

the believer's *submersion into God* and *consumption of God* meant that God Himself would take up residence within the psychosomatic unity of their being. The change of manhood would be so drastic that friends and family would beg the question: "Is this the same man?" (Jn. 9:8-9).

A STARTLING PROPOSITION

WE THUS ARRIVE AT THE CORNERSTONE of a complex theological position—much akin to a battle line drawn in the sand—that Jesus Christ is mankind's essential source for knowledge about God (Jn. 1:18) and knowledge about ourselves (1 Jn. 4:2).[345] This means that the only way for mankind to fulfill our creation mandate of imaging God will be through the supernatural experience of God Himself taking up residence within us. Until Jesus transforms us from the "inside out," humanity will remain weak, broken, and sinful—a mere skeleton of the image we were meant to be.[346] In this sense, God became man for the purpose of turning mankind into a new type of humanity—a change so drastic we transform from being a creature of God into being children of God.[347] When Jesus breathes into humanity *His breath of life* (Gn. 2:7; Jn. 20:22; cf. Acts 1:8), we awaken in spiritual brotherhood to the man who cries out, "I once was blind, but now I see" (Jn. 9:25).

SUPPORTING THE POSITION

THE WORLD'S GREATEST CHRISTIAN MINDS have long wrestled with the meaning of mankind's ability to image God (Ge. 1:26). Traditionally there have been three ways of conceptualizing and describing what the image of God *(Imago Dei)* would entail for humanity. These views are referred to as *substantive, relational,* and *functional.* We will briefly examine each of these more commonly held ways of understanding the image of God before

---

345   The great theologian Andrew Murray wrote: "Jesus came to show to us at once the image of God and our own image." *The Essential Works of Andrew Murray* (Uhrichsville, OH: Barbour, 1962), p. 1380.

346   C. S. Lewis wrote that "God became man to turn creatures into sons: not simply to produce better men of the old kind but to produce a new kind of man." *Mere Christianity*, p. 167.

347   Lewis, p. 175.

proceeding into a somewhat more challenging theological position.

The *substantive view* holds that human beings have a unique and definite characteristic or quality within their makeup, and this same characteristic represents the *Imago Dei*. At one end of the spectrum this would suggest that the image of God is an aspect of humanity's physicality or bodily makeup, while at the other end of the spectrum the image would be more related to a spiritual quality in human nature, mainly reason.[348] Many theologians argued that after the fall in Genesis 9:6, only a relic of the image of God remained in humanity. Furthermore, the locus of the image (although broken) remained as a resident quality within all humans whether or not they choose to recognize God's existence.[349]

The second view is *relational* and focuses more on a quality of mankind that is within our human nature. In this sense, the focus shifts from something substantial about imaging God and turns the attention to the manner in which humanity is intended to experience God within the context of a relationship.[350] Only by studying the Word of God can we realize what humanity was originally created and intended to be—and God Himself in the person of Jesus Christ is the most perfect expression of that revelation (Col. 1:15). The relational view means that rather than imaging God in a structural manner, the *Imago Dei* is more a matter of one's relationship to God as made possible through faith in Christ (Jn. 14:6).

The final view treats the *Imago Dei* as something *functional* and holds that the image consists in something that humanity measurably, tangibly, and constructively does. In this sense, humans image God in an objective way. The biblical support is taken from an association between mankind being made in the image of God (Gen. 1:26a) and the subsequent functional command to "rule over the fish of the sea …." (Gen. 1:26b). The implication of Genesis 1:26 is that mankind's ability to participate in rule and dominion is itself the image of God.[351]

We now turn our attention to a somewhat more challenging treatment of conceptualizing the *Imago Dei*. This view is referred to as *divine presence* and suggests that the *Imago Dei* is a *status* conferred by God onto all humans. In other words, God created human persons to be the physical means by which

---

348   Erickson, p. 460.
349   Erickson, p. 463.
350   Ibid., p. 464.
351   Ibid., p. 466. f

He would display and manifest His divine presence in the world, but God is not necessarily restricted to making His presence known only through humans.[352] This unique and privileged status includes the responsibility of representing (or being an image bearer of) God. The attributes that God gives humanity are the *means to imaging*, but not the image status itself. In this sense, God's original intent was to equip His imagers with both the will (relational) and ability (functional) to carry out His decrees and to "extend Eden over all the earth."[353] Thus, there is indeed an innate quality *within the substantive makeup* of human beings that enables us to image God. In addition, because humans are the primary means by which God manifests His presence on Earth, the *Imago Dei* is intimately linked to the indwelling presence of the Holy Spirit.[354]

JESUS CHRIST – THE TRUE IMAGE OF GOD

AS IMAGE BEARERS OF GOD, the human race is uniquely situated to learn something about God as we simultaneously learn something about ourselves. However, history has demonstrated that along the path of humanity's quest for greater understanding of our inherent nature, we routinely set off in the wrong direction and with a broken compass—we are comparable to a flock of hopelessly lost sheep (Lk. 15:3-7, 19:10). The reason for mankind's perpetual wandering is due to our focus on the *existential* and traditionally held empirical conceptions of *who we think we are* rather than the *essential nature* of humanity as perfectly revealed in the person of Jesus Christ.[355] Apart from divine revelation, the journey of self-discovery will succumb to seeking answers through the severely limited inductive investigation of ourselves and other human beings (Ro. 1:22).[356]

Humanity has long suffered from the ill-fated consequences of imposing upon ourselves *who we think we are* rather than *who we were made to be*.[357]

---

352   Cortez, Marc. *Resourcing Theological Anthropology* (Grand Rapids, MI: Zondervan, 2017), p. 109.
353   Heiser, Michael. *The Unseen Realm* (Bellingham, WA: Lexham Press, 2015), p. 59.
354   Cortez, p. 112.
355   Similar to Millard Erickson, I use the terms *essential* and *existential* humanity to differentiate between humanity from the perspective of God's original and intended creation (essential) and humanity's attempt to study and understand itself apart from God (existential).
356   Erickson, Millard. *Christian Theology* (Grand Rapids, MI: Baker Academic, 2013), p. 671.
357   This observation seems to be consistent with all the major world religions. The Indian sage Ramana Maharshi

The theological implications of this position are staggering, for none of us is humanity as God intended it to be, or as it first came from His hand (Ro. 3:23).[358] By way of illustration, inductive reasoning is akin to a *painting* telling the *painter* the vision for his picture, or a *machine* attempting to explain its inherent functioning mechanism to the *inventor of the machine itself*.[359] In a word, this means that eternity may very well lie in the heart of mankind (Ec. 3:11), yet apart from divine revelation we will remain woefully unable to realize it.

The Bible is full of rich examples of the consequences of inductive reasoning into the limited view of humanity, the skewed sense of our essential nature and the negligent conception of our divinely created image. As a case study, when the disciples took Jesus into their boat *just as he was* (Mk. 4:36), they imposed upon Jesus the restricted framework of their individual and collectively held ideas about *who they thought Jesus was* (Mk. 4:35-41).[360] However, when Jesus calmed the storm and saved their lives (Mk. 4:37-38), the disciples begin to sense there remained a great deal still to learn about *who Jesus actually was* (Mk. 4:41). The tension in this particular biblical account is that the person the disciples *thought Jesus was*, and the Person whom they would *discover Jesus to be*, were altogether different.[361] In other words, the disciples' preconceived and limited understanding of humanity was extended onto the very person who had come to model for them what humanity was intended to be (1Co. 1:11).[362]

The marvelous account of Jesus calming the storm also demonstrates that even one critical moment of Holy Spirit illumination can reveal what we could never discover through the tools of individualistic learning or inductive reasoning (1Co. 2:16). While in the boat, asleep with his disciples, Christ suggests that place in mankind where to varying degrees we remain unknowingly rooted in the goodness of the divine image in which we were

---

explained human suffering in the context of "forgetting who we are," and the Bible likewise contains accounts of people not realizing (or forgetting) who they were destined to become (Es. 4:1-17).

358   Erickson, p. 671.

359   The great Christian mystic and theologian C. S. Lewis used a similar illustration when describing *the cost of discipleship* in his book, *Mere Christianity*.

360   I argue here that the disciples use of the word "teacher" in addressing Jesus, and further the inquiry amongst themselves, "Who is this?" is evidence they had not yet arrived at the realization that Jesus was the "fullness of deity in bodily form" (Col. 2:19).

361   The words of the great Christian mystic A. W. Tozer are most fitting to mention here: "The thoughts that come into your mind when you think about God are the most important thoughts about you." Tozer, A. W. *The Knowledge of the Holy*. (New York: Harper One, 1961), p. 1.

362   Rakestraw, Robert. *Becoming like God: An Evangelical Doctrine of Theosis*. Journal of the Evangelical Theological Society 40.2 (1997).

first created (Gen. 1:31).[363] However, once awakened, the sleeping Christ rebukes the winds and calms the waves (Mk. 4:39), thus supremely revealing that humanity's greatest source of identity and strength will only be found within Him. Finally, the story teaches that although mankind cries out for understanding, there can be no understanding apart from divine revelation, and divine revelation will never be possible apart from accepting Jesus Christ as the God-Man that He said He was.[364]

Finally, the account of Jesus calming the storm is just one of several instances of New Testament authors emphatically teaching that the true *Imago Dei* is constricted to one person—Jesus Christ.[365] The Apostle Paul and the author of Hebrews make the case that *Jesus alone* is the "exact representation of God" (Heb. 1:3) and the only "image of the invisible God" (Col. 1:15). However, although Jesus is indeed the one true *Imago Dei*, these same authors proclaim the good news that mankind can be "transformed into his image" (2Co. 3:18) through the process of "putting on the new self" (Col. 3:10) so that our lives "gradually become brighter and more beautiful as God enters our lives and we become like Him" (2Co. 3:18 MSG). This means that although Jesus Christ is history's only example of the *Imago Dei* present in all its fullness (Col. 2:9), through union with Christ, humanity can participate in the *Imago Dei* and experience the *fullness of what we were meant to be* (2Co. 3:18; Ro. 8:29).[366]

The great theologian C.S. Lewis wrote, "The Son of God became a man to enable men to become sons of God."[367] This means that until the study of mankind uniquely and supremely points to the perfect example set by Jesus Christ (Heb. 2:14-17), we will fail to actualize the awesome image that God intended humanity to be (Ps. 8:4-6). Because God directly created the human race according to His image and likeness (Gen. 1:26-27; 2:7; 1 Cor. 11:7; Jas. 3:9), only God is able to reveal to mankind the image that He wants us to emulate. In other words, God is the Creator and we are His *creation*. The incredible privilege of imaging and representing God is a status conferred upon

---

363   *By varying degrees and unknowingly rooted*, I suggest that although the invisible qualities of God have been plainly visible within creation since the beginning of time (Ro. 1:20), woefully large populations of mankind remain ignorant of His glory. At the other end of the spectrum, even many Christians alive today may not fully realize the extent to which we are called to conform ourselves to the image of Jesus Christ (Ro. 8:29).

364   The distinction of "taking Jesus as who He says He is" is of crucial significance. As I will argue throughout the *support section*, absent knowing Jesus as Lord and Savior in both the fullness of his deity and humanity, mankind will never be able to fully experience the *Imago Dei*.

365   Cortez, p. 114.

366   Cortez makes a similar argument in his chapter on *Divine Presence*. Cortez, pp. 114–115.

367   Lewis, C. S. *Mere Christianity* (New York, NY: Collier Books, 1952), p. 139.

mankind by God. By obvious implication of this realization, every human life is precious and sacred because we are the creatures that God put on Earth to represent Him.[368] Much like a soldier who wants to become like his commanding officer (2Tm. 2:4), mankind must ultimately conform to our Creator in order to become fully alive in the image we were created to be (1Co. 1:11).

WHO AM I?

WHEN MOSES WAS FACED WITH THE seemingly impossible task of leading his people out of bondage and slavery, he asked God a question that so often reflects humanity's inquiries into our nature: "Who am I?" (Ex. 3:11). However, rather than answering the question, God directed Moses to a completely different and far more significant matter. The important question at hand was not *who Moses was* but rather *who God is* (Ex. 3:12-15). In this sense, Moses represents mankind's misdirected quest for meaning and identity. We cry out in vain, "Who am I?" rather than asking God, "Who are you?" Moses speaks for the entire human race in his impaired and broken vestige of what essential humanity was meant to be.

In addition, Moses reflects the futility and impossibility of imaging God apart from God Himself modeling for us *what the image should be like*. In other words, biblical history revealed and demonstrated that God would need to show His creation what the image was meant to be. This means that Jesus' humanity was something quite different than the humanity of sinful human beings. As the supreme and perfect image bearer of God, "Jesus was not merely as human as we are; he was in fact *more human than we are*."[369]

In the context of human development, the implications of Jesus' divinity and humanity result in two staggering conclusions. First is the discovery that although the human race was made in the image of God (Gen. 1:26), apart from Jesus, our ability to know God and fully image our Creator will remain altogether impossible (Jn. 14:6). Second is the promising realization that in Christ, mankind is ultimately transformed into *the likeness of Christ Himself*—the only perfect imager of God the world has ever known (Ro. 8:29; 1Jn. 3:2).

---

368   Heiser, Michael. *The Unseen Realm* (Bellingham, WA: Lexham Press, 2015), p. 59.
369   Erickson, p. 671. My use of italics.

OBJECTIONS AND OPPOSING IDEAS

IN MANY RESPECTS THIS THEOLOGICAL POSITION has brought us into very deep and challenging waters. Without too far a stretch of one's imagination it becomes quite easy to foresee the stark opposition to such claims that apart from Jesus, "Humanity is not human." This notion would suggest that although there remains one human race, there are varying degrees of ideal humanness, and that until one is able to truly image God through the indwelling presence of Christ, that same individual remains less than human.[370] We must therefore treat these difficulties by examining other historical world religions and modern approaches to the *Imago Dei*, in addition to carefully investigating the specific manner in which the human development movement outside the Christian faith bears witness to Jesus Christ.[371]

The modern self-help and human development movement teaches that throughout the course of history there have been certain individuals who have been channels of great power—the spiritual principles they taught during their relatively brief existence within human history managed to influence the lives of millions of people over long periods of time.[372] These figures often loom larger than life and include such household names as the Buddha, Lord Krishna, Mahatma Gandhi, Mother Theresa, and Jesus Christ.[373]

Yet even the enormous power that was realized through the life of Bill W., the co-founder of Alcoholic Anonymous, could arguably be included in the list of great spiritual accomplishments. Bill. W.'s work and dedication to treating alcoholics has positively touched the lives of countless people, and *Life Magazine* lists him as one of the 100 greatest Americans who have ever lived. Bill W. has even been credited with being the originator of the entire self-help,

---

370   I am not specifically treating the status of infants or those without the mental capacity to make the conscious decision to receive Jesus Christ as their Lord and Savior. In summary, I take the position of Erickson in reflecting upon the fact our Lord did not regard children as under condemnation. Given that the mental acuity of adults with severe mental disorder is akin to a child, I extend the same grace to them, with hopeful expectation they will inherit the Kingdom of God (Mt. 18:3, 19:14). Erickson, p. 581.

371   I focus my world religion investigation on primarily the Hindu and Yogic traditions of ancient India in addition to the modern crosspollination of Yogic texts commonly studied in a traditional Western Yoga school. The Self-help and Human Development movement subject matter experts I refer to include the prominent scholars Dr. Wayne Dyer, Dr. Deepak Chopra, and Dr. Michael Hawkins. Collectively, these scholars acknowledge the humanness of Jesus but not the fullness of his deity as proclaimed by the Christian faith (Heb. 1:1-3; Col. 2:9).

372   Hawkins, David R. *Power vs. Force* (New York, NY: Hay House, 2002), p. 180.

373   The significant point here is that rather than being *elevated in his deity* Jesus is seen only in the realm of his humanity. Although Jesus "spoke on his own authority" (Mt. 7:29) he is relegated into the company of those who speak on the authority of others.

self-mastery, and self-improvement movement.[374] From this perspective, many modern spiritual teachers and human development experts make the argument that although Jesus Christ is a great human to emulate (or image), and a man that possessed an extraordinarily high level of spiritual awareness (he was enlightened), he would nevertheless be included alongside other ancient and modern masters of metaphysics and Universal Truth teaching (he was a Guru).[375]

A THIRD JESUS

ANOTHER OBJECTION TO THE CHRISTIAN CONCEPT of the *Imago Dei* is what modern spiritual guru Deepak Chopra has labeled the *Third Jesus Movement*. Rather than addressing the humanity or deity of Jesus, a third model of his life and teaching is presented. The essence of the position is that if you were to meet Jesus in the world today as he was in "real life," there would be a gap between your level of consciousness and his. Closing the gap in consciousness is not a matter of performing more *outward acts of spiritual or religious devotion*. To emulate Jesus and achieve his level of God-consciousness, a disciple must turn their attention inward through the practice of expanding one's awareness through meditation. In this sense, whereas traditional Christianity sees Jesus Christ as the only means to reach the Father (Jn. 14:6), the *Third Jesus Movement* reduces the path of God-consciousness to a matter of increasingly expanding one's level of meditative awareness.[376] Rather than knowing God *through Jesus*, one could foreseeable come to know God by *acting like Jesus*.

Deepak Chopra is the modern mouthpiece of India's great lineage of spiritual teachers who taught that God-consciousness was possible through meditative practices designed to "saturate the brain with a divine presence."[377] An illustration common in traditional Yogic philosophy is that of a diamond

---

374 Hawkins, p. 186.

375 Hawkins argues in *Power vs. Force* that the *teachings* of Jesus Christ, despite his short three-year period of ministry, managed to transform much of Western society, and that man's encounters with these *teachings* have remained at the center of Western history for the last 2,000 years. Yet Hawkins makes this observation independent of the biblical revelation of Jesus Christ, and thus sidesteps the implications of *who Jesus Christ is*. As a case in point, Hawkins lists the spiritual accomplishments of Bill W., the co-founder of AA, alongside the spiritual accomplishments of God Himself in the person of Jesus Christ.

376 Chopra, Deepak. *The Third Jesus* (New York, NY: Three Rivers Press, 2008), p. 44–45.

377 Iyengar, B. K. S. *Light on Life* (New York, NY: Rodale Press, 2005), p. 79.

and a lump of coal. Although God's light shines equally on all His children, due to delusive ignorance and a false belief in separateness, not all of God's children receive and reflect His light alike. The association then becomes clear: Sunlight falls on both a lump of coal and a diamond, but only the diamond is able to absorb and reflect the light in brilliant beauty. Although the carbon in the coal has within it the ability to become a diamond, its sense of isolation from the light prevents the necessary transformation. The spiritual principle involved is that in order to receive and reflect God's light, you must come to realize that God is already at work within you, and this is achieved though the practice of meditation.[378] Enlightenment and God-consciousness is thus a matter of experiencing "that which we heal in ourselves we heal in the world, and that which we heal in the world, we heal in ourselves."[379]

The final objection resides within the historical realm of emerging Christian theology and serves the purpose of consolidating much of society's misperceptions of mankind's ability to image God apart from Jesus Christ. The traditionally held construct of *kenoticism* taught that Jesus Christ—the Second Person of the Trinity—laid aside His divine qualities for human qualities instead. In other words, the incarnation itself consisted of an exchange of his distinctly divine nature for human characteristics.[380] This view of an exchange of divine for human attributes runs parallel to much of historical Yogic philosophy in addition to more modern *Third Jesus Movements*. In this sense, the idea of a successive yet reductionist appeal to God becoming man, then man being "absorbed back into God," is akin to the modern Yogic notion that humans are similar to "drops of water," and that through meditation a spiritual devotee can be absorbed back into the "Ocean of God."[381]

---

378   Gates, Rolf. 200-hour Yoga Teacher Training Course, Santa Cruz, CA, student guide to Yogic philosophy and Asana.

379   Gates.

380   Erickson, p. 668.

381   Erickson succinctly describes *kenoticism* as the idea that "with respect to certain attributes Jesus is God, then he is a human, then God again" (Erickson, p. 668). This description influenced my use of the *successive yet reductionist* illustration of God becoming man (successive) then returning to His divine nature (reductionist – i.e., returning to God). The Yogic concept of "drops of water absorbed into the ocean" was a predominant illustration taught by B. K. S. Iyengar.

REBUTTAL TO OBJECTIONS

THESE OBJECTIONS COLLECTIVELY RESULT IN a pileup of misinformation and minimization of the world's independent, supreme authority on both God and mankind. For it is exactly Jesus Christ's *deity* that allows Him to perfectly represent *essential humanity*. In other words, it takes the Creator to explain the nature of that which is created. There was a two-fold work that Jesus accomplished in His lifetime. On one hand, Jesus had to reveal in His life the likeness and image of God, so that mankind might finally understand what a life in that likeness and image was.[382] Yet Jesus did more than provide humanity with the exact representation of God—Jesus also provided humanity with an image of the ideal human being (Heb. 1:1-3, 5:8-9; 1Co. 11:1).

And herein we crash into our society's predominant roadblock to understanding *who Jesus Christ is* and *what He came to do*. For if Jesus Christ is lumped into the long lineage of other spiritual masters, gurus, and self-help experts, then the point will have been entirely (and perhaps conveniently) missed. In this sense, the danger is not so much in *denying or rejecting* Jesus. Rather, it is accepting Jesus on terms that are in contradiction to those that He established during His ministry on Earth. Thus, the Christian evangelist today must realize that the great majority of objections to the idea that Jesus is mankind's best source for knowledge about God (Jn. 1:18) and mankind (1 Jn. 4:2) is not in direct opposition to the biblical claim itself. Rather, it is sidestepping the issue altogether by assembling a hodgepodge of spiritual teachers—a little of this and a bit of that—and creating onto oneself a false image of a godlike teacher. In other words, the danger is in accepting the *teaching of Jesus* absent the *teacher Himself*. This is all to say that the question of our Lord—"Who do you say I am?"—continues to reverberate through the ages in a rhetorical and haunting tone (Mt. 16:13-15).

---

382   Murray, p. 1380.

TAKING IT TO THE STREET

DR. DAVID HAWKINS' WORK IN THE FIELD of applied kinesiology now serves the purpose of providing modern scientific context for our transition of *Imago Dei* from theory to application. Kinesiological experiments have convincingly proven that there is a significant and decidedly different bodily response to all manner of *original* and *forged creation*.[383] In one particular experiment, subjects tested strong when looking at an original painting and weak when looking at a mechanical (forged) reproduction. Even the most precisely computer-generated reproduction of an original piece of art resulted in the test subject immediately going weak. Perhaps even more intriguing was that this testing outcome was consistent regardless of pictorial content—an original painting of a disturbing object would make the test subject go stronger than a forged copy of a pleasant one.[384]

By way of juxtaposing modern scientific knowledge across the revelation of biblical history, let us consider the implications of Hawkins' remarkable discovery in the context of David and Goliath. When David requested permission from King Saul to fight against Goliath, it was granted on the condition that David "dresses up" in Saul's armor (1Sa. 17:38). David momentarily consented, donning the armor, but then exclaimed, "I cannot go in these.... I am not used to them" (1Sa. 17:39). Reverse engineering this moment in time through the lens of modern kinesiology leads us to a most startling realization. The donning of the armor was akin to forgery—the attempt to alter human identity by making a change from the "outside in" rather than the "inside out."[385] With the armor in place, David went weak. When the armor was removed, David became strong. Although seemingly counterintuitive to the precepts of modern warfare, a hidden spiritual key is discovered. Any meaningful change in a human being's essential nature will only result from a fundamental reconstruction within their *inner man*.[386]

---

383   Hawkins, p. 190. The testing procedure includes a test subject and tester. The tester will press down on the test subject's outstretched arm to determine strength or weakness. Positive stimuli result in the arm going "strong" while negative stimuli result in the arm going "weak." A "strong arm" is firm against resistance while a "weak arm" will immediately fall even with the slightest amount of applied pressure.

384   Hawkins, p. 190.

385   Incidentally, this breakthrough in kinesiology also gives incredible credence to the Lord telling Samuel, "Although people look at the outward appearance, the LORD looks at the heart" (1Sa. 16:7).

386   Needless to say, the implications of modern kinesiology for the Apostle Paul's claim that "we are God's handiwork" is astounding (Eph. 2:10). When mankind looks at the true image of who we are in Jesus Christ, we become strong. When mankind distorts the image we "forge our attempt" and become weak.

And herein we discover the hinge-point to the profoundness of understanding *Imago Dei* in the context of human development. No amount of "armor" will result in a change in the nature and constitution of mankind grand enough to substantiate the true image or likeness of God. In this sense—and indeed this contention may navigate us into uncharted waters—even the isolated adoption of Christ's teachings *absent Christ Himself* would not be sufficient to image God (Jn. 2:23-25; Mt. 12:34).

The Bible teaches that steadfast adherence to religious customs and traditions were not what our Lord required of his followers (Jn. 3:1-7). Rather, Jesus was much like a force field in which his disciples would be drawn into—a Body in which their very cells and molecules would reside within. Jesus knew that the change in mankind required to conform to the true *Imago Dei* was so great that Jesus Himself would need to take up residence within the believer (Lk. 19:5). Whitewashed tombs were not what God was desirous of; a complete death of the *old man* (Ro. 1:18-3:20) and resurrection of the *new man* would be needed (Ro. 3:21-26).

From this perspective a most starling conclusion is reached. In anticipation of our Lord's arrival, mankind remains blind from birth (Jn. 9:1). In this sense, how can a blinded humanity hope to image God apart from the indwelling presence of God Himself? Lest we fool ourselves, blindness only begins to portray the fallen state of mankind; not only are we blind, but neither can we hear or speak (Mk. 7:31-37). The independent hope and exclusive only way for such a depraved being to image a perfect God is for the divine presence of God Himself to live within us.[387]

Although a seemingly radical proposition, the basic premise of this concept was at the heart of our Lord's teaching (Jn. 7:37; 15:1-8). Being the very embodiment of the power by which God makes and sustains the world, Jesus promised that when *grafted onto Him* a new life would begin (Jn. 15:5). Flipping the illustration upside down implies that apart from Jesus we have *no life*. On the positive application of the lesson, professing the Lordship of Jesus and receiving the Holy Spirit leads to *new life*. The Spirit of God within the believer is akin to sunlight that illuminates the air on a bright day. Take away the sun, and you take away the light. To press the metaphor even further—God within us is like the air we breathe. Take away the oxygen, and we are no longer alive.[388]

Lest we remain blind from birth, we now turn our attention to the manner in which Jesus healed those who called on His name in preparation of the miraculous

---

387   This idea was shaped in my mind through the work of Michael Heiser in his book *The Unseen Realm*, pp. 58–60.

388   The sermon Podcast by Bishop Robert Barron on June 4, 2017, helped me frame and conceptualize the ideas and illustrations in this paragraph.

new life that awaits His indwelling presence. Jesus healed the blind man with a combination of *spittle* and *mud*. The spittle represents the divinity of Jesus— the mud His humanity. The merging of the two, when *rubbed into the blind man's eyes,* became the first step in the awesome transformation from blindness to sight. The final step, however, is even richer in spiritual significance. Jesus required that the man go and "wash in the Pool of Siloam" (Jn. 9:7). The word "Siloam" means "sent" and provides immediate correlation to the very purpose of Jesus' life—the God-Man who was "sent" to save mankind (Jn. 3:16). With our Lord's humanity and divinity now assimilated into the blind man's eyes, the final moment of transition into a new life of *Imago Dei* took place when the man submerged himself into Jesus—the One sent from God to enable humanity to faithfully image God Himself.

CHAPTER
TWENTY THREE

A THEOLOGY OF THE HOLY SPIRIT

JESUS CHRIST'S LAST WORDS TO His disciples were, "But you will receive power when the Holy Spirit has come upon you, and you will be my witness in Jerusalem and in all Judea and Samaria, and to the ends of the earth" (Acts 1:8-9 — my emphasis). Although in this context our Lord was specifically addressing the apostles, the Bible teaches that the promise of the Holy Spirit is freely available for every believer in Jesus Christ (Acts 2:38-39). All believers in Jesus receive the gift of the Holy Spirit at the moment of their conversion (Acts 2:38; Romans 5:5; Galatians 3:2). This means that when a believer confesses their sin and asks for God's forgiveness, they become a new person—not by their own deeds, works, or merit, but by the gracious work of God's Holy Spirit (Ephesians 2:9).[389] To use the terminology of our Lord, the believer is "born again" (John 3:3-7).

The Apostle Paul further elaborated on the supernatural "born again" new life of the Christian: "If anyone is in Christ, he is a new creation. The old has passed away; behold, the new has come (2 Corinthians 5:17). The moment the believer looks to Christ as Lord and Savior, the Holy Spirit comes to indwell their body, making it a "temple of the Holy Spirit" (1 Corinthians 6:19-20; cf., 2 Corinthians 6:16). According to Jesus, this transformational experience results in a receipt of power that enables the believer to be a witness of the Gospel message to the ends of the earth. This all boils down to one amazing promise, one astonishing mission, and one breathtaking responsibility for the individual believer and collective Body of Christ.

---

389 Dr. Harold Sala. *Getting Acquainted with the Holy Spirit.* (Mandaluyong City, Manila. OMF Literature, INC., 2017), p. 58.

ARE OUR LORD'S
EXPECTATIONS BEING MET?

I FIND THAT I MUST DRAW on a theological query from the great mind of author and pastor Francis Chan. Based on the inerrant Word of God, we have confidence that the Spirit of God dwells within every believer, which effectually makes every Christian a living and breathing Temple of God's Holy Spirit (1 Corinthians 3:16, 6:19). This being the case, then shouldn't there be a measurable and observable difference between the regenerated person who has the very Spirit of God within them, and another person who does not? [390] Although by conversion Christians can declare that they are born again and dead to sin but alive in Christ (Romans 6:3-8), we must caution ourselves against the possibility that these words have become nothing more than the parroted teaching of biblical doctrine. In other words, if someone outside the Body of Christ began to notice that there was no fundamental change or difference in the life of a converted person, then are believers truly witnessing our faith as our Lord commanded?

The late author and minister Martyn Lloyd-Jones once pointed out that there is a vast difference between being a witness for Jesus and an advocate for Jesus.[391] Whereas a great many people today are quite content to be an advocate of the Christian faith, only a few actively witness their spiritual gifts for the purpose of edifying the Body of Christ. Furthermore, many churches seem to be more concerned with filling pews and developing new programs than in proclaiming the transformational power of a Spirit-filled life.[392] Reasoning from this fact, perhaps now is the time for renewed urgency in addressing the concern of A.W. Tozer: "The whole level of spirituality among us is low— the incentive to seek the higher plateaus in the things of the Spirit is all but gone."[393]

In his acclaimed book, The Forgotten God, Francis Chan argued that "there is a desperate need in the church for the Holy Spirit of God to be given room

---

390 This "theological question" was brought to my attention in Francis Chan's book *The Forgotten God – Reversing Our Tragic Neglect of the Holy Spirit*. (Colorado Springs, CO. David C. Cook. 2009), p. 32.
391 Sala, p. 34. The Blue Letter Bible defines *witness* in the context of Acts 1:8 in the ethical sense as, "Those who after his example have proved the strength and genuineness of their faith in Christ by undergoing a violent death."
392 Sala, p. 31.
393 A.W. Tozer. Quoted in Francis Chan's book, *The Forgotten God – Reversing Our Tragic Neglect of the Holy Spirit*. (Colorado Springs, CO. David C. Cook. 2009), p. 27.

to have His way." [394] Similar to the uneasiness felt by Tozer's observation of the generally low level of spirituality among Christians, Chan's sentiment that the Church is in desperate need of the Holy Spirit ought to compel the Body of Christ to question what's gone wrong. After all, according to the Apostle Paul, the Spirit of God dwells in believers (Romans 8:9), effectually making every individual follower of Christ a physical tabernacle of God's Spirit (1 Corinthians 3:16, 6:19-20). This means that the individual believer's body is the Spirit of God's temple—we are His dwelling place (John 14:23). Continuing this line of reasoning, Paul explained that "just as a body, though one, has many parts, but all its parts form one body, so it is with Christ" (1 Corinthians 12:12). In other words, if each individual believer is a temple, then the spiritual power of the collective Body of Christ should turn the world upside down. On the basis thereof, how are we to reconcile the declaration of the biblical testimony with the troubling observations of such influential ministers of God's Word as Chan and Tozar?

MAKING ROOM FOR THE SPIRIT

IN THE SPORT OF OLYMPIC WEIGHTLIFTING, few masters of the barbell have achieved the worldwide respect and admiration as that of Coach Mike Burgener.[395] In the CrossFit community, legend has it that when Coach Burgener walks into the gym, everyone in attendance on that particular day gain's five pounds on their former personal weightlifting records (a huge increase in strength considering that many weightlifting world records are set in increments of one-half pounds). Coach Burgener says nothing, offers no technical cues, nor demonstrates any particular hidden insights on the fundamental principles of the snatch or clean and jerk. How then do people account for the near instantaneous increase in strength?

Based on the testimony of hundreds of gym owners (each gym owner represents approximately 100 athletes), it can only be attributed to a combination of Mike's presence in the gym and his immediate proximity to each individual athlete.[396] Although seemingly impossible to quantify, ordinary

---

394 Chan, p. 27. Chan's book *Forgotten God* reached the *New York Times* bestseller list top 10 for 10 consecutive weeks.
395 Mike Burgener's oldest son Casey broke the national record for the snatch at the 2004 Olympic Trials and won gold in the 2008 Pan American Championships.
396 In addition to the sport of weightlifting, I have experienced similar testimonies from professional boxers

people and world-class weightlifters alike increase in strength simply because they spend time in the presence of Coach Burgener. In all humility, Coach Burgener explains the phenomenon by saying that "people increase in strength because they think then can." This account certainly begs the question—if people gain physical strength in the presence of a person who compels them to think they can, then how much more should believers manifest the miraculous gifts of the Spirit when God Himself dwells within them?

For our purposes of understanding the work of the Holy Spirit, this particular illustration has immense relevance. In fact, the spiritual principle involved is exactly what we read about in the book of Acts. In describing what happened when John and Peter went on trial before the Sanhedrin, Luke wrote, "When they saw the courage of Peter and John and realized that they were unschooled, ordinary men, they were astonished and they took note that these men had been with Jesus (Acts 4:13 — my emphasis). It was not about books, laws, regulations, or moral lessons (or in the weightlifting analogy, coaching cues, tips, or physical demonstrations). What set Peter and John apart was the fact that they had been with Jesus—and they had stayed with Him (John 1:37-39). And in the process, Jesus had completely transformed their lives.

In the Apostle John's beautiful account of our Lord's conversation with His first two disciples (John 1:35-42), we are witness to the Gospel-centered transformation that awaits those people who stay with Jesus. When our Lord asked the two men, "What do you want?" (John 1:38a), they immediately responded by asking a question of their own: "Rabbi, where are you staying?" (John 1:38b). How interesting to answer a question with a question—not to mention the seemingly mindless quality of the question. To ask where Jesus is staying? Couldn't these two former disciples of John the Baptist have come up with a more profound question? After all, here is the Lord of the universe asking, "What do you want? What are you looking for?" And they answer by asking, "Where are you staying?"

But I propose their instincts were in fact completely right. When Jesus was on the earth, His presence was limited to His physical and spatial locality. In this sense, in order for the first disciples to stay with Jesus, they needed to be physically in His presence. However, for the followers of Christ

---

who have trained under master-level trainers and coaches. Most recently, 6-time world champion Robert "The Ghost" Guerrero commented that his dad's presence ringside (his dad, Ruben Guerrero, is his longtime coach) has propelled him to victories that were otherwise seemingly impossible. My interviews with gym owners took place between the years of 2012 and 2014 during my worldwide travels teaching the CrossFit Goal Setting and Positive Self-talk course.

after His ascension to the Father, we now experience personal fellowship with Him through the Holy Spirit every moment of our life (Romans 8:9-11; Galatians 2:19-20; Titus 3:4-6). This means that Jesus Christ, as much as the Father, is the indwelling presence of God within every regenerated Christian believer—but only through the Spirit of God.[397] To this effect, Paul explained, "Anyone who does not have the Spirit of Christ, that person does not belong to him" (Romans 8:9) and believers are "dead to sin but alive to God" (Romans 6:11—MSG). Paul's logic would seem to suggest that when the Spirit of God dwells within the believer there should be a significant difference between that person and a non-Christian. But is this in fact the case in the life of the individual believer and the Body of Christ?

THE CENTER AND ITS CONTRAST[398]

THE BIBLE TEACHES THAT A life in the Spirit is what God desires for all Christians. At the moment of conversion, the Holy Spirit indwells believers, guiding them, sanctifying them, and empowering them for work in God's Kingdom (Romans 8:2-17). The notion that Christians are *in the Spirit*, and that the *Spirit dwells in them*, was such an important theological idea for the Apostle Paul that he reinforced it three times in his letter to the Romans (Romans 8:9-11), and succinctly culminated his argument with the resounding statement: "For those who are led by the Spirit of God are the children of God" (Romans 8:14).

The Apostle Paul's theology of the Holy Spirit has led Evangelical Christians around the world to share the doctrine that the Spirit is active in the lives of all believers.[399] A believer's first experience with the Spirit of God takes place within their heart the moment they put their faith in Christ. Emphasizing this very point, in his book, *The Small Catechism,* Martin Luther described the initial work of the Holy Spirit in his heart as essential to his conversion experience by saying, "I believe that I cannot by my own reason or strength believe in Jesus Christ, my Lord, or come to Him but the Holy Ghost

---

397 M. Turner in T. Desmond Alexander's *The New Dictionary of Biblical Theology – Holy Spirit.* (Downers Grove, IL. Inter-Varsity Press, 2000), p. 550.

398 The idea for this particular part of the study title and the accompanying organizational framework were brought to my attention in Gregory Boyd's book, *Across the Spectrum* (Grand Rapids, MI: Baker Academic, 2009).

399 Timothy Tennent. *Theology in the context of World Christianity.* (Grand Rapids, MI: Zondervan, 2007), p. 166.

has called me by the gospel."[400] Echoing Luther's sentiment on the Holy Spirit, the great theologian J.I. Packer wrote, "Without the Spirit there would not be a Christian in the world."[401]

The Apostle Paul masterfully treats the issue of the believer's first experience with the Holy Spirit in 1 Corinthians 12:13: "For we were all baptized by one Spirit so as to form one body—whether Jews or Gentiles, slave or free—and we were all given one Spirit to drink." In this theologically packed verse, Paul makes four remarkable points: First, the baptism applies to all believers; second, all believers are baptized by the same Spirit; third, believers are baptized into the Body of Christ; and fourth, the baptism and union with the Body of Christ take place *at the moment of conversion.* This means that when a new believer "confesses with their mouth that Jesus Christ is Lord, and believes in their heart that God raised Jesus from the dead" (Romans 10:9), they receive the indwelling power of the Holy Spirit (John 14:17), a new heart (Titus 3:5), and are incorporated into the Body of Christ (1 Corinthians 12:13).[402] Paul seems to suggest throughout his theological treatment on baptism that Christians become members of Christ's body by being baptized into it by the Spirit—and that this supernatural experience is either equivalent to conversion or simultaneous with it.[403]

This being the case, how do we account for cases in Acts where there was clearly a separation between conversion (or regeneration) and a subsequent baptism of the Spirit? The Pentecostals substantiate much of their doctrine based on the account in Acts 2, which records that on the day of Pentecost the Holy Spirit descended onto the Body of Christ in the form of "tongues of fire" and empowered those that received it for special service and bold witness (Acts 2:2-4). To account for what might otherwise be accepted as the norm, esteemed theologian Millard Erickson argues that Acts covers a transitional period in the life of the church.[404] Although he acknowledges that in certain cases there was indeed a lapse of time between regeneration and the receipt of the Holy Spirit, these instances involved the last of the Old Testament believers who were regenerate because of the revelation they received and their faith in God.[405]

---

400 Quoted in Mollie Ziegler Hemingway's piece "Faith Unbounded," *Christianity Today,* September 9, 2010, p. 74.
401 J.I. Packer, *Knowing God.* (London: Hodder & Stoughton, 1984), p. 79.
402 Dr. Gerry Breshears. Western Seminary TH503 outline on the Holy Spirit.
403 Millard Erickson, *Christian Theology* (Grand Rapids, MI: baker Academic, 2013) p. 801.
404 Erickson, p. 801.
405 Erickson, p. 801.

The issue of an immediate or post-conversion experience with the Spirit (in contrast with a more gradual *filling of the Spirit)* is significant and affects nearly every area of the Christian life. Accessing the biblical arguments on both sides of the equation leads us to a fundamental theological and doctrinal question: Should believers anticipate (and in this sense actively seek out and pray for) a subsequent filling of the Spirit beyond their initial conversion experience? Furthermore, to what degree would this unique and distinct second encounter with the Spirit be objectively recognizable in the manifestation of miraculous spiritual gifts? And perhaps most important, to what extent should speaking in tongues be associated with the first evidence of a Second Baptism?

UNDERSTANDING PENTECOSTALISM

IN THE PENTECOSTAL TRADITION, many hold that a postconversion (or postregeneration) experience, often referred to as, "the baptism in (or with) the Holy Spirit," will take place in the life of the believer.[406] Evidence of this unmistakable moment commonly manifests itself in the believer's life through a full range of gifts and miraculous manifestations of the Spirit that were evident during the era of the New Testament.[407] Pentecostal and Charismatic Christian theology teach that believers should look forward to an experience of the Holy Spirit—and unique sign-gifts of the Spirit—subsequent to their initial conversion.

The *Foundations of Pentecostal Theology* emphasizes, "The Baptism of the Holy Ghost is a definite experience, subsequent to salvation, whereby the Third Person of the Godhead comes upon the believer to anoint and energize him for special service."[408] This same body of doctrine holds that although "baptism with the Holy Ghost was given once and for all, as far as the Church in general is concerned" it does not necessarily mean that every believer is immediately *filled with the Spirit* upon conversion.[409] The Baptism in the Holy Spirit is meant to empower believers for greater acts of service within the Body of Christ. This being the case, the full range of Spirit-empowered gifts of healing, prophecy, tongues, and miraculous powers (1 Corinthians 12:7-

---

406 Tennent. p. 166.
407 Gregory Boyd. *Across the Spectrum.* (Grand Rapids, MI: Baker Publishing, 2009), p. 237.
408 Dr. Gerry Breshears. Western Seminary TH503 outline on the Holy Spirit.
409 Dr. Gerry Breshears. Western Seminary TH503 outline on the Holy Spirit.

11) are available for believers today and should be actively sought after (1 Corinthians 12:31a).

THE GIFTS SHALL CEASE

A MORE CONSERVATIVE BAPTIST THEOLOGY would point to the fact that very often proponents for a Second Baptism and "sign-gifts" tend to overly focus on 1 Corinthians 12:31a, which states, "Now eagerly desire the greater gifts" while completely dismissing the continuing thought of Paul to "seek the most excellent way" (1 Corinthians 12:31b). And what was Paul's "most excellent way?" It was love! Paul emphatically explained that no matter how great the apparent "sign-gift" was in the believer's life, it amounted to nothing if the believer did not have love (1 Corinthians 13:1-3). This means that the real evidence of the Spirit at work in the believer's life is the *fruit of the Spirit itself*—"faith, hope and love. But the greatest of these is love" (1 Corinthians 13:13). Baptists teach that every Christian receives the Spirit at conversion (1 Corinthians 12:13), and that speaking in tongues or any other objective "sign-gift evidence" are not intended to be the normal effectual work of the Spirit within the believer's life. Rather, Christ gives the Spirit the moment He welcomes individuals into God's family through faith and repentance (Acts 2:38).

In addition to addressing the possibility that Paul taught that the gifts would cease, many theologians make a similar argument based on Hebrews 2:3-4, namely that the purpose of the "signs, wonders and various miracles" (Hebrews 2:4a) of the Holy Spirit was to authenticate the revelation of Jesus Christ. Given that the final revelation is now freely available in the completed canon of Scripture, the gifts have ceased. This line of reasoning seems to be supported by the Apostle John who explained that the purpose of our Lord's "signs in the presence of his disciples" was so that Christians would "believe that Jesus is the Messiah" (John 20:30-31). In other words, Cessationist theology would contend that the purpose of the miraculous gifts was to testify to the life and divinity of Christ in addition to our Lord's first apostles (Acts 2:34). This unique and historic purpose having once been fulfilled, the miraculous gifts become unnecessary and subsequently faded out of the Church.[410]

---

410 Erickson, p. 800.

New Testament scholar William Barclay makes a compelling argument for Cessationist theology by suggesting that the miracles of the early church were needed as a guarantee of the truth and power of the Gospel message. Furthermore, the apostles had uniquely benefited from personal contact with Jesus, empowering them for miraculous gifts and service in a way never to be repeated following their death. This, combined with a general atmosphere of expectancy of the Lord's imminent return, contributed to the supernatural presence of spiritual gifts.[411] As an afterthought, Barclay then proposes the question, "But have miracles in fact stopped?" A visit to any first-world emergency room would reveal doctors and surgeons doing *common* things that in apostolic times would have been seen as so *uncommon* they would be immediately regarded as a miracle. In this sense, for Christians, miracles are all around us when we have eyes to see them.

WRESTLING WITH THE EVIDENCE

WE NOW TURN OUR ATTENTION to addressing the implications and considerations raised by both sides of the dispute. However, before doing so I suggest that we set aside for a moment the particular issue of a distinct Second Baptism to wrestle with what appears to be the intimate cause and effect relationship between a subsequent encounter with the Holy Spirit and the evidence of the encounter made manifest through particular spiritual gifts. (As mentioned above, many hold that the initial evidence will be speaking in tongues). In other words, is one possible without the other? The potential danger in holding to a doctrine that teaches that objective and tangible evidence of a Second Baptism is to be expected is that a believer may be unintentionally compelled to focus on the gifts (the evidence) of the experience, rather than the actual encounter with the Holy Spirit Himself.

By way of an illustration, imagine a parent who loves their child so much they are compelled—out of love—to give their child a gift. The child, upon receiving the gift, is then compelled to love the *giver of the gift* more than the gift itself. I believe this is an apt example of the exchange that takes place in the life of the Christian. Our Heavenly Father is eager to pour out into the lives of His children a great many gifts (James 1:17). This means that on one

411   William Barclay. *The Acts of the Apostles New Daily Study Bible.* (Louisville, KY: Westminster John Know Press, 2003), p. 36.

hand, as children of God, we should eagerly anticipate and pray for His gifts. However, on the other hand (and arguably more important) we should seek greater intimacy with God—the *giver of the gift* rather than focusing solely on the gift itself. As Erickson so eloquently pointed out, "It is not a matter of getting more of the Holy Spirit—it is, rather, a matter of His possessing more of our lives."[412]

Returning then to the matter of spiritual gifts, we can glean a great deal of wisdom from a close study of the Apostle Paul's exposition on the matter. First and foremost, the gifts are bestowed on the Body of Christ and are therefore meant for the edification of the *entire Body* rather than the enrichment (or boasting!) of an individual member of the Body (1 Corinthians 12:7). Second, the gifts are intended for use in cooperation with other believers, meaning that not one person has all the gifts (1 Corinthians 12:28-30). This is why Paul explained that each member of the Church is crucial for the Body of the Church to function properly. This logic leads Paul to elaborate on the fact that all the gifts of the Spirit are important (1 Corinthians 12:22-26), and that the Holy Spirit "distributes them just as He determines" (1 Corinthians 12:11).

In 1 Corinthians 12:13, Paul emphasizes the point that *"One Spirit* forms one body."[413] Whether of the more conservative or the liberal theological camp, Paul's emphasis on the "one Spirit" holds remarkable implications in the believer's life. Paul makes the case that the same *"one Spirit"* that raised Jesus from the dead comes to dwell within the believer at the moment of their conversion (Romans 6:10-11). This particular verse should therefore be of resounding *encouragement* and *comfort* for all believers, because without this assurance, a new Christian could be led to think there needs to be a dramatic experience with the Holy Spirit in order for their conversion to "be real." Needless to say, this uncertainty is unhealthy in the life of the Christian and may lead to self-doubt, and even worse, fabricated testimonials about Spirit activity and encounters.

All this being said, it is equally important to heed the fact that Paul expected all Christians to "be filled with the Spirit" (Ephesians 5:18). Paul contrasts being "Spirit filled" with being "wine-filled." The former leads to glorifying God and the Body of Christ, the later to debauchery and foolishness. Being "filled with the Spirit" implies the action is on-going and continual. However,

---

412 Erickson, p. 802.

413 My use of italics in this verse to emphasize the unity of God in the Spirit and to accentuate my argument made throughout the remainder of the paragraph.

rather than being led to think this means that we effectually need "more of the Spirit," I think it means that we are to surrender more of our lives to Him. As Christians, we are called to give the Holy Spirit full control over every area of our life. After all, this in and of itself is the primary gift of the Holy Spirit—the Holy Spirit Himself.[414]

CESSATIONISM AND CONTINUATIONISM — THE HISTORY OF THE CHURCH

OVER THE YEARS THERE HAVE been differing views on the active role of the Holy Spirit continuing to perform miracles such as divine healing, prophecy, and most notably, speaking in tongues. Generally speaking, four different views have been proposed to include *Cessationism, Functional Cessationism, Continuationism,* and *Word-Faith.* For our purposes, a brief overview of the first three positions (the *Word-Faith* movement is outside the scope of our discussion) is helpful in creating a framework for understanding the church's historical positions on Second Baptism and spiritual gifts.

Continuationism holds that while Scripture is God's only trustworthy voice, He continues to speak to Churches and individuals through His Spirit. These unique revelations of His Word must be tested and weighed against the Bible. In addition, God continues to perform miracles (which may include speaking in tongues) and believers should pray for and expect these miracles to be a present reality within their life and the Body of Christ.[415] Continuationism holds that believers in Jesus Christ should expect (and look forward to) an experience of the Holy Spirit after their initial conversion. This distinct second blessing results in the manifestation of spiritual gifts in the believer's life. In the Pentecostal tradition, this experience is commonly referred to as the "Baptism in the Spirit." According to this view, the primary objective evidence of the Holy Spirit baptism is speaking in tongues and empowerment for service in God's Kingdom.[416] Those who hold this view substantiate their position by noting that in Acts 2, the disciples "were filled with the Holy Spirit and began to speak in other tongues as the Spirit enabled them" (Acts 2:4). Because the

---

414 Dr. Gerry Breshears. *Spiritual Gifts Position Paper.* Grace Community Church, Gresham, OR.
415 Breshears. Western Seminary TH503 outline on Holy Spirit.
416 Tennent, p. 167.

disciples had been followers of Jesus for nearly three years, in addition to the fact that in John 20:22, "Jesus breathed on them (the disciples) and said, 'Receive the Holy Spirit," the logical conclusion is that there is a distinct Second Baptism. In other words, John 20:22 clearly establishes one baptism, whereas Acts 2:4 establishes another. The difference in Acts 2:4 (the Second Baptism) is that there is *objective evidence* of the Holy Spirit's work within the believer which is made manifest in *glossalilia*—speaking in unknown human languages.

Perhaps the strongest biblical evidence for Continuationism is the careful exegetical reading of 1 Corinthians 13:8-12. The Cessationist has historically connected the verse, "But when completeness comes, what is in part disappears" (1 Corinthians 13:10), to the close of the biblical canon, and concludes that miraculous gifts are no longer necessary or operational. In other words, the "completeness" in this particular verse is the complete canon of Scripture, which Paul foretold would result in the cessation of prophecy, tongues, and words of knowledge (1 Corinthians 13:8). However, a more through understanding of Paul's theology on spiritual gifts demonstrates that completeness is in fact the eternal state ushered in at the second coming of Christ. Furthermore, when Paul speaks in verse 12 of seeing "face to face," he most likely is referring to the eternal state, subsequent to the return of Christ.[417] Finally, it is vital to pay close attention to Paul's explicitly stated purpose for the gifts: namely, the edification of the Body of Christ (1 Corinthians 12:7). One would be hard-pressed to conclude that the church is no longer in need of edification, and therefore beyond the need of Christians empowered by God's Spirit with unique gifts meant to build up and strengthen His Body.

The Functional Cessationist would hold that the purpose of the sign-gifts of speaking in tongues and miraculous healing most notably authenticated the Apostles (Acts 5:15, 19:12), yet there is no reason to believe that these gifts have ceased today (John 14:12-14; 1 Corinthians 12:31,14:1-18). Furthermore, Functional Cessationism holds that although the Bible is God's only trustworthy voice, believers should "let the Holy Spirit guide our lives" (Galatians 5:16) and leave room within the traditionally held Western Enlightenment worldview that tends to create a wall between the experiential framework of the senses and the supernatural framework of the biblical authors.[418] In other words, when

---

417 Sam Storms. *Practicing the Power.* (Grand Rapids, MI: Zondervan, 2017), p. 246.
418 Tennent, p. 178.

guided by the Bible, believers have more to gain than lose in opening their mind to the idea that the same Holy Spirit who acted supernaturally in the lives of the Apostles and early church is active and alive in similar ways today.

At the other end of the spectrum, many notable theologians believe in Cessationism and that the diffusion of miraculous gifts by the Holy Spirit was confined to the apostolic church and subsequently passed away with it.[419] Because abuses and exaggerations of continuing miraculous experiences with the Holy Spirit are so rampant and abusive in the church, it is better to rely solely on the revealed wisdom of the Bible.[420]

Although the Cessationist view contends that the miraculous gifts were reserved for the Apostles and served the purpose of establishing the church, it is important to note that numerous non-apostolic men and women exercised these gifts including the 70 who were commissioned in Luke 10:9 and at least 108 of the 120 who were gathered in the upper room on the day of Pentecost. Furthermore, the Cessationist's appeal to Ephesians 2:20 that the gifts were for the first century period of time in which the church was being built overlooks the fact that miraculous gifts (specifically the gift of prophecy) were not linked to the apostles and never functioned foundationally.[421]

Theologian Millard Erickson argues for what appears to be a Cessationist view and suggests that even if the Spirit were to actively dispense special gifts in the church today, Christians "are not to set their lives to seeking them." Erickson points to Paul's teaching that the Spirit dispenses the gifts sovereignly, and that He alone will determine the recipients (1 Corinthians 12:11). This being the case, the Spirit may choose to give a believer a special gift regardless of their prayers or expectation of it. Erickson reiterates the fact that Paul's command to be "filled with the Spirit" (Ephesians 5:18) is a *present imperative,* which suggests an ongoing action and experience in the daily life of the believer.

A careful assessment of the totality of the positions (with a special emphasis on the points I feel were unfairly made by Erickson) compels me to lean towards a Continuationism theology. Although I certainly agree with Erickson's view of the sovereignty of the Spirit, it is supremely important to note that according to Paul, in the particular case of miraculous gifts, the Spirit can be quenched

---

419   B.B. Warfield in his book *Counterfeit Miracles* as identified in *Christian Theology,* p. 172.

420   Breshears. Western Seminary TH503 outline on Holy Spirit.

421   Storms, p. 249.

(1 Thessalonians 5:19-22). This is a remarkable thought considering that Paul is speaking about the sovereign Spirit of God who works all things together according to His will. Nevertheless, here Paul warns believers that God has granted Christians the ability to either *"restrict* or *release* what He does in the life of the local church."[422] Furthermore, in 1 Corinthians 14:32, Paul explains, "The spirits of prophets are subject to prophets." This means that the Spirit is happy to align Himself with the believer's expectations for what is possible, and will "not act upon us or through us as if we were puppets." [423] This line of reasoning seems to contradict Erickson and suggests that believers have a responsibility to not just seek the Spirit—but so much of Him that we "fan the flame of the Spirit's fire" (2 Timothy 1:6).

Perhaps the most compelling reason to embrace the active pursuit of the Spirit is our Lord's teaching on the subject. In Luke 11:13, in the context of explaining the magnitude of God's grace, Jesus said, "If you then, who are evil, know how to give good gifts to your children, *how much more will the heavenly Father give the Holy Spirit to those who ask him*" (Luke 11:13 — my emphasis). In application within the believer's life, we have the confidence that God intimately knows our every need and is fully aware of the emptiness in our life. This means that on one hand God knows what we need even before we ask for it, and on the other hand God wants us to ask (Matthew 7:7-11). Weighing all the evidence—with special attention given to our Lord's discourse—leads me to believe that God is far more willing to fill us with His Spirit than we are willing to ask.

EXERCISING OUR FAITH

I BELIVE THAT ALL OF the gifts of the Spirit continue to be given by God to believers today, and are fully operative in the Body of Christ. These gifts may be immediately accompanied by the initial conversion experience; or similar to the way that a physical muscle grows stronger over time, the gifts may develop gradually throughout the believer's lifetime. This being said, I must emphasize the fact that I believe the Holy Spirit indwells believers at the moment of their conversion. The question we may very well consider at

---

422   Storms, p. 180.
423   Storms, p. 180.

this point is what should be expected in the life of the believer *following their conversion*? The answer could not be any clearer—the Bible plainly teaches that following the initial conversion experience and the receipt of the Holy Spirit, the believer is called to a life of increasing sanctification and growing in Christlikeness (2 Thessalonians 2:13; Colossians 3:1,5). Fundamentally, I believe this means that although the Holy Spirit comes to indwell every person at conversion, there is an ongoing experience throughout the believer's new life in Christ of being continually *filled with the Spirit*.

By way of illustration, consider an athlete who enrolls into a CrossFit gym. The moment of conversion takes place during their initial entry and enrollment into the fitness studio. However, the real benefits to the athlete of the program are derived from the daily experience of applying the methodology of constantly varied, functional movement, at high intensity. Some athletes might enjoy rather sudden "breakthroughs" in advanced gymnastic movements or weightlifting skills, whereas others tend to need more time to see any evidence of growth. But in either case, the increase in strength (to borrow theological language—*filling the muscles*) is clearly subsequent to, and a secondary effect of, the initial entry into the gym.

Pressing this illustration into the context of the church, the subsequent filling with the Spirit may be gradual or rather dramatic (1 Corinthians 12:7-11), and occurs as a result of living out the reality of being baptized by the Spirit.[424] This perpetual filling is not to be confused with a distinct second blessing of the Holy Spirit, but rather "an actualization of what we have already received at conversion."[425] This conclusion, however, brings us to face to face with very two very interesting and compelling questions: Should the believer actively pray for, seek out, and make room for the ongoing filling of the Spirit? And if so, what are the functional steps a believer should take in pursuit of an encounter with the Spirit? Returning for a moment to our CrossFit analogy, the athlete desirous of increasing in strength will take great measures to create the appropriate environment in their life to facilitate such growth. Should Christians model and adopt such athletic behavior into our spiritual life?

---

424 Breshears. Western Seminary TH503 outline on Holy Spirit.
425 Breshears. Western Seminary TH503 outline on Holy Spirit.

THE IMPLICATIONS OF THE EASTER INBREATHING

THE APOSTLE JOHN RECORDS A meeting that Jesus had with his disciples that is sometimes referred to as the "Easter Inbreathing." After appearing to His disciples in His resurrected body and showing them His hands and side, Jesus said, "'Peace be with you. As the Father has sent me, even so I am sending you.' And when He had said this, He breathed on them and said to them, 'Receive the Holy Spirit'" (John 20:21-22).[426] It is important to note that although Jesus gave the disciples the Holy Spirit on this particular day, He still commanded them to wait for a secondary experience that would take place when they would be "baptized with the Holy Spirit" (Acts 1:4-5). How can we reconcile what appears to be two distinct baptisms?

I believe that the 11 disciples who were breathed on by Jesus are the archetype of Christians today who receive the Holy Spirit at conversion but remain idle (or even worse, powerless) to *witness their faith*. Although the 11 disciples initially received the Holy Spirit on the Easter Inbreathing, they were filled with the Spirit on the Day of Pentecost. It this sense, it was the second experience with the Holy Spirit that led to a "life-changing encounter that forever transformed them, turning ordinary men into firebrands for God, willing to face harsh criticism, beatings, and dying for the cause of Christ."[427] To recapitulate the series of events, when Jesus met with the disciples behind closed doors, breathed on them, and commanded them to receive the Holy Spirit, they received the Spirit of God in that very moment—representative of the experience believers have today when they first put their faith in Christ. However, when the 11 disciples were baptized by the Holy Spirit on the Day of Pentecost, they had a face-to-face encounter with the Holy Spirit that completely transformed their lives. This being the case, believers today have much to learn from those who *waited for the gift the Father promised.*

---

426 In the context of our Lord's command to "Receive the Holy Spirit", in the *A Manual Grammar of the Greek New Testament*, H. E. Dana points out that Jesus used an aorist tense, the meaning of which is "right now!" In other words, the giving of the Holy Spirit took place immediately, and should not be confused with the idea that Jesus was speaking to a future event. H. E. Dana, *A Manual Grammar of the Greek New Testament* (New York, NY: Macmillan Publishers, 1957), p. 300.

427 Sala, p. 108.

APPLICATION IN LIFE

JESUS MADE IT CLEAR TO his disciples that there must be a "hunger and thirst for God" before that desire can be fulfilled. To this effect, the Apostle John elaborated on our Lord's teaching on the Holy Spirit by recording: "On the last day of the feast, the great day, Jesus stood up and cried out, 'If anyone thirsts, let him come to me and drink. Whoever believes in me, as the Scripture has said, out of his heart will flow rivers of living water'" (John 7:37-38). Christians alive today inhabit the world of the feast—the *great day* in which our Lord's Spirit will be poured out into those who believe (John 7:38-40). This means that believers must have an active and conscious desire for the Holy Spirit, while also praying that "the Spirit would have full control over the will, emotions, and reasoning faculties of the believer." [428]

As a simple illustration from the CrossFit studio, in over 20 years of coaching athletes to achieve their first muscle-up, I have noticed a curious thing. Athletes who had a "hunger and thirst" for their first muscle-up (a very challenging gymnastic movement performed on the high-rings) achieved it in record time compared with people who thought it would never happen. In this sense, I propose there is an intimate connection between obedience, waiting on the Lord, and positive expectancy on the gift of the Holy Spirit. Acts 5:32 speaks of the Spirit "whom God has given to *those who obey Him.*"[429] This magnificent verse testifies to the great truth that believers can experience more of the Spirit, not based on anything that we do, but rather on the type of people that we are. Are we obedient? Do we have faith? Do we wait on our Lord?

Following our Lords command to *patiently wait* on the gift promised by the Father (Acts 1:4), Jesus' last words to His disciples were, "But you will receive power when the Holy Spirit has come upon you, and you will be my witness in Jerusalem and in all Judea and Samaria, and to the ends of the earth" (Acts 1:8-9). Whereas a great many people in the church today are quite content to be an *advocate* of the Christian faith, it seems that very few are actively *witnessing* their faith to the extent that we read about in the New Testament. Therefore, let us note three characteristics of a true *Christian witness* and how they affect our pursuit of the spiritual gifts.

---

428   Kenneth Wuest, "The Holy Spirit in Greek Exposition," *Bibliotheca Sacra, CXIIX.* Quoted in Dr Harold Sala's book, *Getting Acquainted with the Holy Spirit,* p. 119.
429   My use of italics in this verse to emphasize obedience to the Lord resulted in the gift of the Holy Spirit.

In a court of law, a witness testifies on their first-hand knowledge of an experience. In order for something to be admitted as actual evidence (as opposed to hearsay or mere speculation), the witness must be able to declare, "I *know* this to be true" rather than "I *think* this is true." Second, a real witness is not of words, but of deeds (James 2:14-26). Peter and John astonished the Sanhedrin because of their courage (Acts 4:13). In other words, it was *who they were that was significant*, which led the inquisitors to conclude: "These men had been with Jesus" (Acts 4:13b). New Testament scholar William Barclay relates a story in which journalist Sir Henry Morton Stanley, having spent time with evangelist David Livingstone in central Africa, said: "If I had been with him any longer, I would have been compelled to be a Christian—and he never spoke to me about it at all." And perhaps most importantly, the Greek word for *witness* and the word for *martyr* is the same (*martus*). To be a witness means to be loyal to the faith—no matter the cost.[430]

The world that Christians inhabit today moves at an extremely fast pace. In a fiberoptic Internet cable, the speed at which a data packet can travel is nearly 200,000 kilometers per second, (or 124,300 miles per second).[431] Considering the circumference of the Earth is about 40,000 kilometers, this is *mind-boggling fast*. Caught up in the speed of the world around us, is it possible that a believer's expectation for an immediate life-changing encounter with the Holy Spirit at the moment of conversion—or at a time subsequent to conversion—has been unfairly swayed by common culture? In the context of the CrossFit studio, the most discouraging reality athletes must face is the fact that fitness goals often take a very long time to achieve. In many cases, I have discovered that unless athletes are able to experience near immediate evidence of progress, it can be difficult for them to sustain the necessary momentum to eventually achieve—and perhaps even surpass—what they think is possible. In this sense, what is the capacity for a believer today to wait an indefinite period of time for either a distinct second encounter, or a more gradual filling, of the Holy Spirit? And is the principle and expectation of waiting even biblical?

Moving our illustrations of waiting from the CrossFit studio to the Body of Christ, believers must hold within their mind two seemingly conflicting ideas. On one hand, it is important to note that in the New Testament, the coming of the Spirit is the fulfillment of the promise of Jesus: "And remember, I am with you always, to the end of the age" (Matthew 28:20). This means that at the moment of conversion,

---

430   The three qualities of a "Christian Witness" were brought to my attention William Barclay's *The Acts of the Apostles Daily Study Bible.* (Louisville, KY: Westminster John Knox Press, 2017), p. 13.

431   NetworkingGuides.com

Jesus is with us through His Spirit, and in this sense there is no waiting at all. On the other hand, in Acts 1:4, the apostles are specifically commanded to *wait for the coming of the Spirit.* How are we to reconcile what appears to be a "now—then" reality?

I believe that Christians would gain more power and confidence to witness their faith if they followed the example of the apostles and learned to wait for the Lord. In other words, Christians today (in particular Christian athletes within the CrossFit culture) need to develop *skillfulness in stillness.* Amid a world of hurry-up and get things done, we must cultivate space in our heart to slow down and receive. Given that everything about the sport of CrossFit revolves around the principle of *doing more work in less time,* the prophet Isaiah's words are more applicable today than ever before: "Those who wait for the Lord shall renew their strength" (Isaiah 40:31).

In his book *Baptism and Fullness,* author John Stott relates, "The baptism was a unique initiatory experience; the fullness was intended to be the continuing, the permanent result, the norm. As an initiatory event the baptism is not repeatable and cannot be lost, but the fullness can be repeated and in any case needs to be maintained."[432] When I first started in CrossFit in December 2001, the program's founder told me that I should look forward to 20 years of favorable athletic adaptation and steady physical development. Reflecting on the past 20 years of CrossFit training, my increasingly high stack of fitness journals is evidence of the resounding truth of the founder's statement. I can't help but conclude that the relationship between my subjective thoughts and expectations about my progress, and the actual objective measurement of my progress, were intimately connected. In other words, I have a strong sense that my physical progress and growth in the program are directly attributed to my expectations about the possibility for such growth in the first place. Succinctly stated, the thought preceded (and arguably produced) the outcome.

Against this background, it is interesting to note the role of faith in receiving a subsequent encounter with the Holy Spirit following conversion. I find that I must differentiate between different types of faith in order to make this point. All believers exercise the first type of faith, which I refer to as *converting faith*—this faith takes place at the moment of our conversion, and is present in every born-again believer. The second type of faith is a *continuing faith,* which is that daily confidence that God is with us, and that He will never leave or forsake

---

432 John Stott, *Baptism and Fullness* (Downers Grove, IL: InterVarsity Press, 1964), p. 62.

us (Deuteronomy 31:6). In biblical-historical context, Abraham demonstrated *converting faith* when he "obeyed when God called him to leave home and go to another land" (Hebrews 11:8a), and *continuing faith* when he pressed forward each day "without knowing where he was going" (Hebrews 11:8b).

In addition to *converting* and *continuing faith*, I also believe there is a third type of faith that author and pastor Sam Storms has defined as *charismatic faith*, which is a "sudden, supernatural surge of confident assurance that God is going to do something right now, right here."[433] To this effect, it is interesting to note that when Jesus returned to His hometown of Nazareth, He was only able to accomplish a few miracles there because of the people's lack of faith (or perhaps *charismatic faith?*—Matthew 13:54-58). On the other hand, in instances of Jesus healing people, it was commonly accompanied by the fact that they had faith in Him (Luke 7:50, 8:48, 18:42). Given the relationship between faith and healing, it would seem that faith in God's ability to enable a distinct encounter with Him might very well be largely in the hands (or head) of the believer.

It is also important to remember that Paul wrote, "The spirits of prophets are subject to prophets" (1 Corinthians 14:32). Paul's point is that the Holy Spirit does not move through believers as if we were mindless sedentary beings. Rather, the "sovereign Spirit happily subjects Himself to our decisions."[434] In other words, believers who hold in their theological framework the idea that a distinct experience with the Holy Spirit is possible are far more likely to have their expectations and prayers met than someone who believes it's just not going to happen.

Legendary Drug Enforcement Administration (DEA) supervisory Special Agent and Firearms Instructor John Browning told my investigative group, "It's better to have a back-up gun and not need it, then need a back-up gun, and not have one." In the perilous moment that a Law Enforcement Officer finds himself in need of a back-up gun, it means that something has gone horribly amiss, and lives are on the line. Pressing the street-savvy wisdom of Agent Browning into a theological construct, we may very well conclude that it's far better to believe that a powerful encounter with the Holy Spirit is possible after conversion and not experience it during our lifetime—than to discover in the afterlife that while on earth the Holy Spirit was desirous of uniquely empowering us to edify the Body of Christ—yet sadly we never thought to ask.

---

433 Storms, p. 53. The distinctions between, "Three Types of Faith" were brought to my attention by Storm's section on "The Role of Faith" in his masterful book, *Practicing the Power.*
434 Storms, p. 180.

HOLD ON A MINUTE — WHAT ABOUT SPEAKING IN TONGUES?

IN SOME PENTECOSTAL AND CHARISMATIC denominations, a theology gradually developed that taught absent the spiritual gift of speaking in tongues, a believer has not been baptized in the Holy Spirit. This doctrine is based primarily on the fact that speaking in tongues was often accompanied by the outpouring of the Holy Spirit (Acts 2:4, 10:46, 19:6). From this reasoning, one could easily conclude that the outpouring of the Spirit and speaking in tongues should constitute a normal and anticipated experience for everyone. However, this conclusion tragically overlooks the fact that this would mean that anyone who does not speak in tongues is not Spirit-filled—a concept that is clearly not in alignment with the biblical teaching of baptism (1 Corinthians 12:27-31). Furthermore, this position would put a great number of renowned men of God in the category of "not Spirit-filled" including Billy Graham and Charles Spurgeon.[435]

When Paul addressed the matter of speaking in tongues, he asked the question, "Do all speak in tongues?" (1 Corinthians 12:30). As renowned New Testament scholar Harold Sala has pointed out in his book, *Getting Acquainted with the Holy Spirit,* in the Greek language a question can be asked in such a way that the speaker makes it clear that either a "Yes" or a "No" is expected. In the case of the question asked by Paul, the expected answer is "No!"[436] I must reiterate at this point that I do not mean to imply that tongues have ceased, or that a believer and should not actively pray for or exercise this particular gift. Rather, I humbly suggest that the Body of Christ must be careful not to overemphasize the gift of tongues or require it as demonstrable proof of a Spirit-filled life.

God knows His children better than we know ourselves, and when we invite Him to be Lord over our life, our encounter with Him will be as completely unique as the individual believer himself.

---

435 Sala, p. 133.
436 Sala, p. 134.

CONCLUSION

CONCLUDING THOUGHTS
Right Thinking About God

"Be transformed by the renewing of your mind."
– Romans 12:2

THE THOUGHTS IN YOUR MIND about God are the most important thing about you.[437] In other words, if you think incorrectly about God, it is not God who changes. You change for the better or worse and in direct proportion to your better or worse thoughts about God.

Being a *good soldier* and *fighting well, finishing the race, and keeping the faith* are all unequivocally dependent upon your ability to first think rightly about God (2 Timothy 2:3, 4:7).

For the purposes of concluding this book, I encourage you to embrace three foundational ideas about God:

1.   God is entirely devoted to your spiritual advancement.[438]
2.   When you trust God to lead you, He will trust you to lead others.[439]
3.   God is good.[440]

Having faith in the idea that God is good, devoted to your advancement, and desirous of enabling you to lead yourself and others, is tantamount to your success, fulfillment, and happiness. Your entire outlook on life will be instantly changed when your heart knows that God, although exalted in power and majesty, is eager to be your friend, and that He only wants what is best for you.

---

437   The great Christian mystic A.W. Tozer said, "What comes into our mind when we think about God is the most important thing about us."

438   Jeremiah 29:11 promises that the plans God have for you are meant to prosper you, to give you hope in your endeavors and a bright future.

439   2 Samuel 3:1 explains that King David's faith in God and obedience to Him enabled David to become stronger and more capable of leading others both in peacetime and in war.

440   James 1:17 states that every good and perfect gift comes from God, and in Mark 10:18 Jesus Christ said that only God is good.

BIBLIOGRAPHY

Alexander, Desmond and Rosner, Brian. *The New Dictionary of Biblical Theology* (Downers Grove, IL: InterVarsity Press, 2000).

Barron, Robert. *To Light a Fire on the Earth* (New York, NY: Image Books, 2017).

Carson, D. A. and Douglas Moo. "Colossians." In *An Introduction to the New Testament* (Grand Rapids, MI: Zondervan, 2006), pp. 516–531.

Ciampa, R. E. "Galatians." In *The New Dictionary of Biblical Theology*. Edited by Alexander, Desmond and Rosner, Brian (Downers Grove, IL: InterVarsity Press, 2000), pp. 311–315.

Donfried, K. P. "Romans." In *The New Dictionary of Biblical Theology*. Edited by Alexander, Desmond and Brian Rosner, (Downers Grove, IL: InterVarsity Press, 2000), pp. 291–296.

Easwaran, Eknath. *The Bhagavad Gita* (Tomales, CA: Nilgiri Press, 2007).

Erickson, Millard. *Christian Theology* (Grand Rapids, MI: Baker Academic, 2013).

France, R. T. "Hebrews." In *The Expositor's Bible Commentary*. Edited by Longman, Tremper III and David E. Garland (Grand Rapids, MI: Zondervan, 2008), pp. 19–195.

Hooper, Richard. *Jesus, Buddha, Krishna & Lao Tzu: The Parallel Sayings* (Charlottesville, VA: Hampton Roads, 2007).

Johnson, Alan. "Revelation." In *The Expositor's Bible Commentary*. Edited by Longman, Tremper and Garland, David E. (Grand Rapids, MI: Zondervan, 2008), pp. 573–789.

Laney, Carl. "Colossians." In *Essential Bible Background* (CreateSpace, 2016), pp. 210–213.

Laney, Carl. "Hebrews." In *Essential Bible Background* (CreateSpace, 2016), pp. 237–240.

Laney, Carl. "1 and 2 Corinthians." In *Essential Bible Background* (Create Space, 2016), pp. 189–198.

Lane, W. L. "Hebrews." In The *Dictionary of the Later New Testament and Its Developments*. Edited by Martin, Ralph P. and Davids, Peter H. (Downers Grove, IL: InterVarsity Press, 1997), pp. 443–458.

Lewis, C. S. *Mere Christianity* (New York, NY: Collier Books, 1952).

Mackie, Timothy. "Galatians." In *Read Scripture: Illustrated Summaries of Biblical Books* (Portland, OR: The Bible Project, 2017), p. 110.

Mackie, Timothy. "Hebrews." In *Read Scripture: Illustrated Summaries of Biblical Books* (Portland, OR: The Bible Project, 2018), p. 130–131.

O'Brien, P. T. "Colossians." In *The Dictionary of Paul and His Letters*. Edited by Hawthorne, Gerald F., Ralph P. Martin, and Daniel G. Reid (Downers Grove, IL: InterVarsity Press, 1993), pp. 147–153.

Rapa, Robert. "Galatians." In *The Expositor's Bible Commentary*. Edited by Longman, Tremper III and David E. Garland, (Grand Rapids, MI: Zondervan, 2008), pp. 549–640.

Still, Todd. "Colossians." In *The Expositor's Bible Commentary*. Edited by Longman, Tremper and Garland, David E. (Grand Rapids, MI: Zondervan, 2008), pp. 265–360.

Tennent, Timothy. *Theology in the Context of World Christianity* (Grand Rapids, MI: Zondervan, 2007).

Thiselton, A. C. "1 Corinthians." In *The New Dictionary of Biblical Theology*. Edited by Alexander T. Desmond Alexander and Brian S. Rosner. (Downers Grove, IL: InterVarsity Press, 2000), pp. 297–306.

Tozer, A. W. *The Knowledge of the Holy* (New York, NY: Harper One, 1961).

Tuck, Gary. "Revelation." In *The Arguments of the Books of the New Testament* (Western Seminary San Jose, 2016), pp. 197–209.

Tuck, Gary. *Revelation Book (A Readers Guide to the Book of Revelation),* (Western Seminary San Jose, 2019), pp. 1–81.

Tuck, Gary. "Colossians." In *The Arguments of the Books of the New Testament* (Western Seminary San Jose, 2016), pp. 133–137.

Tuck, Gary. "Hebrews." In *The Arguments of the Books of the New Testament* (Western Seminary San Jose, 2016), pp. 159–169.

Tuck, Gary. "Galatians." In *The Arguments of the Books of the New Testament,* pp. 112–119.

Tuck, Gary. "First Corinthians." In *The Arguments of the Books of the New Testament,* pp. 95–104.

Tuck, Gary. "Romans." In *The Arguments of the Books of the New Testament,* pp. 83–94.

Verbrugge, Verlyn. "1 Corinthians." In *The Expositor's Bible Commentary.* Edited by Longman, Tremper III and David E. Garland. (Grand Rapids, MI: Zondervan, 2008), pp. 241–414.

ALSO FROM BESTSELLING AUTHOR GREG AMUNDSON

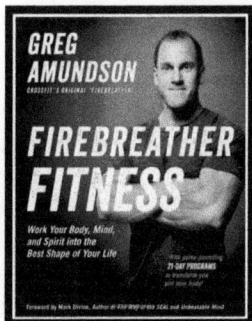

Greg Amundson's effective guides to functional fitness, nutrition, goal-setting, pain tolerance, honing purpose and focus, and exerting control over your mental state are designed to help meet any challenge. Packed with practical advice, vetted training methods, and Amundson's guided workout programs, *Firebreather Fitness* is a must-have resource for athletes, coaches, law enforcement and military professionals, and anyone interested in pursuing the high-performance life. Includes a foreword from *New York Times* bestselling author Mark Divine.

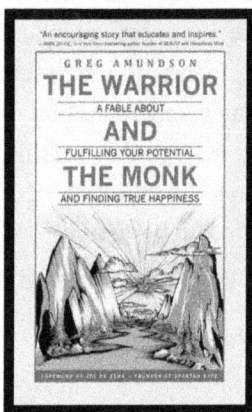

The *Warrior and The Monk* tells the extraordinary story of a young warrior who seeks the counsel of a wise monk on the universal quest to find true happiness. This is Greg Amundson's #1 Amazon multi-category bestselling book.

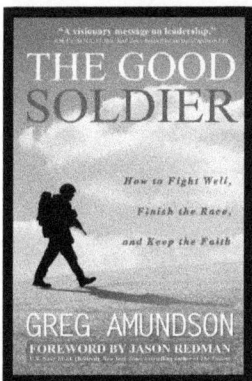

From #1 bestselling author Greg Amundson comes the nations first biblical theology on leadership through the perspective of the warrior archetype. Greg's book *The Good Soldier* opens the Bible in a fresh and relevant new way, and provides actionable steps that you can take to fight well, finish the race, and keep the faith. This is the leadership book that is redefining what it means to be a leader and a modern day warrior.

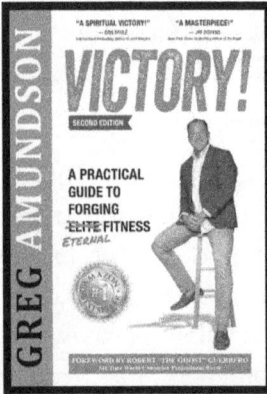

Greg Amundson's book *VICTORY* offers people of all faiths powerful strategies and practical guidelines for bringing health, happiness, fitness, and purpose into their lives and the lives of others. Renowned for his ability to merge fitness and faith, Greg offers a proven methodology for establishing life-affirming beliefs, understanding Divine wisdom, tapping into the power of prayer, integrating physical fitness with spiritual practice, and optimizing the power of mental and physical nutrition.

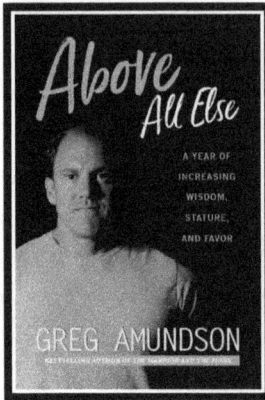

In a unique and groundbreaking new voice, Greg Amundson merges biblical truth with modern day lessons on leadership, positive psychology, and the warrior spirit. Each day of the year, you will be scripturally guided through the key principles and teachings from the Bible, resulting in a more intimate relationship with God and greater understanding of His Word. Greg's message will help you internalize disciplined practices and ways of thinking that are central to developing your full potential, and achieving your greatest dreams and goals. Greg's integration of the Mind, Body, and Spirit offers a unique perspective to keep you thriving in all aspects of your life.

ABOUT THE AUTHOR

An alumnus of the University of California at Santa Cruz (BA Legal Theory) and Western Seminary (MA Ministry and Leadership), Greg Amundson has spent nearly twenty years in warrior professions to include assignments as a Special Weapons and Tactics Team Operator (SWAT) and Sniper in Santa Cruz County, a Captain in the United States Army, a Special Agent with the Drug Enforcement Administration (DEA) on the Southwest Border and an Agent on the highly effective Border Enforcement Security Taskforce (BEST) Team.

In addition to his extensive government work, Greg is recognized as a thought leader in the field of integrated wellness practices, and is a prolific author and speaker whose message has positively influenced the lives of thousands of spiritual seekers. A former owner of the nation's first CrossFit gym, Greg has traveled around the world teaching functional fitness and self-mastery principles for over nineteen years.

Greg is an ecclesiastically endorsed and ordained minister, a Krav Maga Black Belt with Krav Maga Worldwide and the Krav Maga Association of America, and an honor graduate of the Los Angeles Police Department Handgun Instructor School (HITS). Greg currently serves as a Reserve Peace Officer and Law Enforcement Chaplain in Santa Cruz. Greg is a four-time #1 Amazon bestselling author, and the founder of Eagle Rise Publishing, a Christian focused publishing platform that has produced numerous bestselling books. Connect with Greg at www.GregoryAmundson.com.

KEYNOTES AND SEMINARS

Greg Amundson is one of North America's most electric, encouraging, and motivating professional speakers. Greg has logged more than 10,000 hours of dynamic public speaking on topics including leadership, intrinsic motivation, holistic wellness practices, functional fitness, warrior spirit, and God's Love. Greg speaks around the Country to Law Enforcement Departments on integrating disciplined warrior practices to foster increased Officer Safety while simultaneously generating stronger community relationships. A plank owner of the highly regarded Eagle Rise Speakers Bureau, Greg is renowned for his ability to transcend boundaries and speak to the heart of Spirituality. His use of captivating storytelling results in a profound and transformational learning experience.

To book Greg Amundson at your next conference or in-house event please visit www.GregoryAmundson.com.

www.ingramcontent.com/pod-product-compliance
Lightning Source LLC
LaVergne TN
LVHW011219080426
835509LV00005B/207